CONTAINMENT AND THE COLD WAR

CONTAINMENT AND THE COLD WAR:

American Foreign Policy since 1945

Edited by
THOMAS G. PATERSON
University of Connecticut

66246

ADDISON-WESLEY PUBLISHING COMPANY
Reading, Massachusetts
Menlo Park, California • London • Don Mills, Ontario

This book is in the Addison-Wesley
SERIES IN HISTORY

Consulting Editor
Robin W. Winks

For Virginia and Bill Cain,
always an encouragement

PREFACE

Books grow out of many minds. This one developed from my interest in Cold War diplomacy and from discussions with students in my history of American foreign relations courses at the University of Connecticut. We have been struck, as have the authors in this book and its bibliography, by the persistence and predominance of the containment doctrine in American foreign policy. Central to the major debates on containment since the 1940's has been one of its chief architects, George F. Kennan. By focusing on the containment doctrine, Kennan, and the vigorous debates involving both, we can understand the continuities and changes in international relations since 1945.

My students at the University of Connecticut deserve my appreciation for their questions and thoughts. James Mylott diligently helped me compile an extensive bibliography. Edmund Wehrle, a colleague and friend writing an important study of international relations in Asia, has exchanged ideas and material with me which demonstrate parallels between Europe and Asia in the Cold War. George F. Kennan and his staff have been generous and gracious to me and my students. Walter LaFeber and Allen Yarnell made useful suggestions for improving the book. Alice Gangaway and Janet Payne produced typographical order out of my chaotic first draft. Thanks go also to the authors and publishers of the works reprinted herein.

Storrs, Connecticut   T. G. P.
Summer, 1972

CONTENTS

INTRODUCTION

PART 1 CONTAINMENT FORMULATED

1. Harry S. Truman
   "The Truman Doctrine". 12
2. George F. Kennan
   "Firm Containment and Unalterable Counter-Force". 18

PART 2 CONTAINMENT DEBATED

3. Walter Lippmann
   "A Defective Policy" 41
4. John Foster Dulles
   "From Negative Containment to Liberation" 52
5. William A. Williams
   "A Policy Boomerangs". 56
6. George F. Kennan
   "A Rebuttal and an Apology" 64
7. Lloyd C. Gardner
   "Will the Real Mr. 'X' Please Stand Up?" 85
8. Eduard M. Mark
   "What Kind of Containment?". 96

PART 3 CONTAINMENT OR DISENGAGEMENT IN THE 1950s:
        THE ISSUE IN EUROPE

9. George F. Kennan,
   "Demilitarizing the Cold War". 117
10. Dean Acheson,
    "Disengagement Equals Isolationism" 131
11. Henry A. Kissinger,
    "Can the United States Trust Russia?" 139
12. George F. Kennan,
    "Facing Reality: Disengagement Defended". 142

PART 4 CONTAINMENT OR DISENGAGEMENT IN THE 1960s:
THE ISSUE IN ASIA

13. Townsend Hoopes,
    "Cold Warriors under Kennedy and Johnson" 161
14. George F. Kennan,
    "Vietnam and Containment" 171
15. Dean Rusk,
    "The Containment of China" 181
16. David P. Mozingo,
    "Containment in Asia Reconsidered" 187

PART 5 SOMETHING OLD, SOMETHING NEW?: THE 1970s

17. J. William Fulbright,
    "The Frayed and Tattered Truman Doctrine and the Future". . . . 208

SUGGESTIONS FOR FURTHER READING 241

INTRODUCTION

President Harry S. Truman spoke dramatically and confidently to a special joint session of Congress on March 12, 1947. "I believe," the President declared, "that it must be the policy of the United States to support free peoples who are resisting attempted subjugation by armed minorities or by outside pressures." His words soon became known as the "Truman Doctrine." A few months later, in July, the well-respected *Foreign Affairs* journal carried an article titled "The Sources of Soviet Conduct," mysteriously authored by a Mr. "X." He asserted that the "main element of any United States policy toward the Soviet Union must be that of a long-term, patient but firm and vigilant containment of Russian expansive tendencies." America, he insisted, must adopt a "policy of firm containment, designed to confront the Russians with unalterable counter-force at every point where they show signs of encroaching upon the interests of a peaceful and stable world." Columnist Arthur Krock of the *New York Times* quickly identified the author as George F. Kennan, then head of the newly formed Policy Planning Staff of the Department of State.

Truman and Kennan articulated the "containment doctrine," although the two leaders did not collaborate and did not agree on the means to implementation. Both organized ideas which had existed in official Washington for months, but which had not been heretofore so succinctly and simply stated. Both men attempted to dismantle the complaint of some Americans before 1947 that the United States had no foreign policy, but rather a hodgepodge of uncoordinated reactions to specific international crises. The contrast with the American image of the strong-willed, single-minded, and totalitarian thrust of Soviet diplomacy was stark. Like many other Americans, Truman and Kennan were reaching for a positive and assertive foreign policy that would dispel American complaints and challenge the Soviet Union at the same time.

Behind their appeals for containment lay years of squabbles with the

1

Soviet Union. Neither Soviet-American tension nor containment were altogether new after World War II. In 1918, American troops participated in a joint expedition to contain or crush the Bolshevik Revolution. Washington sent aid to non-Bolshevik forces and helped blockade economically the fledgling Communist government. Until 1933, the United States refused to recognize the Soviet Union, although American businessmen eagerly traded with and invested in Russia. In 1933, worried by Japanese expansion in China and desirous of selling American products abroad to offset the depressed markets at home, President Franklin D. Roosevelt extended recognition. Yet this diplomatic effort did not remove divisive issues; trade improved little, Americans protested Russian propaganda, anticipated loans fell through, and the viciousness of Stalin's purges and callous treatment of starving Russians sickened Americans. More shocking was the Nazi-Soviet pact of 1939, which left a weak Poland helpless between two giants. Some Americans began to speak of "Red Fascism," finding little difference between the German Nazi and the Russian Communist regimes. It was the common exaggerated assumption that the Soviet Union was evil, if not barbarian, and could not be trusted in international affairs.

Yet when Germany attacked Russia in mid-1941, the United States extended Lend-Lease aid to the beleaguered Russian nation. A somewhat shaky Soviet-American accommodation developed. It was a marriage of convenience or of similar national interests to defeat Hitler's Germany. During the second world war, Americans set aside temporarily their virulent anti-communism and the Soviets cooled their anti-capitalist rhetoric. Americans appreciated and felt guilty about the fact that the Russians, losing lives and property heavily, carried the burden of the European war until the Normandy invasion of mid-1944. The Russians had asked for the opening of a second front earlier, and the United States had promised it in 1942. But delays, largely the making of Winston Churchill, scotched the cross-channel attack until 1944. The Soviets were deeply annoyed. They were also embittered by Anglo-American discussions with German officers in the Italian theater who unsuccessfully sought surrender in early 1945. Stalin could only think that the Allies were contemplating a separate peace.

Tensions built up near the close of the war as each major power jockeyed for an advantageous postwar position. Wartime conferences, especially Yalta in 1945, resolved little. Russian troops, charging toward Germany, marched through and occupied much of Eastern Europe. American troops occupied Western Europe, Italy, and with the help of the atomic bomb, Japan. Both Russia and America had spheres of influence and each was doing what it wished in its own sphere. When Washington complained about Russian influence in Rumania, Moscow would mention American influence in Italy and Japan, and Britain's influence in Greece. The atomic bomb itself was an awesome new weapon, and some American diplomats like Secretary of State James F. Byrnes hoped that it would frighten the Russians into diplomatic concessions. Lend-Lease aid to Russia ended abruptly in May, 1945, and with some accuracy, Soviet leaders believed that it was a form of American diplomatic pressure. As Washington gradually cut off foreign aid to the Soviet sphere, trade began to decline. Although the great powers had established the United Nations Organization and had agreed to zones in Germany, acrimony visited both arrangements, and hopes for a postwar peace crumbled.

Postwar crises developed with mounting alarm. Poland became a symbol of the collapse of the wartime alliance as Russia manhandled the Polish government. America, unwilling to grant arguments that Poland was vital to Soviet security and had in the 1930s been so weak, conservative, and anti-Soviet as to invite Germany to march through toward Moscow, insisted on "free elections" and a representative government. Russia could only believe that Washington followed a double standard by insisting on meddling in countries neighboring Russia, but crying loudly if Russia questioned American behavior in Latin America, Italy, or Japan. Also in Iran, the former Allies clashed over oil and spheres of influence in 1945–1946, with the United States eventually gaining the upper hand. Nor could the two powers agree on controlling atomic weapons in 1946. In Greece during the same year, Communist-led rebels challenged the British-backed Athens regime, and Washington officials saw the civil war as Moscow-inspired. Turkey appeared threatened by Soviet appeals for joint control of the Black Sea Straits. Some Americans predicted that Russia would attack Western Europe, still weak from the war's devastation. By 1947, then, a frustrated and prostrate world was divided; Russia and America glared at each other; and the Truman Administration began formulating a grand doctrine to explain the crises, to confront the Soviet Union, and to assert its intention of establishing an American-oriented international order.

George F. Kennan seemed especially qualified to help formulate the containment doctrine. Born in Milwaukee in 1904 to well-to-do parents, Kennan went to Princeton University in the early twenties and led the independent life instilled in him by his family. A "loner," Kennan seemed uncomfortable among Princeton's fashionable Eastern elite. "I left college as obscurely as I had entered it," he later recalled. He joined the Foreign Service in 1926, because "I did not know what else to do," and began his distinguished career in diplomacy. He thrived under the Service's discipline, "protective paternalism," professional style, and sense of responsibility. He took on confidence as he mastered foreign languages and the menial tasks of a vice-consul in Geneva, Hamburg, and Estonia in the late 1920s.

Although the United States had not recognized Russia, the State Department had the foresight to begin training Russian specialists. Chosen for this select group, which included Charles "Chip" Bohlen, Kennan began studying the Russian language, literature, and history in Berlin. When the United States established its first American embassy in Moscow in 1933–1934, Kennan became Third Secretary. He felt frustrated by the inconveniences of the American living quarters and was hospitalized by illness in 1935. He recalled later that his years in Moscow, 1933–1937, were "unavoidably a sort of liberal education in the horrors of Stalinism," and his intellectual revulsion against Marxism grew simultaneously. As he said, "I had never gone through a 'Marxist period.'" He found Russian Marxism violative of the principles of individualism, hard work for personal reward, moderation, and moral rigor. He nurtured too an ill-defined love of "Western civilization," which was at least the opposite of the "collectivism" in Russia. Ambassador William C. Bullitt impressed Kennan, particularly after Bullitt began his movement toward the hard line, "a line," wrote Kennan, "which most of us in the embassy wholeheartedly supported but which FDR, caring little about the specific issues involved, had no intention whatsoever of adopting." Kennan was bitterly disappointed when Joseph Davies replaced Bullitt in 1937, because the new ambassador did not share the "hard line" toward Moscow, often bypassed the embassy staff, and seemed to Kennan to be more a headline-seeking politician than a careful diplomat. Kennan thereafter distrusted politicians and public opinion, and considered them an unfortunate intrusion in foreign affairs that were best left to professionals.

After a year in Washington at the "Russian desk," Kennan headed for Prague as a diplomatic secretary in 1938, and stayed there until the outbreak of World War II. Assigned to posts in Berlin and Lisbon until 1943, Kennan returned to Moscow in 1944 as "minister-counselor" and chargé d'affaires in the embassy. He held an important position under Ambassador W. Averell Harriman, yet Kennan felt frustrated. He did not believe that Washington was conscious enough of how unfit Russia was as an ally. He believed Americans cultivated mistaken hopes about the postwar peace because they had faith in the good intentions of the Soviet Union. By 1946, he was writing that Russia was expansionist, deceitful, uncompromising, warlike, and bent on disrupting American life. Some critics would later complain that Kennan ignored the role the United States played in creating such Soviet behavior.

In February, 1946, he wrote a long telegram to Washington during the absence of Ambassador Harriman. As Kennan recorded in his autobiography: "The more I thought about this message, the more it seemed to be obvious that this was 'it.' For eighteen months I had done little else but pluck people's sleeves, trying to make them understand the nature of the phenomenon with which we in the Moscow embassy were daily confronted and which our government and people had to learn to understand if they were to have any chance of coping successfully with the problems of the postwar world." Indeed, "They had asked for it. Now, by God, they would have it." Strongly antagonistic toward Russia, Kennan's telegram created a sympathetic stir in Washington, and he was brought there to lecture at the National War College and to head the new Policy Planning Staff of the Department of State. Elevated at last to a position of considerable influence, Kennan wrote the "X" article and carried his ideas beyond the State Department to the American people. The obscure Midwesterner had become the preeminent philosopher-diplomat of containment.

The containment doctrine fixed itself as the most consistent and commanding official principle of American foreign policy since World War II. But neither Truman, Kennan, nor other architects of the Cold War, were precise in their language or conceptualization in 1947. They set themselves and the containment doctrine up for various interpretations and persistent debate, especially after the Soviet-American confrontation changed, China emerged as a contending world power, and nationalist revolutions challenged international stability. Most Americans nevertheless clung tightly to containment, applying it globally. Yet they were forced by critics to defend the principle in the 1950s against calls for "disengagement," and in the 1960s against more widespread appeals for withdrawal from Vietnam.

The debate centered on a number of troubling questions. First, what was the threat to be contained? Was it an aggressive Soviet state contemplating military attack, and where? Or was it "Communism" or Communist parties eating away from within vulnerable nations? Or was the threat China and its support for wars of national liberation? Or, was it revolution? Or finally, was it a combination of these threats?

That set of questions suggested another about implementation. Were economic, military, political, or propagandistic means, for example, to be employed to contain the threat? Truman Doctrine aid to Greece and Turkey, Marshall Plan assistance to Western Europe, Radio Free Europe, and the North Atlantic Treaty Organization (NATO) demonstrated the various ways containment could be implemented. The debate largely focused on the efficacy of military vs. economic means.

Two other questions begged for clarity. First, is containment defensive or offensive? Action or reaction? Should America wait until it detected a threat and then react, or should it take preventive measures? Second, were there geographical or chronological limits to containment? Should the doctrine be applied selectively or universally? In Asia as well as in Europe? In the 1940s as well as in the 1960s?

The answers have not come easily for Americans, who immersed themselves in the confusing environment of Indochinese politics and foreign relations in the 1960s. Indeed, the debate continues, often in shrill tones, in the 1970s. By studying this debate and George F. Kennan's central place in it since 1947, we can attempt to understand the many twists and turns of the Cold War and the uncertainties of the United States in international affairs today. We can begin to determine not only what happened, and is happening, but what has gone wrong.

Part One

CONTAINMENT FORMULATED

Introduction
CONTAINMENT FORMULATED

When the British appealed in late February, 1947, for substantial aid to crush a rebellion against the British- and American-endorsed Athens regime in Greece, American officials were not unprepared for an immediate response. For the period 1945–1946, American aid flowed to Greece and American warships visited Greek (and Turkish) ports as symbols of support. In the fall of 1946, President Truman had informed the American Ambassador to Athens that Greece was an area of vital interest to the United States, and at about the same time, Secretary of State James F. Byrnes, in cutting foreign aid off from Eastern Europe, specifically mentioned Greece and Turkey as American "friends" which should be assisted. What always bothered Washington was the reactionary and corrupt character of the Athens government and its inability to defeat the Greek rebels.

Greece was in economic chaos after the war, her countryside laid waste by the German army. But the government in Athens was too corrupt, inept, and conservative to master the reconstruction problem. The Greek government remained in office largely because the British backed it with money and troops. Greek resistance fighters had organized against Germany in 1941–42, and by 1944 had control of a major part of Greece. Communists were counted among their number, and many of them advanced into leadership positions when the political aim of the resistance (EAM) turned its attention to the Athens regime and demanded long overdue social and economic improvements. Hoping to salvage something, the rebels disarmed in February, 1945, and waited to participate in a new government. They waited in vain, because the British-supported conservatives brutally attempted to repress the EAM. An election in March, 1946, returned the conservatives to power. The EAM had seemingly forfeited a last chance to act politically by boycotting the election; the insurgents took up arms again. A bloody civil war ensued, and the Greek rebels received aid from Yugoslavia. Although the Greek rebels and Communists had minimal ties to Russia, Washington, eager to understand an ugly crisis it could not control, assumed that the Greek civil war was Moscow's handiwork. As 1947 began, Americans thought that the Greek turmoil was part of a Soviet international plot of Communist expansion.

In early 1947, the Greek problem escalated. Britain could no longer muster the funds necessary to maintain troops in foreign territories, including Greece. The American Ambassador's reports became more frantic. Washington called for reform, and when some reorganization of the inefficient government resulted, American observers expressed satisfied relief. Meanwhile, Russia continued to berate Turkey verbally for refusing to establish joint control of the strategic Dardanelles to the Black Sea.

Shortly after his dramatic Truman Doctrine address to Congress on March 12, the President commented that he had wanted to announce such a far-reaching position several months earlier, but had to wait for a "fitting moment." In his speech he sounded a bell of immediate panic. But the Truman Doctrine looked beyond Greece and Turkey. As one adviser put it, the address was an "all-out" speech of simple and strong anti-Communist language. When questioned by Secretary of State George C. Marshall about that emphasis, the President replied that a vigorous statement was required in order to get the Greek-Turkish aid bill ($400 million) through Congress. So Truman spoke of "two ways of life" and advocated, without using the word, the "containment" of Communism, apparently anywhere. The anti-Communist rhetoric of crisis worked in Congress, and America intervened in the Greek civil war. The Greek rebels were routed by 1949 by a combination of American aid and the Yugoslav refusal to provide further assistance and sanctuary. Greece entered years of conservative military-oriented governments.

Historians have noted that Truman's speech is interesting not only for what it said, but for what it ignored. It was a moving address of imprecise words like "free" and facile analogies with World War II. Truman, however, did not mention the long-standing Greek rebellion growing out of legitimate grievances against a corrupt government partially manipulated by imperialist Britain. Nor did he indicate the increasing postwar American activity in the Middle and Near East as a prelude to the new intervention. He neglected to mention the traditional Russian-

Turkish squabble over the Dardanelles and Turkey's unilateral closing of the Straits to Russia during the war. Importantly for the developing Cold War, Truman gave no evidence of a Soviet presence in Greece, but nevertheless constantly suggested it. There was, of course, no evidence because Russia sent only minimal aid, if any at all, and had abandoned the Greek Communists. The President chose to deliver a speech of emotion, designed not to educate, but to arouse and excite. He did so, and thereby gave the Cold War a superficial analysis. The simple "either-or" Truman Doctrine made a complex world intelligible. At last, sighed many Americans, the United States had a defined goal in its foreign policy which would hopefully reverse the trend of international relations which had been deteriorating since 1945.

About one year before Truman delivered his "doctrine," George F. Kennan sent a long and influential telegram to Washington from Moscow. Like officials in the United States, Kennan was disturbed by what he considered to be a militant, expansionist Soviet foreign policy. His February 22, 1946, telegram stated that Russia would pay only "lip service" to international cooperation and would use Communist parties as an "underground operating directorate of world communism." Kennan further noted that Russia would seldom compromise; in fact, its foreign policy would be "negative and destructive in character, designed to tear down sources of strength beyond the reach of Soviet control." In summary, wrote Kennan, "we have here a political force committed fanatically to the belief that with [the] US there can be no permanent *modus vivendi.* . . ."

Yet Kennan closed his message with less alarmist language. He wrote that Russia would not risk major war because it was weaker than the "Western World" and had not yet concluded its domestic experiment. America could, he added, counter the Soviet Union's postwar expansion and appeal by constructive propaganda efforts at home and abroad. At the same time, "much depends on [the] health and vigor of our own society." Kennan did not spell out in the telegram the tenets of the containment doctrine he espoused in 1947, and he did not mention "force." Indeed, his emphasis seemed to be that Russia was a "political" threat. Yet the 8000-word statement could be variously interpreted, and Washington officials read it with relish and excitement, for Kennan seemed to have captured their own moods and fears. They chose to emphasize those parts of the telegram that described an alarming, contentious, and aggressive Russia which somehow had to be stopped.

Whether Kennan intended to or not, he fed exaggerated fears that an international Communist thrust, directed from Moscow, sought to subvert the world.

Secretary of the Navy James V. Forrestal was especially impressed with Kennan's long telegram and his many other informative, yet vigorous cables from Moscow. Forrestal brought Kennan to Washington and helped set him up as the head of the State Department's Policy Planning Staff in early 1947. He invited Kennan to elaborate on his ideas of Soviet behavior, and on January 31, 1947, Kennan submitted to the Secretary a paper titled "Psychological Background of Soviet Foreign Policy." It was this paper which became the famous "X" article in the July, 1947, issue of *Foreign Affairs.* The editor of this Council on Foreign Relations magazine had asked Kennan for an article, Kennan successfully requested the State Department to give the piece a security clearance, and the author became anonymously Mr. "X."

Appearing as it did shortly after the launching of the Truman Doctrine (although written and widely circulated in the government before it), the "X" article was interpreted as government policy, especially after the *New York Times* reported that the author of the essay was none other than the director of the Policy Planning Staff. Aid to Greece and Turkey seemed to many to be the practical application of the theoretical formulation of containment in Kennan's article. In the 1950s and 1960s, especially in his *Memoirs, 1925–1950* (1967), Kennan argued that he had profound reservations about the Truman Doctrine's universal language and military aid. Yet in 1947 Kennan did not publicly divorce himself from Truman's Cold War offensive. He helped feed the American belief that the United States held the requisite power to challenge an unbending Russia, and he helped stimulate American alarm and later hysteria. Importantly, it was not Kennan, but other less reflective leaders, who would implement containment after 1947. Kennan and his "Sources of Soviet Conduct" became a foundation of American Cold War diplomacy—willingly or not. Combined with the Truman Doctrine, the "X" article helped set the mood, philosophy, and direction of American foreign policy.

The Truman Doctrine
HARRY S. TRUMAN

The gravity of the situation which confronts the world today necessitates my appearance before a joint session of the Congress.

The foreign policy and the national security of this country are involved.

One aspect of the present situation, which I present to you at this time for your consideration and decision, concerns Greece and Turkey.

The United States has received from the Greek Government an urgent appeal for financial and economic assistance. Preliminary reports from the American Economic Mission now in Greece and reports from the American Ambassador in Greece corroborate the statement of the Greek Government that assistance is imperative if Greece is to survive as a free nation.

I do not believe that the American people and the Congress wish to turn a deaf ear to the appeal of the Greek Government.

Greece is not a rich country. Lack of sufficient natural resources has always forced the Greek people to work hard to make both ends meet. Since 1940, this industrious, peace loving country has suffered invasion, four years of cruel enemy occupation, and bitter internal strife.

When forces of liberation entered Greece they found that the retreating Germans had destroyed virtually all the railways, roads, port facilities, communications, and merchant marine. More than a thousand villages had been burned. Eighty-five percent of the children were tubercular. Livestock, poultry, and draft animals had almost disappeared. Inflation had wiped out practically all savings.

As a result of these tragic conditions, a militant minority, exploiting

Public Papers of the Presidents of the United States: Harry S. Truman, 1947. Washington: Government Printing Office, 1953, pp. 176-180.

human want and misery, was able to create political chaos which, until now, has made economic recovery impossible.

Greece is today without funds to finance the importation of those goods which are essential to bare subsistence. Under these circumstances the people of Greece cannot make progress in solving their problems of reconstruction. Greece is in desperate need of financial and economic assistance to enable it to resume purchases of food, clothing, fuel and seeds. These are indispensable for the subsistence of its people and are obtainable only from abroad. Greece must have help to import the goods necessary to restore internal order and security so essential for economic and political recovery.

The Greek Government has also asked for the assistance of experienced American administrators, economists and technicians to insure that the financial and other aid given to Greece shall be used effectively in creating a stable and self-sustaining economy and in improving its public administration.

The very existence of the Greek state is today threatened by the terrorist activities of several thousand armed men, led by Communists, who defy the government's authority at a number of points, particularly along the northern boundaries. A Commission appointed by the United Nations Security Council is at present investigating disturbed conditions in northern Greece and alleged border violations along the frontier between Greece on the one hand and Albania, Bulgaria, and Yugoslavia on the other.

Meanwhile, the Greek Government is unable to cope with the situation. The Greek army is small and poorly equipped. It needs supplies and equipment if it is to restore authority to the government throughout Greek territory.

Greece must have assistance if it is to become a self-supporting and self-respecting democracy.

The United States must supply this assistance. We have already extended to Greece certain types of relief and economic aid but these are inadequate.

There is no other country to which democratic Greece can turn.

No other nation is willing and able to provide the necessary support for a democratic Greek government.

The British Government, which has been helping Greece, can give no further financial or economic aid after March 31. Great Britain finds itself under the necessity of reducing or liquidating its commitments in several parts of the world, including Greece.

We have considered how the United Nations might assist in this crisis. But the situation is an urgent one requiring immediate action, and the United Nations and its related organizations are not in a position to extend help of the kind that is required.

It is important to note that the Greek Government has asked for our aid in utilizing effectively the financial and other assistance we may give to Greece, and in improving its public administration. It is of the utmost importance that we supervise the use of any funds made available to Greece, in such a manner that each dollar spent will count toward making Greece self-supporting, and will help to build an economy in which a healthy democracy can flourish.

No government is perfect. One of the chief virtues of a democracy, however, is that its defects are always visible and under democratic processes can be pointed out and corrected. The government of Greece is not perfect. Nevertheless it represents 85 percent of the members of the Greek Parliament who were chosen in an election last year. Foreign observers, including 692 Americans, considered this election to be a fair expression of the views of the Greek people.

The Greek Government has been operating in an atmosphere of chaos and extremism. It has made mistakes. The extension of aid by this country does not mean that the United States condones everything that the Greek Government has done or will do. We have condemned in the past, and we condemn now, extremist measures of the right or the left. We have in the past advised tolerance, and we advise tolerance now.

Greece's neighbor, Turkey, also deserves our attention.

The future of Turkey as an independent and economically sound state is clearly no less important to the freedom-loving peoples of the world than the future of Greece. The circumstances in which Turkey finds itself today are considerably different from those of Greece. Turkey has been spared the disasters that have beset Greece. And during the war, the United States and Great Britain furnished Turkey with material aid.

Nevertheless, Turkey now needs our support.

Since the war Turkey has sought additional financial assistance from Great Britain and the United States for the purpose of effecting that modernization necessary for the maintenance of its national integrity.

That integrity is essential to the preservation of order in the Middle East.

The British Government has informed us that, owing to its own difficulties, it can no longer extend financial or economic aid to Turkey.

As in the case of Greece, if Turkey is to have the assistance it needs, the United States must supply it. We are the only country able to provide that help.

I am aware of the broad implications involved if the United States extends assistance to Greece and Turkey, and I shall discuss these implications with you at this time.

One of the primary objectives of the foreign policy of the United States is the creation of conditions in which we and other nations will be able to work out a way of life free from coercion. This was a fundamental issue in the war with Germany and Japan. Our victory was won over countries which sought to impose their will, and their way of life, upon other nations.

To ensure the peaceful development of nations, free from coercion, the United States has taken a leading part in establishing the United Nations. The United Nations is designed to make possible lasting freedom and independence for all its members. We shall not realize our objectives, however, unless we are willing to help free peoples to maintain their free institutions and their national integrity against aggressive movements that seek to impose upon them totalitarian regimes. This is no more than a frank recognition that totalitarian regimes imposed upon free peoples, by direct or indirect aggression, undermine the foundations of international peace and hence the security of the United States.

The peoples of a number of countries of the world have recently had totalitarian regimes forced upon them against their will. The Government of the United States has made frequent protests against coercion and intimidation, in violation of the Yalta agreement, in Poland, Rumania, and Bulgaria. I must also state that in a number of other countries there have been similar developments.

At the present moment in world history nearly every nation must choose between alternative ways of life. The choice is too often not a free one.

One way of life is based upon the will of the majority, and is distinguished by free institutions, representative government, free elections, guarantees of individual liberty, freedom of speech and religion, and freedom from political oppression.

The second way of life is based upon the will of a minority forcibly imposed upon the majority. It relies upon terror and oppression, a controlled press and radio, fixed elections, and the suppression of personal freedoms.

I believe that it must be the policy of the United States to support free peoples who are resisting attempted subjugation by armed minorities or by outside pressures.

I believe that we must assist free peoples to work out their own destinies in their own way.

I believe that our help should be primarily through economic and financial aid which is essential to economic stability and orderly political processes.

The world is not static, and the *status quo* is not sacred. But we cannot allow changes in the *status quo* in violation of the Charter of the United Nations by such methods as coercion, or by such subterfuges as political infiltration. In helping free and independent nations to maintain their freedom, the United States will be giving effect to the principles of the Charter of the United Nations.

It is necessary only to glance at a map to realize that the survival and integrity of the Greek nation are of grave importance in a much wider situation. If Greece should fall under the control of an armed minority, the effect upon its neighbor, Turkey, would be immediate and serious. Confusion and disorder might well spread throughout the entire Middle East.

Moreover, the disappearance of Greece as an independent state would have a profound effect upon those countries in Europe whose peoples are struggling against great difficulties to maintain their freedoms and their independence while they repair the damages of war.

It would be an unspeakable tragedy if these countries, which have struggled so long against overwhelming odds, should lose that victory for which they sacrificed so much. Collapse of free institutions and loss of independence would be disastrous not only for them but for the world. Discouragement and possibly failure would quickly be the lot of neighboring peoples striving to maintain their freedom and independence.

Should we fail to aid Greece and Turkey in this fateful hour, the effect will be far reaching to the West as well as to the East.

We must take immediate and resolute action.

I therefore ask the Congress to provide authority for assistance to Greece and Turkey in the amount of $400,000,000 for the period ending June 30, 1948. In requesting these funds, I have taken into consideration the maximum amount of relief assistance which would be furnished to Greece and Turkey out of the $350,000,000 which I recently requested that the Congress authorize for the prevention of starvation and suffering in countries devasted by the war.

In addition to funds, I ask the Congress to authorize the detail of

American civilian and military personnel to Greece and Turkey, at the request of those countries, to assist in the tasks of reconstruction, and for the purpose of supervising the use of such financial and material assistance as may be furnished. I recommend that authority also be provided for the instruction and training of selected Greek and Turkish personnel.

Finally, I ask that the Congress provide authority which will permit the speediest and most effective use, in terms of needed commodities, supplies, and equipment, of such funds as may be authorized.

If further funds, or further authority, should be needed for the purposes indicated in this message, I shall not hesitate to bring the situation before Congress. On this subject the Executive and Legislative branches of the Government must work together.

This is a serious course upon which we embark.

I would not recommend it except that the alternative is much more serious.

The United States contributed $341,000,000,000 toward winning World War II. This is an investment in world freedom and world peace.

The assistance that I am recommending for Greece and Turkey amounts to little more than 1/10 of 1 percent of this investment. It is only common sense that we should safeguard this investment and make sure that it was not in vain.

The seeds of totalitarian regimes are nurtured by misery and want. They spread and grow in the evil soil of poverty and strife. They reach their full growth when the hope of a people for a better life has died.

We must keep that hope alive.

The free peoples of the world look to us for support in maintaining their freedoms.

If we falter in our leadership, we may endanger the peace of the world—and we shall surely endanger the welfare of this Nation.

Great responsibilities have been placed upon us by the swift movement of events.

I am confident that the Congress will face these responsibilities squarely.

2

Firm Containment
and Unalterable Counter-Force

GEORGE F. KENNAN

The political personality of Soviet power as we know it today is the product of ideology and circumstances: ideology inherited by the present Soviet leaders from the movement in which they had their political origin, and circumstances of the power which they now have exercised for nearly three decades in Russia. There can be few tasks of psychological analysis more difficult than to try to trace the interaction of these two forces and the relative rôle of each in the determination of official Soviet conduct. Yet the attempt must be made if that conduct is to be understood and effectively countered.

It is difficult to summarize the set of ideological concepts with which the Soviet leaders came into power. Marxian ideology, in its Russian-Communist projection, has always been in process of subtle evolution. The materials on which it bases itself are extensive and complex. But the outstanding features of Communist thought as it existed in 1916 may perhaps be summarized as follows: (a) that the central factor in the life of man, the factor which determines the character of public life and the "physiognomy of society," is the system by which material goods are produced and exchanged; (b) that the capitalist system of production is a nefarious one which inevitably leads to the exploitation of the working class by the capital-owning class and is incapable of developing adequately the economic resources of society or of distributing fairly the material goods produced by human labor; (c) that capitalism contains the seeds of its own destruction and must, in view of the inability of the capital-owning class to adjust itself to economic change, result eventually and inescapably in a revolutionary transfer of power to the working class; and (d) that imperialism, the final phase of capitalism, leads directly to war and revolution.

"X" (George F. Kennan), "The Sources of Soviet Conduct," *Foreign Affairs,* XXV (July 1947), 566-582. Reprinted by permission from *Foreign Affairs.* Copyright © by Council on Foreign Relations, Inc., New York.

The rest may be outlined in Lenin's own words: "Unevenness of economic and political development is the inflexible law of capitalism. It follows from this that the victory of Socialism may come originally in a few capitalist countries or even in a single capitalist country. The victorious proletariat of that country, having expropriated the capitalists and having organized Socialist production at home, would rise against the remaining capitalist world, drawing to itself in the process the oppressed classes of other countries."[1] It must be noted that there was no assumption that capitalism would perish without proletarian revolution. A final push was needed from a revolutionary proletariat movement in order to tip over the tottering structure. But it was regarded as inevitable that sooner or later that push be given.

For 50 years prior to the outbreak of the Revolution, this pattern of thought had exercised great fascination for the members of the Russian revolutionary movement. Frustrated, discontented, hopeless of finding self-expression—or too impatient to seek it—in the confining limits of the Tsarist political system, yet lacking wide popular support for their choice of bloody revolution as a means of social betterment, these revolutionists found in Marxist theory a highly convenient rationalization for their own instinctive desires. It afforded pseudo-scientific justification for their impatience, for their categoric denial of all value in the Tsarist system, for their yearning for power and revenge and for their inclination to cut corners in the pursuit of it. It is therefore no wonder that they had come to believe implicitly in the truth and soundness of the Marxian-Leninist teachings, so congenial to their own impulses and emotions. Their sincerity need not be impugned. This is a phenomenon as old as human nature itself. It has never been more aptly described than by Edward Gibbon, who wrote in "The Decline and Fall of the Roman Empire": "From enthusiasm to imposture the step is perilous and slippery; the demon of Socrates affords a memorable instance how a wise man may deceive himself, how a good man may deceive others, how the conscience may slumber in a mixed and middle state between self-illusion and voluntary fraud." And it was with this set of conceptions that the members of the Bolshevik Party entered into power.

Now it must be noted that through all the years of preparation for revolution, the attention of these men, as indeed of Marx himself, had been centered less on the future form which Socialism[2] would take than on the necessary overthrow of rival power which, in their view, had to precede the introduction of Socialism. Their views, therefore, on the positive program to be put into effect, once power was attained, were for

the most part nebulous, visionary and impractical. Beyond the nationali-
zation of industry and the expropriation of large private capital holdings
there was no agreed program. The treatment of the peasantry, which
according to the Marxist formulation was not of the proletariat, had
always been a vague spot in the pattern of Communist thought; and it
remained an object of controversy and vacillation for the first ten years
of Communist power.

The circumstances of the immediate post-revolution period—the
existence in Russia of civil war and foreign intervention, together with
the obvious fact that the Communists represented only a tiny minority
of the Russian people—made the establishment of dictatorial power a
necessity. The experiment with "war Communism" and the abrupt attempt to eliminate private production and trade had unfortunate economic consequences and caused further bitterness against the new
revolutionary régime. While the temporary relaxation of the effort to
communize Russia, represented by the New Economic Policy, alleviated
some of this economic distress and thereby served its purpose, it also
made it evident that the "capitalistic sector of society" was still prepared
to profit at once from any relaxation of governmental pressure, and
would, if permitted to continue to exist, always constitute a powerful
opposing element to the Soviet régime and a serious rival for influence
in the country. Somewhat the same situation prevailed with respect to
the individual peasant who, in his own small way, was also a private
producer.

Lenin, had he lived, might have proved a great enough man to
reconcile these conflicting forces to the ultimate benefit of Russian society, though this is questionable. But be that as it may, Stalin, and those
whom he led in the struggle for succession to Lenin's position of leadership, were not the men to tolerate rival political forces in the sphere of
power which they coveted. Their sense of insecurity was too great. Their
particular brand of fanaticism, unmodified by any of the Anglo-Saxon
traditions of compromise, was too fierce and too jealous to envisage any
permanent sharing of power. From the Russian-Asiatic world out of
which they had emerged they carried with them a skepticism as to the
possibilities of permanent and peaceful coexistence of rival forces. Easily
persuaded of their own doctrinaire "rightness," they insisted on the
submission or destruction of all competing power. Outside of the Communist Party, Russian society was to have no rigidity. There were to be
no forms of collective human activity or association which would not be
dominated by the Party. No other force in Russian society was to be

permitted to achieve vitality or integrity. Only the Party was to have structure. All else was to be an amorphous mass.

And within the Party the same principle was to apply. The mass of Party members might go through the motions of election, deliberation, decision and action; but in these motions they were to be animated not by their own individual wills but by the awesome breath of the Party leadership and the overbrooding presence of "the word."

Let it be stressed again that subjectively these men probably did not seek absolutism for its own sake. They doubtless believed—and found it easy to believe—that they alone knew what was good for society and that they would accomplish that good once their power was secure and unchallengeable. But in seeking that security of their own rule they were prepared to recognize no restrictions, either of God or man, on the character of their methods. And until such time as that security might be achieved, they placed far down on their scale of operational priorities the comforts and happiness of the people entrusted to their care.

Now the outstanding circumstance concerning the Soviet régime is that down to the present day this process of political consolidation has never been completed and the men in the Kremlin have continued to be predominantly absorbed with the struggle to secure and make absolute the power which they seized in November 1917. They have endeavored to secure it primarily against forces at home, within Soviet society itself. But they have also endeavored to secure it against the outside world. For ideology, as we have seen, taught them that the outside world was hostile and that it was their duty eventually to overthrow the political forces beyond their borders. The powerful hands of Russian history and tradition reached up to sustain them in this feeling. Finally, their own aggressive intransigence with respect to the outside world began to find its own reaction; and they were soon forced, to use another Gibbonesque phrase, "to chastise the contumacy" which they themselves had provoked. It is an undeniable privilege of every man to prove himself right in the thesis that the world is his enemy; for if he reiterates it frequently enough and makes it the background of his conduct he is bound eventually to be right.

Now it lies in the nature of the mental world of the Soviet leaders, as well as in the character of their ideology, that no opposition to them can be officially recognized as having any merit or justification whatsoever. Such opposition can flow, in theory, only from the hostile and incorrigible forces of dying capitalism. As long as remnants of capitalism were officially recognized as existing in Russia, it was possible to place on them, as an internal element, part of the blame for the maintenance of a dictatorial form of society. But as these remnants were liquidated, little by little, this justification fell away; and when it was indicated officially that they had been finally destroyed, it disappeared altogether. And this fact created one of the most basic of the compulsions which came to act upon the Soviet régime: since capitalism no longer existed in Russia and since it could not be admitted that there could be serious or widespread opposition to the Kremlin springing spontaneously from the liberated masses under its authority, it became necessary to justify the retention of the dictatorship by stressing the menace of capitalism abroad.

This began at an early date. In 1924 Stalin specifically defended the retention of the "organs of suppression," meaning, among others, the army and the secret police, on the ground that "as long as there is a capitalist encirclement there will be danger of intervention with all the consequences that flow from that danger." In accordance with that theory, and from that time on, all internal opposition forces in Russia have consistently been portrayed as the agents of foreign forces of reaction antagonistic to Soviet power.

By the same token, tremendous emphasis has been placed on the original Communist thesis of a basic antagonism between the capitalist and Socialist worlds. It is clear, from many indications, that this emphasis is not founded in reality. The real facts concerning it have been confused by the existence abroad of genuine resentment provoked by Soviet philosophy and tactics and occasionally by the existence of great centers of military power, notably the Nazi régime in Germany and the Japanese Government of the late 1930's, which did indeed have aggressive designs against the Soviet Union. But there is ample evidence that the stress laid in Moscow on the menace confronting Soviet society from the world outside its borders is founded not in the realities of foreign antagonism but in the necessity of explaining away the maintenance of dictatorial authority at home.

Now the maintenance of this pattern of Soviet power, namely, the pursuit of unlimited authority domestically, accompanied by the cultivation of the semi-myth of implacable foreign hostility, has gone far to shape the actual machinery of Soviet power as we know it today. Internal organs of administration which did not serve this purpose withered on the vine. Organs which did serve this purpose became vastly swollen. The security of Soviet power came to rest on the iron discipline of the Party, on the severity and ubiquity of the secret police, and on the uncompromising economic monopolism of the state. The "organs of suppression," in which the Soviet leaders had sought security from rival forces, became in large measure the masters of those whom they were designed to serve. Today the major part of the structure of Soviet power is committed to the perfection of the dictatorship and to the maintenance of the concept of Russia as in a state of siege, with the enemy lowering beyond the walls. And the millions of human beings who form that part of the structure of power must defend at all costs this concept of Russia's position, for without it they are themselves superfluous.

As things stand today, the rulers can no longer dream of parting with these organs of suppression. The quest for absolute power, pursued now for nearly three decades with a ruthlessness unparalleled (in scope at least) in modern times, has again produced internally, as it did externally, its own reaction. The excesses of the police apparatus have fanned the potential opposition to the régime into something far greater and more dangerous than it could have been before those excesses began.

But least of all can the rulers dispense with the fiction by which the maintenance of dictatorial power has been defended. For this fiction has been canonized in Soviet philosophy by the excesses already committed in its name; and it is now anchored in the Soviet structure of thought by bonds far greater than those of mere ideology.

So much for the historical background. What does it spell in terms of the political personality of Soviet power as we know it today?

Of the original ideology, nothing has been officially junked. Belief is maintained in the basic badness of capitalism, in the inevitability of its destruction, in the obligation of the proletariat to assist in that destruction and to take power into its own hands. But stress has come to be laid primarily on those concepts which relate most specifically to the Soviet régime itself: to its position as the sole truly Socialist régime in a dark and misguided world, and to the relationships of power within it.

The first of these concepts is that of the innate antagonism between capitalism and Socialism. We have seen how deeply that concept has become imbedded in foundations of Soviet power. It has profound implications for Russia's conduct as a member of international society. It means that there can never be on Moscow's side any sincere assumption of a community of aims between the Soviet Union and powers which are regarded as capitalist. It must invariably be assumed in Moscow that the aims of the capitalist world are antagonistic to the Soviet régime, and therefore to the interests of the peoples it controls. If the Soviet Government occasionally sets its signature to documents which would indicate the contrary, this is to be regarded as a tactical manoeuvre permissible in dealing with the enemy (who is without honor) and should be taken in the spirit of *caveat emptor.* Basically, the antagonism remains. It is postulated. And from it flow many of the phenomena which we find disturbing in the Kremlin's conduct of foreign policy: the secretiveness, the lack of frankness, the duplicity, the wary suspiciousness, and the basic unfriendliness of purpose. These phenomena are there to stay, for the foreseeable future. There can be variations of degree and of emphasis. When there is something the Russians want from us, one or the other of these features of their policy may be thrust temporarily into the background; and when that happens there will always be Americans who will leap forward with gleeful announcements that "the Russians have changed," and some who will even try to take credit for having brought about such "changes." But we should not be misled by tactical manoeuvres. These characteristics of Soviet policy, like the postulate from which they flow, are basic to the internal nature of Soviet power, and will be with us, whether in the foreground or the background, until the internal nature of Soviet power is changed.

This means that we are going to continue for a long time to find the Russians difficult to deal with. It does not mean that they should be considered as embarked upon a do-or-die program to overthrow our society by a given date. The theory of the inevitability of the eventual fall of capitalism has the fortunate connotation that there is no hurry about it. The forces of progress can take their time in preparing the final *coup de grâce.* Meanwhile, what is vital is that the "Socialist fatherland"— that oasis of power which has been already won for Socialism in the person of the Soviet Union—should be cherished and defended by all good Communists at home and abroad, its fortunes promoted, its enemies badgered and confounded. The promotion of premature, "adventuristic" revolutionary projects abroad which might embarrass Soviet power in any way would be an inexcusable, even a counter-revolutionary act. The cause of Socialism is the support and promotion of Soviet power, as defined in Moscow.

This brings us to the second of the concepts important to contemporary Soviet outlook. That is the infallibility of the Kremlin. The Soviet concept of power, which permits no focal points of organization outside the Party itself, requires that the Party leadership remain in theory the sole repository of truth. For if truth were to be found elsewhere, there would be justification for its expression in organized activity. But it is precisely that which the Kremlin cannot and will not permit.

The leadership of the Communist Party is therefore always right, and has been always right ever since in 1929 Stalin formalized his personal power by announcing that decisions of the Politburo were being taken unanimously.

On the principle of infallibility there rests the iron discipline of the Communist Party. In fact, the two concepts are mutually self-supporting. Perfect discipline requires recognition of infallibility. Infallibility requires the observance of discipline. And the two together go far to determine the behaviorism of the entire Soviet apparatus of power. But their effect cannot be understood unless a third factor be taken into account: namely the fact that the leadership is at liberty to put forward for tactical purposes any particular thesis which it finds useful to the cause at any particular moment and to require the faithful and unquestioning acceptance of that thesis by the members of the movement as a whole. This means that truth is not a constant but is actually created, for all intents and purposes, by the Soviet leaders themselves. It may vary from week to week, from month to month. It is nothing absolute and immutable—nothing which flows from objective reality. It is only the most recent manifestation of the wisdom of those in whom the ultimate wisdom is supposed to reside, because they represent the logic of history. The accumulative effect of these factors is to give to the whole subordinate apparatus of Soviet power an unshakeable stubbornness and steadfastness in its orientation. This orientation can be changed at will by the Kremlin but by no other power. Once a given party line has been laid down on a given issue of current policy, the whole Soviet governmental machine, including the mechanism of diplomacy, moves inexorably along the prescribed path, like a persistent toy automobile wound up and headed in a given direction, stopping only when it meets with some unanswerable force. The individuals who are the components of this machine are unamenable to argument or reason which comes to them from outside sources. Their whole training has taught them to mistrust and discount the glib persuasiveness of the outside world. Like the white dog before the phonograph, they hear only the "master's voice." And if they are to be called off from the purposes last dictated to them, it is the master who must call them off. Thus the foreign representative cannot hope that his words will make any impression on them. The most that he can hope is that they will be transmitted to those at the top, who are capable of changing the party line. But even those are not likely to be swayed by any normal logic in the words of the bourgeois representative. Since there can be no appeal to common purposes, there can be no appeal to common mental approaches. For this reason, facts speak louder than words to the ears of the Kremlin; and words carry the greatest weight when they have the ring of reflecting, or being backed up by, facts of unchallengeable validity.

But we have seen that the Kremlin is under no ideological compulsion to accomplish its purposes in a hurry. Like the Church, it is dealing in ideological concepts which are of long-term validity, and it can afford to be patient. It has no right to risk the existing achievements of the revolution for the sake of vain baubles of the future. The very teachings of Lenin himself require great caution and flexibility in the pursuit of Communist purposes. Again, these precepts are fortified by the lessons of Russian history: of centuries of obscure battles between nomadic forces over the stretches of a vast unfortified plain. Here caution, circumspection, flexibility and deception are the valuable qualities; and their value finds natural appreciation in the Russian or the oriental mind. Thus the Kremlin has no compunction about retreating in the face of superior force. And being under the compulsion of no timetable, it does not get panicky under the necessity for such retreat. Its political action is a fluid stream which moves constantly, wherever it is permitted to move, toward a given goal. Its main concern is to make sure that it has filled every nook and cranny available to it in the basin of world power. But if it finds unassailable barriers in its path, it accepts these philosophically and accommodates itself to them. The main thing is that there should always be pressure, unceasing constant pressure, toward the desired goal. There is no trace of any feeling in Soviet psychology that that goal must be reached at any given time.

These considerations make Soviet diplomacy at once easier and more difficult to deal with than the diplomacy of individual aggressive leaders like Napoleon and Hitler. On the one hand it is more sensitive to contrary force, more ready to yield on individual sectors of the diplomatic front when that force is felt to be too strong, and thus more rational in the logic and rhetoric of power. On the other hand it cannot be easily defeated or discouraged by a single victory on the part of its opponents. And the patient persistence by which it is animated means that it can be effectively countered not by sporadic acts which represent the momentary whims of democratic opinion but only by intelligent long-range policies on the part of Russia's adversaries—policies no less steady in their purpose, and no less variegated and resourceful in their application, than those of the Soviet Union itself.

In these circumstances it is clear that the main element of any United States policy toward the Soviet Union must be that of a long-term, patient but firm and vigilant containment of Russian expansive tendencies. It is important to note, however, that such a policy has nothing to do with outward histrionics: with threats or blustering or superfluous gestures of outward "toughness." While the Kremlin is basically flexible in its reaction to political realities, it is by no means unamenable to considerations of prestige. Like almost any other government, it can be placed by tactless and threatening gestures in a position where it cannot afford to yield even though this might be dictated by its sense of realism. The Russian leaders are keen judges of human psychology, and as such they are highly conscious that loss of temper and of self-control is never a source of strength in political affairs. They are quick to exploit such evidences of weakness. For these reasons, it is a *sine qua non* of successful dealing with Russia that the foreign government in question should remain at all times cool and collected and that its demands on Russian policy should be put forward in such a manner as to leave the way open for a compliance not too detrimental to Russian prestige.

In the light of the above, it will be clearly seen that the Soviet pressure against the free institutions of the western world is something that can be contained by the adroit and vigilant application of counter-force at a series of constantly shifting geographical and political points, corresponding to the shifts and manoeuvres of Soviet policy, but which cannot be charmed or talked out of existence. The Russians look forward to a duel of infinite duration, and they see that already they have scored great successes. It must be borne in mind that there was a time when the Communist Party represented far more of a minority in the sphere of Russian national life than Soviet power today represents in the World community.

But if ideology convinces the rulers of Russia that truth is on their side and that they can therefore afford to wait, those of us on whom that ideology has no claim are free to examine objectively the validity of that premise. The Soviet thesis not only implies complete lack of control by the west over its own economic destiny, it likewise assumes Russian unity, discipline and patience over an infinite period. Let us bring this apocalyptic vision down to earth, and suppose that the western world finds the strength and resourcefulness to contain Soviet power over a period of ten to fifteen years. What does that spell for Russia itself?

The Soviet leaders, taking advantage of the contributions of modern technique to the arts of despotism, have solved the question of obedience within the confines of their power. Few challenge their authority; and even those who do are unable to make that challenge valid as against the organs of suppression of the state.

The Kremlin has also proved able to accomplish its purpose of building up in Russia, regardless of the interests of the inhabitants, an industrial foundation of heavy metallurgy, which is, to be sure, not yet complete but which is nevertheless continuing to grow and is approaching those of the other major industrial countries. All of this, however, both the maintenance of internal political security and the building of heavy industry, has been carried out at a terrible cost in human life and in human hopes and energies. It has necessitated the use of forced labor on a scale unprecedented in modern times under conditions of peace. It has involved the neglect or abuse of other phases of Soviet economic life, particularly agriculture, consumers' goods production, housing and transportation.

To all that, the war has added its tremendous toll of destruction, death and human exhaustion. In consequence of this, we have in Russia today a population which is physically and spiritually tired. The mass of the people are disillusioned, skeptical and no longer as accessible as they once were to the magical attraction which Soviet power still radiates to its followers abroad. The avidity with which people seized upon the slight respite accorded to the Church for tactical reasons during the war was eloquent testimony to the fact that their capacity for faith and devotion found little expression in the purposes of the régime.

In these circumstances, there are limits to the physical and nervous strength of people themselves. These limits are absolute ones, and are binding even for the cruelest dictatorship, because beyond them people cannot be driven. The forced labor camps and the other agencies of constraint provide temporary means of compelling people to work longer hours than their own volition or mere economic pressure would dictate; but if people survive them at all they become old before their time and must be considered as human casualties to the demands of dictatorship. In either case their best powers are no longer available to society and can no longer be enlisted in the service of the state.

Here only the younger generation can help. The younger generation, despite all vicissitudes and sufferings, is numerous and vigorous;

and the Russians are a talented people. But it still remains to be seen what will be the effects on mature performance of the abnormal emotional strains of childhood which Soviet dictatorship created and which were enormously increased by the war. Such things as normal security and placidity of home environment have practically ceased to exist in the Soviet Union outside of the most remote farms and villages. And observers are not yet sure whether that is not going to leave its mark on the over-all capacity of the generation now coming into maturity.

In addition to this, we have the fact that Soviet economic development, while it can list certain formidable achievements, has been precariously spotty and uneven. Russian Communists who speak of the "uneven development of capitalism" should blush at the contemplation of their own national economy. Here certain branches of economic life, such as the metallurgical and machine industries, have been pushed out of all proportion to other sectors of economy. Here is a nation striving to become in a short period one of the great industrial nations of the world while it still has no highway network worthy of the name and only a relatively primitive network of railways. Much has been done to increase efficiency of labor and to teach primitive peasants something about the operation of machines. But maintenance is still a crying deficiency of all Soviet economy. Construction is hasty and poor in quality. Depreciation must be enormous. And in vast sectors of economic life it has not yet been possible to instill into labor anything like that general culture of production and technical self-respect which characterizes the skilled worker of the west.

It is difficult to see how these deficiencies can be corrected at an early date by a tired and dispirited population working largely under the shadow of fear and compulsion. And as long as they are not overcome, Russia will remain economically a vulnerable, and in a certain sense an impotent, nation, capable of exporting its enthusiasms and of radiating the strange charm of its primitive political vitality but unable to back up those articles of export by the real evidences of material power and prosperity.

Meanwhile, a great uncertainty hangs over the political life of the Soviet Union. That is the uncertainty involved in the transfer of power from one individual or group of individuals to others.

This is, of course, outstandingly the problem of the personal position of Stalin. We must remember that his succession to Lenin's pinnacle of preëminence in the Communist movement was the only such transfer of individual authority which the Soviet Union has experienced. That transfer took 12 years to consolidate. It cost the lives of millions of people and shook the state to its foundations. The attendant tremors were felt all through the international revolutionary movement, to the disadvantage of the Kremlin itself.

It is always possible that another transfer of preëminent power may take place quietly and inconspicuously, with no repercussions anywhere. But again, it is possible that the questions involved may unleash, to use some of Lenin's words, one of those "incredibly swift transitions" from "delicate deceit" to "wild violence" which characterize Russian history, and may shake Soviet power to its foundations.

But this is not only a question of Stalin himself. There has been, since 1938, a dangerous congealment of political life in the higher circles of Soviet power. The All-Union Congress of Soviets, in theory the supreme body of the Party, is supposed to meet not less often than once in three years. It will soon be eight full years since its last meeting. During this period membership in the Party has numerically doubled. Party mortality during the war was enormous; and today well over half of the Party members are persons who have entered since the last Party congress was held. Meanwhile, the same small group of men has carried on at the top through an amazing series of national vicissitudes. Surely there is some reason why the experiences of the war brought basic political changes to every one of the great governments of the west. Surely the causes of that phenomenon are basic enough to be present somewhere in the obscurity of Soviet political life, as well. And yet no recognition has been given to these causes in Russia.

It must be surmised from this that even within so highly disciplined an organization as the Communist Party there must be a growing divergence in age, outlook and interest between the great mass of Party members, only so recently recruited into the movement, and the little self-perpetuating clique of men at the top, whom most of these Party members have never met, with whom they have never conversed, and with whom they can have no political intimacy.

Who can say whether, in these circumstances, the eventual rejuvenation of the higher spheres of authority (which can only be a matter of time) can take place smoothly and peacefully, or whether rivals in the quest for higher power will not eventually reach down into these politicially immature and inexperienced masses in order to find support for their respective claims? If this were ever to happen, strange consequences could flow for the Communist Party: for the membership at large has been exercised only in the practices of iron discipline and obedience and not in the arts of compromise and accommodation. And if disunity were ever to seize and paralyze the Party, the chaos and weakness of Russian society would be revealed in forms beyond description. For we have seen that Soviet power is only a crust concealing an amorphous mass of human beings among whom no independent organizational structure is tolerated. In Russia there is not even such a thing as local government. The present generation of Russians have never known spontaneity of collective action. If, consequently, anything were ever to occur to disrupt the unity and efficacy of the Party as a political instrument, Soviet Russia might be changed overnight from one of the strongest to one of the weakest and most pitiable of national societies.

Thus the future of Soviet power may not be by any means as secure as Russian capacity for self-delusion would make it appear to the men in the Kremlin. That they can keep power themselves, they have demonstrated. That they can quietly and easily turn it over to others remains to be proved. Meanwhile, the hardships of their rule and the vicissitudes of international life have taken a heavy toll of the strength and hopes of the great people on whom their power rests. It is curious to note that the ideological power of Soviet authority is strongest today in areas beyond the frontiers of Russia, beyond the reach of its police power. This phenomenon brings to mind a comparison used by Thomas Mann in his novel "Buddenbrooks." Observing that human institutions often show the greatest outward brilliance at a moment when inner decay is in reality farthest advanced, he compared the Buddenbrook family, in the days of its greatest glamour, to one of those stars whose light shines most brightly on this world when in reality it has long since ceased to exist. And who can say with assurance that the strong light still cast by the Kremlin on the dissatisfied peoples of the western world is not the powerful afterglow of a constellation which is in actuality on the wane? This cannot be proved. And it cannot be disproved. But the possibility remains (and in the opinion of this writer it is a strong one) that Soviet power, like the capitalist world of its conception, bears within it the seeds of its own decay, and that the sprouting of these seeds is well advanced.

It is clear that the United States cannot expect in the foreseeable future to enjoy political intimacy with the Soviet régime. It must continue to regard the Soviet Union as a rival, not a partner, in the political arena. It must continue to expect that Soviet policies will reflect no abstract love of peace and stability, no real faith in the possibility of a permanent happy coexistence of the Socialist and capitalist worlds, but rather a cautious, persistent pressure toward the disruption and weakening of all rival influence and rival power.

Balanced against this are the facts that Russia, as opposed to the western world in general, is still by far the weaker party, that Soviet policy is highly flexible, and that Soviet society may well contain deficiencies which will eventually weaken its own total potential. This would of itself warrant the United States entering with reasonable confidence upon a policy of firm containment, designed to confront the Russians with unalterable counter-force at every point where they show signs of encroaching upon the interests of a peaceful and stable world.

But in actuality the possibilities for American policy are by no means limited to holding the line and hoping for the best. It is entirely possible for the United States to influence by its actions the internal developments, both within Russia and throughout the international Communist movement, by which Russian policy is largely determined. This is not only a question of the modest measure of informational activity which this government can conduct in the Soviet Union and elsewhere, although that, too, is important. It is rather a question of the degree to which the United States can create among the peoples of the world generally the impression of a country which knows what it wants, which is coping successfully with the problems of its internal life and with the responsibilities of a World Power, and which has a spiritual vitality capable of holding its own among the major ideological currents of the time. To the extent that such an impression can be created and maintained, the aims of Russian Communism must appear sterile and quixotic, the hopes and enthusiasm of Moscow's supporters must wane, and added strain must be imposed on the Kremlin's foreign policies. For the palsied decrepitude of the capitalist world is the keystone of Communist philosophy. Even the failure of the United States to experience the early economic depression which the ravens of the Red Square have been predicting with such complacent confidence since hostilities ceased would have deep and important repercussions throughout the Communist world.

By the same token, exhibitions of indecision, disunity and internal disintegration within this country have an exhilarating effect on the whole Communist movement. At each evidence of these tendencies, a thrill of hope and excitement goes through the Communist world; a new jauntiness can be noted in the Moscow tread; new groups of foreign supporters climb on to what they can only view as the band wagon of international politics; and Russian pressure increases all along the line in international affairs.

It would be an exaggeration to say that American behavior unassisted and alone could exercise a power of life and death over the Communist movement and bring about the early fall of Soviet power in Russia. But the United States has it in its power to increase enormously the strains under which Soviet policy must operate, to force upon the Kremlin a far greater degree of moderation and circumspection than it has had to observe in recent years, and in this way to promote tendencies which must eventually find their outlet in either the break-up or the gradual mellowing of Soviet power. For no mystical, Messianic movement—and particularly not that of the Kremlin—can face frustration indefinitely without eventually adjusting itself in one way or another to the logic of that state of affairs.

Thus the decision will really fall in large measure in this country itself. The issue of Soviet-American relations is in essence a test of the over-all worth of the United States as a nation among nations. To avoid destruction the United States need only measure up to its own best traditions and prove itself worthy of preservation as a great nation.

Surely, there was never a fairer test of national quality than this. In the light of these circumstances, the thoughtful observer of Russian-American relations will find no cause for complaint in the Kremlin's challenge to American society. He will rather experience a certain gratitude to a Providence which, by providing the American people with this implacable challenge, has made their entire security as a nation dependent on their pulling themselves together and accepting the responsibilities of moral and political leadership that history plainly intended them to bear.

NOTES

1. "Concerning the Slogans of the United States of Europe," August 1915. Official Soviet edition of Lenin's works.

2. Here and elsewhere in this paper "Socialism" refers to Marxist or Leninist Communism, not to liberal Socialism of the Second International variety.

Part Two

CONTAINMENT DEBATED

Introduction

CONTAINMENT DEBATED

Shortly after the Truman Doctrine speech and the appearance of the "X" article, veteran journalist Walter Lippmann wrote a series of articles in his "Today and Tomorrow" column for the *Washington Post.* He essentially treated the speech and article as a unit. Lippmann's collected articles were published in late 1947 as *The Cold War,* a book which helped lodge "Cold War" as a description of the postwar Soviet-American deadlock. Lippmann's critique stung Kennan and the latter devoted considerable effort in his *Memoirs* to refute it. Lippmann believed that the "X" article was too wishful and too imprecise. More importantly, the chief issue in the postwar world was not the containment of Communism, but rather the withdrawal of foreign troops (British, American, and Soviet) from Europe. Rid Europe of these armies and establish Germany as a nonaligned nation, and Russia's security concerns would be satiated. Russia could then evacuate its soldiers from Eastern Europe. In opposition to Kennan, Lippmann insisted that pragmatic national interest and security, not ideology, made Soviet foreign policy tick.

The journalist also predicted that the United States, to fulfill the containment doctrine, would have to support puppet regimes and might even overextend its power because containment did not discriminate geographically. It was a "strategic monstrosity." American resources and patience would be tested and tried without limit. He considered some areas peripheral to American national interest, and military aid to Greece and Turkey were for him an example of Washington's defective policy. The Marshall Plan, espoused in June, 1947, was, however, for both Lippmann and Kennan, a sounder means to fulfill containment. But these thoughtful men differed in a number of ways, as a comparison of the "X" article and *The Cold War* demonstrate. Kennan himself admitted in 1967 that Lippmann's critique constituted an "excellent and penetrating" treatise.

Another critique of containment arose heatedly in the 1952 presidential campaign when John Foster Dulles, speculated to be the next Republican Secretary of State under the popular Dwight D. Eisenhower, advocated "liberation." Dulles indeed became the new Secretary (1953–1959). Before his selection he molded the Republican Party platform to read that the Truman Administration (which Dulles had advised in 1945–1953 as a partner in bipartisanship) had "squandered the unprecedented power and prestige which were ours at the close of World War II." Containment, it protested, was negative and had not worked. Worse still, America had "no foreign policy." The Democrats "swing erratically from timid appeasement to reckless bluster." Containment, concluded the platform, was "negative, futile and immoral," and it "abandons countless human beings to a despotism and godless terrorism. . . ."

Eastern Europe, as Dulles said often, had to be liberated. The "liberation" of the "captive world," asserted Dulles, would be a major foreign policy goal of the Republican administration. But how could such a policy be implemented? Dulles was seldom precise. Somewhat like Kennan, Dulles was saying that America had the power and should have the desire to change Russia through pressure. Louis Halle, once a member of the Policy Planning Staff, wrote in *The Cold War as History* (1967) that liberation was in essence not a negation of containment but an extension of it. Kennan had written in the "X" article that a kind of natural process of internal decay would always grip the Soviet empire. Through liberation, Dulles was hoping to speed up the process and to explain the happy result. Containment was a holding action for the most part; liberation would constitute an offense. That is one interpretation. Another is that liberation was an empty campaign phrase to gather votes through an emotional appeal. Another is that containment and liberation were incompatible because containment was designed not to roll back existing Soviet influence in territories, but to halt any further expansion.

The latter interpretation was George F. Kennan's, and he was openly critical of Dulles' inflammatory comments. Washington, insisted Kennan, should do nothing that "purports to affect directly the governmental system in another country, no matter what the provocation may seem." Meddling in Eastern European countries could only make their independence more precarious. Kennan said he, of course, wanted liberation too, but with more patient means. When Dulles demanded "positive loyalty" to the Eisenhower Administration's policies, Kennan resigned from the Foreign Service in 1953. It must have been a grievous decision for Kennan, especially because it followed another personal setback in 1952. President Truman appointed Kennan Ambassador to the Soviet Union, and few doubted that Kennan was the best qualified man ever sent to the Moscow embassy. But within a few months, Soviet officials declared him *persona non grata* and demanded his recall. Kennan had done the unconscionable for a careful professional diplomat. He had offended the Russians in September, 1952, by commenting in Berlin (as reported by the *New York Times*) that "his isolation in the Soviet capital today is worse than that he experienced as an interned United States diplomat in Germany after Pearl Harbor when the Nazis declared war on the United States." The Russians bitterly resented this comparison with the Nazis. Kennan came home and became a member of the Institute for Advanced Study at his alma mater Princeton, and watched international relations from the "outside."

"Liberation" proved to be little more than a slogan. When the Hungarian Revolution of 1956 struck against Soviet imperialism, Dulles could do little to liberate helpless Hungary. The Eisenhower Administration in the 1950s actually extended containment through a variety of treaties (SEATO and Baghdad, for example) and interventions (Guatemala in 1954 and Lebanon in 1958), although Dulles did consider the Soviet-American agreement for withdrawal from Austria in 1955 a victory for liberation. Dulles wrote a widely-read article for *Life* magazine in 1952. Emmet John Hughes, a *Life* editor who helped Dulles prepare "A Policy of Boldness," recalled in 1952 that it was "extraordinarily difficult to persuade him to give clarity and substance either to his critiques of 'containment' or to his exhortations on 'liberation.' " Liberation remained vague and ultimately the property of Eastern European émigré groups, Radio Free Europe, and the "Captive Nations" resolution. Containment survived the liberation attack relatively unscathed.

A more scholarly analysis of containment came from Professor William Appleman Williams, who has conducted a running debate with American Cold War diplomacy since the 1940s. His *American-Russian Relations, 1781–1947* (1952) scored Kennan for ignoring in his "X" article capitalist hostility to Soviet Russia. The armed Allied intervention in the Russian civil war in 1918, among other forms of pressure, gave the victorious Soviet leaders sound reasons for fearing the West. In other words, Russia's uncooperative foreign policy was due in part to the uncooperativeness and antipathy of capitalist nations throughout the twentieth century, according to Williams. Kennan dismissed Soviet language about the hostile world as mere rhetoric designed to arouse support for dictatorial authority at home; Williams believed, on the other hand, that such language reflected Soviet fears of the West. Williams also argued that Kennan's use of the word "force" could be interpreted only in a military sense. Rather than mellow the Soviet Union, containment actually hurried Soviet military and economic preparations, strengthening that Communist power. Kennan's statement that the Kremlin worked "under the compulsion of no timetable" was thereby rendered useless, concluded Williams. Williams continued this analysis in an article for *The Nation* magazine in 1956.

Although Kennan attempted to clarify his meaning of containment in numerous writings after his retirement from the Foreign Service, not until 1967 and the publication of his Pulitzer Prize and National Book Award winning *Memoirs,* did he systematically rebut his critics. Kennan then admitted that he had been imprecise and confusing in the "X" article. But he insisted that his formulation of containment was quite different from the intent and formulation of the Truman Doctrine, especially its military aid thrust. There is contemporary evidence that Kennan was hesitant about Truman's Cold War military emphasis. Kennan opposed the seeming permanence of American troops in Japan and Germany, and wanted to negotiate security treaties with Russia over both defeated nations. He opposed the development of the H-Bomb in 1949–1950, and he argued for tactical military units for limited wars rather than a large-scale military build-up for major conflicts. He questioned the need for a military alliance like NATO, and advocated a less formal military arrangement for Western Europe.

At the same time, however, Kennan supported the Rio Pact for Latin America, constantly spoke of the Soviet presence in Eastern Europe as a military one, and reprinted the "X" article in his popular *American Diplomacy, 1900–1950* (1951) without elaboration or clarification. At mid-century he wrote publicly on behalf of containment without indicating decided differences with the Truman Administration's foreign policies. A troubling question still puzzles many readers of Kennan's *Memoirs:* Even if Kennan did not intend or agree with *all* the means utilized by Truman to administer his Cold War policies, did Kennan not offer a very broad doctrine and essentially concede the basic notion that Russia (and/or Communism?) was an aggressive uncompromising threat which had to be dealt with through counterforce almost everywhere?

One historian who remains unconvinced by Kennan's belated explanation is Professor Lloyd C. Gardner of Rutgers University, who devotes
a chapter of his *Architects of Illusions* (1970) to Secretary of the Navy
James V. Forrestal and George F. Kennan in tandem. Gardner suggests
a Forrestal-Kennan "collaboration" or a confluence of ideas and sometimes less than deliberate mutual assistance. Kennan owed his ascent
from the Moscow Embassy to Forrestal's active but apparently unsolic-
ited help. Forrestal himself eagerly attended Kennan's lectures at the
National War College and popularized the diplomat's ideas among
Washington's foreign policy elite. And the Navy Secretary "used" Kennan's account of Soviet behavior to buttress his case for extending
American naval power to the Mediterranean Sea. Gardner notes further
that the two men wore the label "realist," but actually nurtured at the
same time an "idealism" which held that America was the heralded
vanguard of the "free world." That "idealism" is measured in part by
recognizing, as Gardner does, the moral condemnations of Soviet policy
sprinkled throughout Kennan's works. With this "idealism" and "collaboration," Kennan could not place geographical or chronological limitations on the containment doctrine, according to Gardner. Once
unleashed, Kennan's ideas were utilized by ardent Cold Warriors, and
Kennan could only watch and eventually protest.

Even more so than Lloyd Gardner, Eduard M. Mark of the University of Connecticut questions Kennan's *Memoirs.* Mark analyzes the
confusing meaning of the words "political" and "military." He further
quotes the influential Kennan from the period 1949–1950 to note that at
mid-century Kennan advocated "military" containment. Kennan never
thought war would come to Europe (Russia was not a military threat
there), and thus he saw no need for formal military alliances on the
continent. But Kennan did assume, as in the case of the Korean War,
that Soviet expansionism would have to be halted in the rest of the world
and by military means. Then too, a significant part of the containment
thesis, Mark writes, was the "break-up or mellowing" of the Soviet state.
Mark stresses "break-up" and concludes that the American means to
achieve such a goal could not be easily circumscribed. Containment, in
this sense then, was as universal as the Truman Doctrine. Why, asks
Mark, did Kennan not attempt to counter publicly the alleged misinter-
pretations of his ideas before 1950, if he believed them so wrong?

3

A Defective Policy
WALTER LIPPMANN

We must begin with the disturbing fact, which anyone who will reread the article can verify for himself, that Mr. X's conclusions depend upon the optimistic prediction that the "Soviet power . . . bears within itself the seeds of its own decay, and that the sprouting of these seeds is well advanced"; that if "anything were ever to occur to disrupt the unity and the efficacy of the Party as a political instrument, Soviet Russia might be changed overnight (*sic*) from one of the strongest to one of the weakest and most pitiable of national societies"; and "that Soviet society may well (*sic*) contain deficiencies which will eventually weaken its own total potential."

Of this optimistic prediction Mr. X himself says that it "cannot be proved. And it cannot be disproved." Nevertheless, he concludes that the United States should construct its policy on the assumption that the Soviet power is inherently weak and impermanent, and that this un-proved assumption warrants our entering "with reasonable confidence upon a policy of firm containment, designed to confront the Russians with unalterable counterforce at every point where they show signs of encroaching upon the interests of a peaceful and a stable world."

I do not find much ground for reasonable confidence in a policy which can be successful only if the most optimistic prediction should prove to be true. Surely a sound policy must be addressed to the worst and hardest that may be judged to be probable, and not to the best and easiest that may be possible.

From Walter Lippmann, *The Cold War: A Study in U.S. Foreign Policy.* New York: Harper, 1947, pp. 11-22, 29-31, 33-35, 39, 58-60. Reprinted by permission of Harper & Row, Publishers, Inc. Copyright 1947 by Walter Lippmann.

As a matter of fact, Mr. X himself betrays a marked lack of confidence in his own diagnosis. For no sooner had he finished describing the policy of firm containment with unalterable counterforce at every point where the Russians show signs of encroaching, when he felt he must defend his conclusions against the criticism, one might almost say the wise crack, that this is a policy of "holding the line and hoping for the best." His defense is to say that while he is proposing a policy of holding the line and hoping for the best, "in actuality the possibilities for American policy are by no means limited to holding the line and hoping for the best." The additional possibilities are not, however, within the scope of the authority of the Department of State: "the aims of Russian communism must appear sterile and quixotic, the hopes and enthusiasms of Moscow's supporters must wane, and added strain must be imposed on the Kremlin's foreign policies" if "the United States can create among the peoples of the world generally the impression of a country which knows what it wants, which is coping successfully with the problems of its internal life and with the responsibilities of a world power, and which has a spiritual vitality capable of holding its own among the major ideological currents of the time."

This surely is a case of bolstering up the wishful thinking of "hoping for the best"—namely, the collapse of the Soviet power—by an extra strong dose of wishful thinking about the United States. There must be something deeply defective in Mr. X's estimates and calculations. For on his own showing the policy cannot be made to work unless there are miracles and we get all the breaks.

In Mr. X's estimates there are no reserves for a rainy day. There is no margin of safety for bad luck, bad management, error and the unforeseen. He asks us to assume that the Soviet power is already decaying. He exhorts us to believe that our own highest hopes for ourselves will soon have been realized. Yet the policy he recommends is designed to deal effectively with the Soviet Union "as a rival, not a partner, in the political arena." Do we dare to assume, as we enter the arena and get set to run the race, that the Soviet Union will break its leg while the United States grows a pair of wings to speed it on its way?

Mr. X concludes his article on Soviet conduct and American policy by saying that "the thoughtful observer of Russian-American relations will . . . experience a certain gratitude to a Providence which, by providing the American people with this implacable challenge, has made their entire security as a nation dependent upon their pulling themselves together and accepting the responsibilities of moral and political leadership that history plainly intended them to bear." Perhaps. It may be that Mr. X has read the mind of Providence and that he knows what history plainly intended. But it is asking a good deal that the American people should stake their "entire security as a nation" upon a theory which, as he himself says, cannot be proved and cannot be disproved.

Surely it is by no means proved that the way to lead mankind is to spend the next ten or fifteen years, as Mr. X proposes we should, in reacting at "a series of constantly shifting geographical and political points, corresponding to the shifts and maneuvers of Soviet policy." For if history has indeed intended us to bear the responsibility of leadership, then it is not leadership to adapt ourselves to the shifts and maneuvers of Soviet policy at a series of constantly shifting geographical and political points. For that would mean for ten or fifteen years Moscow, not Washington, would define the issues, would make the challenges, would select the ground where the conflict was to be waged, and would choose the weapons. And the best that Mr. X can say for his own proposal is that if for a long period of time we can prevent the Soviet power from winning, the Soviet power will eventually perish or "mellow" because it has been "frustrated."

This is a dismal conclusion. Mr. X has, I believe, become bogged down in it because as he thought more and more about the conduct of the Soviet, he remembered less and less about the conduct of the other nations of the world. For while it may be true that the Soviet power would perish of frustration, if it were contained for ten or fifteen years, this conclusion is only half baked until he has answered the crucial question which remains: can the western world operate a policy of containment? Mr. X not only does not answer this question. He begs it, saying that it will be very discouraging to the Soviets if the western world finds the strength and resourcefulness to contain the Soviet power over a period of ten or fifteen years.

Now the strength of the western world is great, and we may assume that its resourcefulness is considerable. Nevertheless, there are weighty reasons for thinking that the kind of strength we have and the kind of resourcefulness we are capable of showing are peculiarly unsuited to operating a policy of containment.

How, for example, under the Constitution of the United States is Mr. X going to work out an arrangement by which the Department of State has the money and the military power always available in sufficient amounts to apply "counterforce" at constantly shifting points all over the world? Is he going to ask Congress for a blank check on the Treasury and for a blank authorization to use the armed forces? Not if the American constitutional system is to be maintained. Or is he going to ask for an appropriation and for authority each time the Russians "show signs of encroaching upon the interests of a peaceful and stable world"? If that is his plan for dealing with the maneuvers of a dictatorship, he is going to arrive at the points of encroachment with too little and he is going to arrive too late. The Russians, if they intend to encroach, will have encroached while Congress is getting ready to hold hearings.

A policy of shifts and maneuvers may be suited to the Soviet system of government, which, as Mr. X tells us, is animated by patient persistence. It is not suited to the American system of government.

It is even more unsuited to the American economy which is unregimented and uncontrolled, and therefore cannot be administered according to a plan. Yet a policy of containment cannot be operated unless the Department of State can plan and direct exports and imports. For the policy demands that American goods be delivered or withheld at "constantly shifting geographical and political points corresponding to the shifts and maneuvers of Soviet policy."

Thus Mr. X and the planners of policy in the State Department, and not supply and demand in the world market, must determine continually what portion of the commodities produced here may be sold in the United States, what portion is to be set aside for export, and then sold, lent, or given to this foreign country rather than to that one. The Department of State must be able to allocate the products of American industry and agriculture, to ration the goods allocated for export among the nations which are to contain the Soviet Union, and to discriminate among them, judging correctly and quickly how much each nation must be given, how much each nation can safely be squeezed, so that all shall be held in line to hold the line against the Russians.

If then the Kremlin's challenge to American society is to be met by the policy which Mr. X proposes, we are committed to a contest, for ten or fifteen years, with the Soviet system which is planned and directed from Moscow. Mr. X is surely mistaken, it seems to me, if he thinks that a free and undirected economy like our own can be used by the diplomatic planners to wage a diplomatic war against a planned economy at a series of constantly shifting geographical and political points. He is proposing to meet the Soviet challenge on the ground which is most favorable to the Soviets, and with the very instruments, procedures, and weapons in which they have a manifest superiority.

I find it hard to understand how Mr. X could have recommended such a strategic monstrocity. For he tells us, no doubt truly, that the Soviet power "cannot be easily defeated or discouraged by a single victory on the part of its opponents," and that "the patient persistence by which it is animated" means that it cannot be "effectively countered" by "sporadic acts." Yet his own policy calls for a series of sporadic acts: the United States is to apply "counterforce" where the Russians encroach and when they encroach.

On his own testimony no single victory will easily defeat or discourage the patient persistence of the Kremlin. Yet Mr. X says that the United States should aim to win a series of victories which will cause the Russians to "yield on individual sectors of the diplomatic front." And then what? When the United States has forced the Kremlin to "face frustration indefinitely" there will "eventually" come "either the breakup or the gradual mellowing of the Soviet power."

There is, however, no rational ground for confidence that the United States could muster "unalterable counterforce" at all the individual sectors. The Eurasian continent is a big place, and the military power of the United States, though it is very great, has certain limitations which must be borne in mind if it is to be used effectively. We live on an island continent. We are separated from the theaters of conflict by the great oceans. We have a relatively small population, of which the greater proportion must in time of war be employed in producing, transporting and servicing the complex weapons and engines which constitute our military power. The United States has, as compared with the Russians, no adequate reserves of infantry. Our navy commands the oceans and we possess the major offensive weapons of war. But on the ground in the interior of the Eurasian continent, as we are learning in the Greek mountains, there may be many "individual sectors" where only infantry can be used as the "counterforce."

These considerations must determine American strategy in war and, therefore, also in diplomacy, whenever the task of diplomacy is to deal with a conflict and a contest of power. The planner of American diplomatic policy must use the kind of power we do have, not the kind we do not have. He must use that kind of power where it can be used. He must avoid engagements in those "individual sectors of the diplomatic front" where our opponents can use the weapons in which they have superiority. But the policy of firm containment as defined by Mr. X ignores these tactical considerations. It makes no distinction among sectors. It commits the United States to confront the Russians with counterforce "at every point" along the line, instead of at those points which we have selected because, there at those points, our kind of sea and air power can best be exerted.

American military power is peculiarly unsuited to a policy of containment which has to be enforced persistently and patiently for an indefinite period of time. If the Soviet Union were an island like Japan, such a policy could be enforced by American sea and air power. The United States could, without great difficulty, impose a blockade. But the Soviet Union has to be contained on land, and "holding the line" is therefore a form of trench warfare.

Yet the genius of American military power does not lie in holding positions indefinitely. That requires a massive patience by great hordes of docile people. American military power is distinguished by its mobility, its speed, its range and its offensive striking force. It is, therefore, not an efficient instrument for a diplomatic policy of containment. It can only be the instrument of a policy which has as its objective a decision and a settlement. It can and should be used to redress the balance of power which has been upset by the war. But it is not designed for, or adapted to, a strategy of containing, waiting, countering, blocking, with no more specific objective than the eventual "frustration" of the opponent.

The Americans would themselves probably be frustrated by Mr. X's policy long before the Russians were.

The policy of containment, which Mr. X recommends, demands the employment of American economic, political, and in the last analysis, American military power at "sectors" in the interior of Europe and Asia. This requires, as I have pointed out, ground forces, that is to say reserves of infantry, which we do not possess.

The United States cannot by its own military power contain the expansive pressure of the Russians "at every point where they show signs of encroaching." The United States cannot have ready "unalterable counterforce" consisting of American troops. Therefore, the counterforces which Mr. X requires have to be composed of Chinese, Afghans, Iranians, Turks, Kurds, Arabs, Greeks, Italians, Austrians, of anti-Soviet Poles, Czechoslovaks, Bulgars, Yugoslavs, Albanians, Hungarians, Finns and Germans.

The policy can be implemented only by recruiting, subsidizing and supporting a heterogeneous array of satellites, clients, dependents and puppets. The instrument of the policy of containment is therefore a coalition of disorganized, disunited, feeble or disorderly nations, tribes and factions around the perimeter of the Soviet Union.

To organize a coalition among powerful modern states is, even in time of war and under dire necessity, an enormously difficult thing to do well. To organize a coalition of disunited, feeble and immature states, and to hold it together for a prolonged diplomatic siege, which might last for ten or fifteen years, is, I submit, impossibly difficult. . . .

It will be evident, I am sure, to the reader who has followed the argument to this point that my criticism of the policy of containment, or the so-called Truman Doctrine, does not spring from any hope or belief that the Soviet pressure to expand can be "charmed or talked out of existence." I agree entirely with Mr. X that we must make up our minds that the Soviet power is not amenable to our arguments, but only "to contrary force" that "is felt to be too strong, and thus more rational in the logic and rhetoric of power."

My objection, then, to the policy of containment is not that it seeks to confront the Soviet power with American power, but that the policy is misconceived, and must result in a misuse of American power. For as I have sought to show, it commits this country to a struggle which has for its objective nothing more substantial than the hope that in ten or fifteen years the Soviet power will, as the result of long frustration, "break up" or "mellow." In this prolonged struggle the role of the United States is, according to Mr. X, to react "at a series of constantly shifting geographical and political points" to the encroachments of the Soviet power.

The policy, therefore, concedes to the Kremlin the strategical initiative as to when, where and under what local circumstances the issue is to be joined. It compels the United States to meet the Soviet pressure at these shifting geographical and political points by using satellite states, puppet governments and agents which have been subsidized and supported, though their effectiveness is meager and their reliability uncertain. By forcing us to expend our energies and our substance upon these dubious and unnatural allies on the perimeter of the Soviet Union, the effect of the policy is to neglect our natural allies in the Atlantic community, and to alienate them.

They are alienated also by the fact that they do not wish to become, like the nations of the perimeter, the clients of the United States in whose affairs we intervene, asking as the price of our support that they take the directives of their own policy from Washington. They are alienated above all by the prospect of war, which could break out by design or accident, by miscalculation or provocation, if at any of these constantly shifting geographical and political points the Russians or Americans became so deeply engaged that no retreat or compromise was possible. In this war their lands would be the battlefield. Their peoples would be divided by civil conflict. Their cities and their fields would be the bases and the bridgeheads in a total war which, because it would merge into a general civil war, would be as indecisive as it was savage.

We may now ask why the official diagnosis of Soviet conduct, as disclosed by Mr. X's article, has led to such an unworkable policy for dealing with Russia. It is, I believe, because Mr. X has neglected even to mention the fact that the Soviet Union is the successor of the Russian Empire and that Stalin is not only the heir of Marx and of Lenin but of Peter the Great, and the Czars of all the Russias.

For reasons which I do not understand, Mr. X decided not to consider the men in the Kremlin as the rulers of the Russian State and Empire, and has limited his analysis to the interaction of "two forces": "the ideology inherited by the present Soviet leaders from the movement in which they had their political origin" and the "circumstances of the power which they have now exercised for nearly three decades in Russia."

Thus he dwells on the indubitable fact that they believe in the Marxian ideology and that "they have continued to be predominantly absorbed with the struggle to secure and make absolute the power which they seized in November 1917." But with these two observations alone he cannot, and does not, explain the conduct of the Soviet government in this postwar era—that is to say its aims and claims to territory and to the sphere of influence which it dominates. The Soviet government has been run by Marxian revolutionists for thirty years; what has to be explained by a planner of American foreign policy is why in 1945 the Soviet government expanded its frontiers and its orbit, and what was the plan and pattern of its expansion. That can be done only by remembering that the Soviet government is a Russian government and that this Russian government has emerged victorious over Germany and Japan.

Having omitted from his analysis the fact that we are dealing with a victorious Russia—having become exclusively preoccupied with the Marxian ideology, and with the communist revolution—it is no wonder that the outcome of Mr. X's analysis is nothing more definite, concrete and practical than that the Soviets will encroach and expand "at a series of constantly shifting geographical and political points." Mr. X's picture of the Soviet conduct has no pattern. It is amorphous. That is why his conclusions about how we should deal with the Soviets have no pattern, and are also amorphous. . . .

The westward expansion of the Russian frontier and of the Russian sphere of influence, though always a Russian aim, was accomplished when, as, and because the Red Army defeated the German army and advanced to the center of Europe. It was the mighty power of the Red Army, not the ideology of Karl Marx, which enabled the Russian government to expand its frontiers. It is the pressure of that army far beyond the new frontiers which makes the will of the Kremlin irresistible within the Russian sphere of influence. It is the threat that the Red Army may advance still farther west—into Italy, into western Germany, into Scandinavia—that gives the Kremlin and the native communist parties of western Europe an abnormal and intolerable influence in the affairs of the European continent.

Therefore, the immediate and the decisive problem of our relations with the Soviet Union is whether, when, on what conditions the Red Army can be prevailed upon to evacuate Europe.

I am contending that the American diplomatic effort should be concentrated on the problem created by the armistice—which is on how the continent of Europe can be evacuated by the three non-European armies which are now inside Europe. This is the problem which will have to be solved if the independence of the European nations is to be restored. Without that there is no possibility of a tolerable peace. But if these armies withdraw, there will be a very different balance of power in the world than there is today, and one which cannot easily be upset. For the nations of Europe, separately and in groups, perhaps even in unity, will then, and then only, cease to be the stakes and the pawns of the Russian-American conflict. . . .

All the other pressures of the Soviet Union at the "constantly shifting geographical and political points," which Mr. X is so concerned about—in the Middle East and in Asia—are, I contend, secondary and subsidiary to the fact that its armed forces are in the heart of Europe. It is to the Red Army in Europe, therefore, and not to ideologies, elections, forms of government, to socialism, to communism, to free enterprise, that a correctly conceived and soundly planned policy should be directed. . . .

We may now consider how we are to relate our role in the United Nations to our policy in the conflict with Russia. Mr. X does not deal with this question. But the State Department, in its attempt to operate under the Truman Doctrine, has shown where that doctrine would take us. It would take us to the destruction of the U. N.

The Charter and the organization of the United Nations are designed to maintain peace *after* a settlement of the Second World War has been arrived at. Until there is a settlement of that war, the United Nations does not come of age: it is growing up, it is at school, it is learning and practicing, it is testing its procedure, gaining experience. During this period, which will not come to an end until the great powers have agreed on peace treaties, the United Nations cannot deal with disputes that involve the balance of power in the world. The balance of power has to be redressed and settled in the peace treaties by the great powers themselves, principally, as I have tried to show, by the withdrawal of their armies from the continent of Europe.

Until such a settlement is reached, the United Nations has to be protected by its supporters from the strains, the burdens, the discredit, of having to deal with issues that it is not designed to deal with.

The true friends of the United Nations will, therefore, be opposed to entangling the world organization in the Soviet-American conflict. No good and nothing but harm can come of using the Security Council and the Assembly as an arena of the great dispute, or of acting as if we did not realize the inherent limitations of the Charter and thought that somehow we could by main force and awkwardness use the United Nations organization to overawe and compel the Russians. All that can come of that is to discredit the United Nations on issues that it cannot settle and thus to foreclose the future of the U. N., which can begin only if and when these issues have been settled.

Judging by the speeches in the Greek affair of the British and the American delegates, Sir Alexander Cadogan and Mr. Herschel Johnson appear to be acting on instructions which treat the U. N. as expendable in our conflict with Russia. It is a great pity. Nothing is being accomplished to win the conflict, to assuage it, or to settle it. But the U. N., which should be preserved as the last best hope of mankind that the conflict can be settled and a peace achieved, is being chewed up. The seed corn is being devoured.

Why? Because the policy of containment, as Mr. X has exposed it to the world, does not have as its objective a settlement of the conflict with Russia. It is therefore implicit in the policy that the U. N. has no future as a universal society, and that either the U. N. will be cast aside like the League of Nations, or it will be transformed into an anti-Soviet coalition. In either event the U. N. will have been destroyed.

At the root of Mr. X's philosophy about Russian-American relations and underlying all the ideas of the Truman Doctrine there is a disbelief in the possibility of a settlement of the issues raised by this war. Having observed, I believe quite correctly, that we cannot expect "to enjoy political intimacy with the Soviet regime," and that we must "regard the Soviet Union as a rival, not a partner in the political arena," and that "there can be no appeal to common purposes," Mr. X has reached the conclusion that all we can do is to "contain" Russia until Russia changes, ceases to be our rival, and becomes our partner.

The conclusion is, it seems to me, quite unwarranted. The history of diplomacy is the history of relations among rival powers, which did not enjoy political intimacy, and did not respond to appeals to common purposes. Nevertheless, there have been settlements. Some of them did not last very long. Some of them did. For a diplomat to think that rival and unfriendly powers cannot be brought to a settlement is to forget what diplomacy is about. There would be little for diplomats to do if the world consisted of partners, enjoying political intimacy, and responding to common appeals.

4

From Negative Containment to Liberation

JOHN FOSTER DULLES

If you will think back over the past six years, you will see that our policies have largely involved emergency action to try to "contain" Soviet Communism by checking it here or blocking it there. We are not working, sacrificing and spending in order to be able to live *without* this peril— but to be able to live *with* it, presumably forever.

Early in 1947 Mr. Truman announced, under emergency conditions, the so-called "Truman Doctrine" to save Greece and Turkey.

Later in 1947 we provided emergency economic aid to France and Italy to meet violent Communist subversion in these countries. This was the first instalment of the Marshall Plan which was further developed in 1948 to meet Soviet political warfare in Europe.

Later in 1948 we negotiated the North Atlantic Treaty to meet what some thought was an imminent Soviet military threat to Western Europe.

In 1949 we hurriedly inaugurated a Military Assistance Program to give the Western European countries some arms.

In June 1950 we responded hastily to the North Korean attack upon the Republic of Korea, and we then plunged into a vast armament program for ourselves and for our Western allies.

In all these matters our actions were merely reactions to some of the many Soviet threats. As such, they have been reasonably successful. But that is only a small part of the story. Since 1945, when World War II fighting ended, the Soviet Communists have won control over all or parts of 12 countries in Asia and Central Europe with populations of about 600 million. Their mood today is one of triumphant expectancy: "Which will be the next addition to our camp?" The free world is full of foreboding: "Which of us will be the next victim?"

Our present negative policies will never end the type of sustained offensive which Soviet Communism is mounting; they will never end the peril nor bring relief from the exertions which devour our economic,

From John Foster Dulles, "A Policy of Boldness," *Life,* XXXII (May 19, 1952), 146 ff. Reprinted by permission.

political and moral vitals. Ours are treadmill policies which, at best, might perhaps keep us in the same place until we drop exhausted.

As former Ambassador Minocher R. Masani of India recently put the matter tersely: "Defenses seem constantly improvised—a hole plugged here, a leak stopped there. . . . Clearly, mere containment is no longer enough." The ambassador added to his reproach by recalling that of Demosthenes, addressed to the Athenians in 351 B.C.:

> Shame on you, Athenians . . . for not wishing to understand that in war one must not allow oneself to be at the command of events, but to forestall them. . . . You make war against Philip like a barbarian when he wrestles. . . . If you hear that Philip has attacked in the Chersonese, you send help there; if he is at Thermopylae, you run there; and if he turns aside you follow him to right and left, as if you were acting on his orders. Never a fixed plan, never any precautions; you wait for bad news before you act. . . .

As we stop fretting and start thinking, the first problem to tackle is the strictly military one. It comes in the form of a paradox: for we must seek a military formula more effective than any devised to date—that we may no longer be so overridingly preoccupied with purely military necessity. . . .

There is one solution and only one: that is for the free world to develop the will and organize the means to retaliate instantly against open aggression by Red armies, so that, if it occurred anywhere, we could and would strike back where it hurts, by means of our choosing. . . .

Once the free world has established a military defense, it can undertake what has been too long delayed—a political offense.

It is ironic and wrong that we who believe in the boundless power of human freedom should so long have accepted a static political role. It is also ironic and wrong that we who so proudly profess regard for the spiritual should rely so utterly on material defenses while the avowed materialists have been waging a winning war with social ideas, stirring humanity everywhere.

There are three truths which we need to recall in these times:

1) The dynamic prevails over the static; the active over the passive. We were from the beginning a vigorous, confident people, born with a sense of destiny and of mission. That is why we have grown from a small and feeble nation to our present stature in the world.

2) Nonmaterial forces are more powerful than those that are merely material. Our dynamism has always been moral and intellectual rather than military or material. During most of our national life we had only

a small military establishment and during the last century we had to borrow money abroad to develop our expanding economy. But we always generated political, social and industrial ideas and projected them abroad where they were more explosive than dynamite.

3) There is a moral or natural law not made by man which determines right and wrong and in the long run only those who conform to that law will escape disaster. This law has been trampled by the Soviet rulers, and for that violation they can and should be made to pay. This will happen when we ourselves keep faith with that law in our practical decisions of policy.

We should let these truths work in and through us. We should be *dynamic,* we should use *ideas* as weapons; and these ideas should conform to *moral* principles. That we do this is right, for it is the inevitable expression of a faith—and I am confident that we still do have a faith. But it is also expedient in defending ourselves against an aggressive, imperialistic despotism. For even the present lines will not hold unless our purpose goes beyond confining Soviet Communism within its present orbit.

Consider the situation of the 20-odd non-Western nations which are next door to the Soviet world. These exposed nations feel that they have been put in the "expendable" class, condemned in perpetuity to be the ramparts against which the angry waves of Soviet Communism will constantly hurl themselves. They are expected to live precariously, permanently barred from areas with which they normally should have trade, commerce and cultural relations. They cannot be enthusiastic about policies which would merely perpetuate so hazardous and uncomfortable a position. Today they live close to despair because the United States, the historic leader of the forces of freedom, seems dedicated to the negative policy of "containment" and "stalemate."

As a matter of fact, some highly competent work is being done, at one place or another, to promote liberation. Obviously such activities do not lend themselves to public exposition. But liberation from the yoke of Moscow will not occur for a very long time, and courage in neighboring lands will not be sustained, *unless the United States makes it publicly known that it wants and expects liberation to occur.* The mere statement of that wish and expectation would change, in an electrifying way, the mood of the captive peoples. It would put heavy new burdens on the jailers and create new opportunities for liberation.

Here are some specific acts which we could take:

1) We could make it clear, on the highest authority of the President and the Congress, that U.S. policy seeks as one of its peaceful goals the

eventual restoration of genuine independence in the nations of Europe and Asia now dominated by Moscow, and that we will not be a party to any "deal" confirming the rule of Soviet despotism over the alien peoples which it now dominates.

2) We could welcome the creation in the free world of political "task forces" to develop a freedom program for each of the captive nations. Each group would be made up of those who are proved patriots, who have practical resourcefulness and who command confidence and respect at home and abroad.

3) We could stimulate the escape from behind the Iron Curtain of those who can help to develop these programs.

4) The activities of the Voice of America and such private committees as those for Free Europe and Free Asia could be coordinated with these freedom programs. The agencies would be far more effective if given concrete jobs to do.

5) We could coordinate our economic, commercial and cultural relations with the freedom programs, cutting off or licensing intercourse as seemed most effective from time to time.

6) We could end diplomatic relations with present governments which are in fact only puppets of Moscow, if and when that would promote the freedom programs.

7) We could seek to bring other free nations to unite with us in proclaiming, in a great new Declaration of Independence, our policies toward the captive nations.

We do not want a series of bloody uprisings and reprisals. There can be peaceful separation from Moscow, as Tito showed, and enslavement can be made so unprofitable that the master will let go his grip. Such results will not come to pass overnight. But we can know, for history proves, that the spirit of patriotism burns unquenched in Poles, Czechs, Hungarians, Romanians, Bulgarians, Chinese and others, and we can be confident that within two, five or 10 years substantial parts of the present captive world can peacefully regain national independence. That will mark the beginning of the end of Soviet despotism's attempt at world conquest.

5

A Policy Boomerangs

WILLIAM A. WILLIAMS

One of the most neglected, yet illuminating, aspects of the history of the cold war is the recent decline in the United States of Sir Winston Churchill's prestige as a strategist of foreign affairs. His coincident retirement from active politics has little causative relationship with this eclipse of his influence. Rather the explanation lies in his argument that Soviet strength has increased the chances of avoiding a major war. American policy-makers and their cabal of experts at first tried to overlook such heretical mutterings from the man who delivered the keynote address of the cold war back in March, 1946. But Churchill refused to bow to the new priests of his old orthodoxy. In March, 1955, he asserted his revisionism in terms which made it impossible to misunderstand him, even though, as subsequent events have demonstrated, he could be ignored.

"It may be," he observed, "that we shall, by a process of sublime irony, have reached a stage in this story where safety will be the sturdy child of terror." This remark was so devastating to the assumptions and rationalizations of the policies of containment and liberation (which Kennan now admits are "two sides of the same coin") that American leaders made a concerted effort to stuff it down the memory hole as quickly as possible. Churchill's facility and weakness for the dramatic phrase did him a disservice in this instance, for those who did comment on the speech concentrated on twisting the phrase about "the sturdy child of terror" into an endorsement of the ideas of "Negotiation from Strength" and "Peace through Power."

Churchill was making a radically different point, of course. He was saying, in short, that the policies of containment and liberation have worked, but for reasons and by a logic exactly the opposite of those advanced by their originator and supporters. If this is in fact the case, then the practical conclusion which follows is both very clear and vastly significant. It means that a narrow and militant anti-Soviet policy works to increase the power, influence and prestige of the Soviet Union

William A. Williams, "Irony of Containment," *The Nation,* CLXXXII (May 5, 1956), 376-379. Reprinted by permission.

throughout the world. And startling though it may seem, the record of the last ten years offers considerable support for such an interpretation. It would appear worthwhile to examine this hypothesis, moreover, because neither official policy-makers nor their advisors seem able, either independently or in collaboration, to reach a consensus on this key question. There are, as the *New York Times* pointed out a year ago, two competing interpretations of the relationship between American policy and current events in Russia. The containment-liberation crowd asserts that American pressure, impinging upon the basic weaknesses of the Soviet system, is directly and primarily responsible for the recent modifications in Russian policy. But another group argues that these changes have come from within, as a consequence of Russia's recovery from wartime devastation and its subsequent progress. This second view, of course, has important implications for any analysis, though its proponents do not acknowledge or discuss such ramifications. By and large, therefore, the existing dispute does not deal directly with the central issue.

This confusion is painfully and obviously apparent in the public side of the debate. Secretary Dulles touched it off with his remarks that the Soviet economy was "on the point of collapsing" and that the system was "bankrupt," thus implying that containment was about to produce liberation. This analysis provoked Kennan to make a very sharp retort—"I don't recognize the world Mr. Dulles is talking about"—even though the comment rendered a rather damning judgment on his own policy of containment. Dulles graciously retreated, as if in repayment for Kennan's earlier resignation, and acknowledged that the international situation was still bad even though there had been some improvement.

Most of those who have supported containment (which includes about 99 per cent of the nation's leaders) have sided with Kennan in the ensuing discussion. They, too, seem oblivious to the implications of such a position for their earlier actions. Thus Senator O'Mahoney asserted at the close of 1955 that "world peace is further away now" than at any time since the end of the Korean War. As late as April 4 of this year, Harry Truman agreed, seeing the Russians "more dangerous now than ever before." Averell Harriman, who seems to view himself as a combination of the Samuel Adams and the George Washington of the cold war, contradicts and confutes himself in the same speech. First he cries out that American policy has failed, but then he goes on, in a swirl of language that obscures the logic-chopping, to assert that the only thing that can save us is more of the same.

Still others, who are generally credited with more subtle minds than either Truman or Harriman, advance equally curious arguments. Clifton Daniel, who just won a prize for his handling of the news in Russia, offered one novel interpretation while on a recent *Meet the Press* panel, arguing that all our troubles started when the Eisenhower Administration got too tough with the Russians, thus forcing them to retaliate by becoming more devilish than ever. The most charitable explanation of the *Times* assistant foreign editor's performance (and, very likely, the correct one) is that he really understands the "sublime irony" of containment to which Churchill referred, but hesitated publicly to pull the rug out from under his cantankerous father-in-law. Certainly Daniel is quite aware that Dwight D. Eisenhower has been far less belligerent toward the Russians than was Harry S. Truman.

Adlai Stevenson has done no better than Daniel, and with less excuse. It takes considerable research, for example, to come up with a more confounding bit of analysis than the following gem supplied by the Bard of Michigan Avenue. "I hardly need point out," he commented recently, "that for this nation to walk to the verge of war three times in three years while drastically reducing our military defenses for domestic political advantage can only be counted as 'suicidal folly.' " The implicit meaning of his comment is that it would have been quite all right to walk to the brink of war three times in three years if only we had *not* reduced our armaments.

All these examples, and countless more which could be cited, emphasize the need to establish the actual relationship between the American policy of containment-liberation and the development of Russian domestic and foreign policy. For if it is true, as Churchill suggests, that containment has worked to strengthen Russia by reinforcing ideological and nationalistic forces, then it would seem wise to abandon such a policy as the essential first step in developing a viable program for coexistence. Such an analysis needs to begin with a review of the relative power of America and Russia at the time when Kennan formulated, and Truman accepted, the doctrine of containment.

The central feature of this comparative power alignment, of course, was America's unilateral possession of the technological and military capacity to produce and deliver atomic bombs. Beyond this, the United States had a navy larger than the combined fleets of the rest of the world; an army trained, equipped and battle-conditioned with the most advanced and mobile weapons; the world's only undamaged industrial plant and unharmed managerial and labor force; and possession of, or access to, a great number of military and economic bases extending from Germany on around the Soviet Union to Japan.

It is customary, at this juncture, for official spokesmen to point out indignantly that the United States demobilized whereas the Soviet Union did not. Even if this assertion were true in the sense in which it is presented, which it is not, it would still be necessary to assess relative power after such disarmament. But the facts of demobilization do not fit the official shibboleth. America disarmed, as this writer overheard an admiral remark in 1947, in the sense that it got a bazooka under one arm, a B-B gun under the other, and then dropped the B-B gun. On another level, much is made of the navy's Operation Mothball, in which the fleet was supposedly zipped up in cellulose storage bags. Not only is this false in an absolute sense; it ignores the fact that Russia's deep-water fleet was not even capable of challenging what was left of the Royal Navy. At the center of the analysis, however, stand three unalterable facts: America's monopoly of nuclear weapons and a strategic bombing force; its colossal and undamaged industrial strength; its excellent geopolitical situation.

Russia did not occupy so fortunate a position at the end of the war. Perhaps the most distorted and misunderstood aspect of its power position concerned its occupation of Eastern Europe. In the first place, as Senator Russell pointed out, those countries "were all devastated as badly or worse than our allies." On balance, moreover, the area was weaker than Western Europe, even under the best of circumstances. Moscow's policy of ruthlessly draining those nations to supply Russia's immediate needs served, furthermore, to increase their dissatisfaction with Soviet occupation. These considerations led General Gruenther to discount even the possibility of Russia using them as a springboard for an attack on the West prior to 1952, and even then he estimated that the chances of such action were so small as to be meaningless.

The evidence of absolute and relative weakness becomes even more dramatic when one examines the situation then existing in Russia itself. The contrast with the United States was stark and undeniable: no atomic armaments; no strategic-bombing force; no blue-water navy; a devastated and over-strained industrial and transportation system; a mangled agriculture; a depleted labor force; and a sad, weary and lethargic population. As for the army, General Gruenther reported that it mustered less than three million men in 1947. Nor was it being equipped with new arms that matched America's, for the Russian economy was being converted to production for peacetime reconstruction, and output was down.

In their unguarded moments, America's own cold warriors have let slip the fact of Russia's relative weakness at the time. Kennan himself acknowledged, in the famous "X" article, that Russia, "as opposed to the Western world in general, is still by far the weaker party." As late as 1950, Harriman reported that the "economic strength is all on the side of the free countries"; and Secretary Acheson added that Moscow had "nothing to match E. R. P. and the Point IV concept in the economic field . . . nothing to match the North Atlantic Treaty concept in the field of defense."

Perhaps the most impressive evidence comes from the two top Soviet leaders' revelation of Stalin's formal request for a six-billion-dollar loan from the citadel of capitalism, and Molotov's recent remark that no one in the Kremlin even dreamed, as of 1945–46, that Russia's position could conceivably be so strong in a mere ten years. Small wonder it was, then, that Senator Taft (let alone Henry Wallace) was so reviled by the Republican and Democratic bipartisans for containment when he commented, back in those days, that "it has sometimes seemed to me that the Russian threat is over-estimated."

Instead of long-term credits and candid negotiations, the Russians got Kennan's containment, Truman's doctrine and Dulles' liberation. Emphasizing the grave and immediate danger of Russian power, and arguing that Soviet leadership had to expand in order to keep itself in power, Kennan minced no words in stating the purpose of American policy. The United States, he concluded, "has it in its power to increase enormously the strains under which Soviet policy must operate, to force upon the Kremlin a far greater degree of moderation and circumspection than it has had to observe in recent years, and in this way to promote tendencies which must eventually find their outlet in either the break-up or the gradual mellowing of Soviet power."

Nine years later Kennan argued that he had been misunderstood. "I did not," he claimed, "want people to take a despairing and dramatic view of Soviet relations, as many of them were inclined to do." And he went on to deny that his policy recommendations had any implicit or causative relationship to the militant and militarized policy which followed upon his advice of 1945–47. He did not explain, however, why he had waited so long to get around to clearing up the confusion about what he had meant.

Now it is wrong, of course, to maintain that Kennan was solely responsible for American policy toward Russia after 1945. For one thing, he did not have that kind of power. But he did have tremendous influence: directly with such figures in the Truman Administration as Harriman and Forrestal; and indirectly through the medium of his "X" article, which became the ideological and intellectual touchstone of American thinking on relations with Russia. And, while it is true that Harry Truman was not a man to let a bureaucrat make policy, he was, as he recently remarked, a man "who never went in for half measures." Once he accepted the argument and objectives of containment, it was not surprising that he put it into operation as a Monroe Doctrine for the world.

It is pertinent, in view of this story and Kennan's more recent protestations of innocence, to review the language and tone of the "X" article. For contrary to what he says in 1955, his own words of 1946 would seem to qualify as "despairing and dramatic." Kennan first described the Soviets as "fierce," "jealous" and characterized by "aggressive intransigence." Then he asserted that they were only "sensitive to contrary force, more ready to yield on individual sectors of the diplomatic front when that force is felt to be too strong." And he concluded by describing their policy as moving "inexorably along the prescribed path, like a persistent toy automobile wound up and headed in a given direction, stopping only when it meets with some unanswerable force," or when it runs into "superior force" or "unassailable barriers in its path." His recommendation to "confront the Russians with unalterable counter force" was based on the assumption that the United States "had in its power . . . to force upon the Kremlin" a general compliance with American will.

Either Kennan can not accurately set down on paper what he really had in his mind, or he sought, in his recent apologia, to minimize his own responsibility during the last decade. Whatever the answer, it is certain that the makers of American foreign policy took Kennan's 1946 language at its face value. Abroad, therefore, they embarked upon a program of forcing the Soviet Union to accept extreme terms of settlement. At home, meanwhile, they "bombarded the American people," in the words of one sober and ideologically impeccable student, "with a 'hate the enemy' campaign rarely seen in our history; never, certainly, in peacetime."

There ensued a widespread competition among American leaders (in which, it should be mentioned, Kennan participated) to see which of them could lay down the most all-encompassing prospectus for Russia's salvation. Secretary Acheson's pre-Korea speech at Berkeley in 1950 would seem, on balance, to have been the winner of this American Century Sweepstakes. Acheson laid down seven prerequisites that the Russians would have to meet, not for peace, but as conditions for negotiation. Since compliance with these demands would have reduced the Soviet bargaining posture to that of supplication, it is hardly surprising that Moscow described Acheson's "total diplomacy" as a policy of demanding unconditional surrender as the price of not fighting a war. A year after his Berkeley speech, Acheson unintentionally revealed the psychology of American policy. For although they were directed at Russia, his words cast a glaring light on Washington's attitude: "As long as there is a great disparity of power which makes negotiation seem to be unnecessary to one side, that causes them to believe they can accomplish their purpose without it."

According to Kennan's theory, application of this kind of American power was supposed to produce, *in weak and fearful response*, either the mellowing or the collapse of the Soviet system. What actually happened was somewhat different. First, the Soviet Union reacted with a forced march to meet strength with strength; and second, once it had achieved this objective, it began to employ its vitality and confidence to reform and rationalize at home, which in turn extended its influence abroad.

Appearing as a classic and literal verification of Marx's most apocalyptic prophecy, the policy of containment strengthened the hand of every die-hard Marxist and every extreme Russian nationalist among the Soviet leadership. Those who defend containment as a necessity for America must also admit the validity of Stalin's argument that it was necessary for him to meet strength with strength, for justification by necessity knows no bounds of geography, ideology or morality. Thus the subtle interpretations of a Eugene Varga were brushed aside in Russia just as the sophisticated analyses of a Lewis Mumford were ignored in the United States.

Armed with the language and actions of containment, which underwrote and extended his existing power, Stalin could and did drive the Soviet people to the brink of collapse and, no doubt, to the thought of open resistance. But the dynamic of revolt was always blocked, even among those who did have access to the levels of authority, by the fact of containment and the open threat of liberation. Thus protected by his avowed enemies, Stalin was able to force his nation through extreme deprivations and extensive purges to the verge of physical and psychological exhaustion. But he also steered it through the perils of reconstruction to the security of nuclear parity with the United States.

There is considerable evidence that Stalin understood how narrowly he had skirted catastrophe, and sensed the need to relax the tempo and the rigor of Soviet life. And his successors, appalled even as hardened revolutionaries by the costs of two such forced marches in one lifetime, were both philosophically and psychologically inclined, and politically able, to move in that direction much more rapidly and extensively. That they did so as a consequence of their own strength seems established by comparing the timing of such reforms with Russia's absolute and relative power positions as of 1945–47 and 1954–56.

Thus this review of the record appears to verify Churchill's insight about the irony of containment. In his own inimitable and fumbling way, moreover, Secretary Dulles has further substantiated this analysis. For he remarked, not long ago, that the present relaxation of tension was assured by American policy at Geneva. He seemed unaware, however, that such a comment implied the bankruptcy of the containment-liberation policy. But it does in fact do just that, for it was Eisenhower's assurance of peace, not the "get tough" language of Kennan, Acheson, Truman and Dulles, that convinced the Russians they could relax and embark upon reforms at home.

But Churchill's use of the adjective "sublime" must be questioned, for the costs of containment to Russia and the United States, let alone the rest of the world, can only with sarcasm be described as "sublime." It would seem more fitting to refer to it as the harsh irony of containment. Not only is this more accurate, but such a phrase might serve as a useful reminder to American leaders as they work out a program for coexistence.

It is even possible, and perhaps worthwhile, to suggest that the history of containment points a moral for the practice of coexistence. Nor need we be disturbed or disappointed that Thucydides saw it shining through his study of an earlier war. Indeed, we can let his statement of it stand for our time, too. It is very simple. It is also very true. Its only weakness is that those who would live by it must have great courage and self-containment. It reads as follows: "The greatest exercise of power lies in its restraint."

6

A Rebuttal and an Apology
GEORGE F. KENNAN

I seem to recall that at some time during the first weeks of 1947, while I was still at the War College, Mr. Dean Acheson, then serving as Under Secretary of State, called me to his office and told me that General George Marshall, who had only recently assumed the office of Secretary of State, had in mind the establishment within the department of some sort of a planning unit—something to fill, at least in part, the place of the Divisions of Plans and Operations to which he was accustomed in the War Department. It was likely, Mr. Acheson indicated, that I would be asked to head this new unit when my tour of duty at the War College was completed. I gained no very clear understanding of what was involved; I am not sure that Mr. Acheson had gained a much clearer one from General Marshall. But that some such thing was in store for me, I understood.

I was, therefore, less surprised than I might otherwise have been when, on February 24, Mr. Acheson again summoned me to his office, told me of the crisis of policy that had arisen for us as a result of the decision of the British government to abandon its special support for Greece, and asked me to participate in the deliberations of a special committee that was being established to study the whole problem of assistance to Greece and Turkey.

The committee met that same evening (February 24), as I recall it, under the chairmanship of my old friend and colleague of Riga and Moscow days Loy Henderson, who was now chief of the Division of Near Eastern Affairs in the department. It was my own recollection that we had before us, on that occasion, the task of recommending whether to respond affirmatively at all to the problem posed for us by the British withdrawal, or whether to leave the Greeks and Turks to their own devices. Henderson's recollection (and in the divergence between the two you have a good example of the danger of relying on pure memory,

From George F. Kennan, *Memoirs, 1925–1950.* Boston: Atlantic-Little, Brown, 1967, pp. 313-324, 354-367. Reprinted by permission of Atlantic-Little, Brown and Co. Copyright 1967 by George F. Kennan.

unsupported by written evidence, as a source for diplomatic history) was that this question, so far as the Department of State was concerned, had already been decided in principle by the Acting Secretary of State and himself over the preceding weekend and that the task of the committee was to outline in more detail the course of action that should be recommended to the President and General Marshall (then in Moscow) and to make suggestions as to how it should be explained and justified to other governmental departments, to the Congress (whose action would obviously be necessary to give it effect), and to the public. However this may be (and I gladly yield to Henderson's recollection as more likely to be right than my own), I gave it as my opinion that we had no choice but to accept the challenge and to extend the requisite aid; this was the consensus of the group as a whole; an appropriate recommendation was drawn up; and I returned to my home late that evening with the stimulating impression of having participated prominently in a historic decision of American foreign policy. If, on this occasion, I somewhat overrated the effect of my own voice, it would not be the last time that egotism, and the attention my words seemed often to attract on the part of startled colleagues, would deceive me as to the measure of my real influence on the process of decision-taking.

Mr. Joseph Jones, in his excellent book *The Fifteen Weeks* [1955], has described in great and faithful detail the various discussions, consultations, clearances, and literary struggles that took place within the government in the ensuing days before the President was in a position to present to the Congress, two weeks later, his famous Truman Doctrine message. It was (I learn from Mr. Jones's book) on the day before the State Department's final draft of this message went to the White House, presumably about March 6, that I came over to the department to have a look at the paper. What I saw made me extremely unhappy. The language to which I took particular exception was not the product of Henderson's pen or of any of his associates in the geographic divisions. It had been produced, at the initiative of the department's public relations office, in a subcommittee of the State-War-Navy Coordinating Committee (SWNCC), which evidently felt itself under the necessity of clothing the announced rationale for the President's decision in terms more grandiose and more sweeping than anything that I, at least, had ever envisaged. (More about that later.) I remonstrated, by my own recollection, to Henderson. Mr. Jones says I also remonstrated to Mr. Acheson; and I have no doubt that I did, although I do not specifically recall it. I produced, in any event, some alternative language, though I have no record of what it was. Whether these remonstrations met with much understanding in substance, I cannot remember. In any case, they came too late. No one wanted to repeat the agony of collective drafting that had been invested over the preceding days in the production of this historic piece of paper.

Faced, as any autobiographer is, with the danger of mistaking hindsight for recollection, I am fortunate in finding among my papers one that not only sets forth in detail the reasons, as I saw them at the time, why it was desirable that our government should respond to the challenge of the British move but also explains, by clear implication, the reasons for my unhappiness over the wording of the President's message. We in the faculty of the War College used the Greek crisis, just at that time, as the basis for a problem which we assigned to various committees of the students. We asked them, in effect, to supply some of the individual components of the President's decision on this question. Twice, on the heels of the President's presentation to Congress, I discussed this problem informally before the student body. On the first of these occasions, March 14, two days after presentation of the President's message, I commented on the terms of the War College problem itself. On March 28, after the student answers were in, I discussed the solutions to it and gave the reasons why I, personally, had felt that we had been right to accept the challenge of the British action. It is the stenographic records of these two statements that I find in my papers.

First, as to my understanding of the background of the decision: I accepted the conclusion, to which many others in the government had arrived, that (and I use the words of the War College presentation) "if nothing were done to stiffen the backs of the non-Communist elements in Greece at this juncture the Communist elements would soon succeed in seizing power and in establishing a totalitarian dictatorship along the lines already visible in other Balkan countries." I did not view the prospect of such a Communist takeover as "*in itself* any immediate and catastrophic setback to the Western world." I considered that the Russians and their Eastern European associates were poorly set up to take responsibility either for the governing of Greece or for the support of the Greek economy. Eventually, I thought, all this might boomerang on them in the form of serious economic difficulties and other problems, which the West might even ultimately exploit to good advantage. But Communist rule, I thought, "would probably be successfully consolidated in the long run and might some day have most unfortunate strategic consequences from the standpoint of any military adversary of the

Soviet Union." And more important still were the probable repercussions which such a development would have on neighboring areas.

In this last connection, I took up first the question of Turkey. I pointed out that the situation of Turkey differed quite fundamentally from that of Greece. There was no serious Communist penetration in Turkey—no comparable guerrilla movement. The Turks had nothing to fear but fear. "If . . . the Turks do not lose their nerves, if they keep their internal political life relatively clean and orderly and refuse to become involved in negotiations with the Russians on a bilateral basis over complicated questions such as that of the Straits, they will probably continue to enjoy a temporary and precarious immunity to Russian pressure." But, I pointed out, should they be increasingly encircled by Communist-dominated entities, it would plainly be harder for them to maintain this stance. Aid to Greece was therefore important as a support for stability in Turkey as well.

It should be noted that this view of the problem of Turkey afforded no rationale for the mounting of a special aid program for Turkey itself. The accent was put on internal morale and on firmness of diplomatic stance, not on military preparations. It was for this reason that I was not happy to find in the draft of the President's message to Congress a proposal for aid to Turkey as well as to Greece. I suspected that what was intended primarily was military aid, and that what had really happened was that the Pentagon had exploited a favorable set of circumstances in order to infiltrate a military aid program for Turkey into what was supposed to be primarily a political and economic program for Greece. Since it was important, in my view, that the Soviet threat be recognized for what it was—primarily a political one and not a threat of military attack—it seemed unfortunate that the picture of what was needed in Greece should be confused by association with something that was not needed—or, if needed, was needed for entirely different purposes —in Turkey.

To return to the exposé at the War College: From Turkey, I moved on to the subject of the Middle East. What would be the repercussions there of a Communist takeover in Greece? Here again my conclusions were somewhat different from those of other people. I did not underrate the seriousness of Russian-Communist penetration among the restless intelligentsia of the Moslem capitals. But I questioned the ultimate ability of the Russians to disaffect and dominate the entire Moslem world. Not only was their ideology in conflict with the Moslem faith, but they were just not that good. Even in northern Iran and among the Kurds their recent performance, as political intriguers, had not been impressive. If they were to expand still further in this area they would "soon encounter the far more vigorous political society of Arabia itself and contiguous areas, where the fire of Moslem ideology burns with a purer and fiercer flame, and where resistance to Communist political pressure would be of a far sterner quality than in the lands to the north and east." It was not, then, for the long term that I feared the fillip to Soviet penetration of the Middle East which a Communist coup in Greece would certainly provide. But I had to recognize that the immediate repercussions might be ones unsettling to such fragile stability as the region then enjoyed. And this in turn might have effects in relation to the situation in an area even more important from the standpoint of our security: Western Europe.

It was hard to overestimate, in those days of uncertainty and economic difficulty, the cumulative effects of sensational political events. People were influenced, as I pointed out on that occasion to the War College, not just by their desires as to what *should* happen but by their estimates of what *would* happen. People in Western Europe did not, by and large, want Communist control. But this did not mean that they would not trim their sails and even abet its coming if they gained the impression that it was inevitable. This was why the shock of a Communist success in Greece could not be risked.

In Western Europe, too, I added, it was not likely that Communist domination could last indefinitely. But while it lasted, it could do great damage.

> Because floodwaters must—by the laws of nature—some day subside is no reason that one should welcome them on his place. . . . We have no cause to assume that Europe as we know it—and as we need it—would never recover from the blow which even a brief period of Russian control would deal to her already weakened traditions and institutions. . . . The waves of Communist authority might some day recede but we could have no reason to expect that American prestige and influence could easily reenter the territories thus liberated. . . .

I went on, then to point out that if we were to leave Europe to the Communists, the resulting problem of security for the United States "might not be one of external security alone."

> Remember that in abandoning Europe we would be abandoning not only the fountainheads of most of our own culture and tradition; we would also be abandoning almost all the other areas in the world where progressive

representative government is a working proposition. We would be placing ourselves in the position of a lonely country, culturally and politically. To maintain confidence in our own traditions and institutions we would henceforth have to whistle loudly in the dark. I am not sure that whistling could be loud enough to do the trick.

I know that there are many people—and probably some among you—who will reply indignantly that I am selling short the strength and soundness of our institutions—who will maintain that American democracy has nothing to fear from Europe's diseases and nothing to learn from Europe's experiences.

I wish I could believe that that were true. I wish I could believe that the human impulses which give rise to the nightmares of totalitarianism were ones which Providence had allocated only to other peoples and to which the American people had been graciously left immune. Unfortunately, I know that that is not true. After all, most of us are only Europeans once or twice removed; and some of us are less removed than that. There are openly totalitarian forces already working in our society. Do you think that they could fail to derive new confidence and new supporters from such a series of developments? And it is not even with these small existing groups of extremists that the real danger lies. The fact of the matter is that there is a little bit of the totalitarian buried somewhere, way down deep, in each and every one of us. It is only the cheerful light of confidence and security which keeps this evil genius down at the usual helpless and invisible depth. If confidence and security were to disappear, don't think that he would not be waiting to take their place. Others may lull themselves to sleep with the pleasing assumption that the work of building freedom in this country was accomplished completely and for all time by our forefathers. I prefer to accept the word of a great European, the German poet, Goethe, that freedom is something that has to be reconquered every day. And in that never-ending process of reconquest, I would hate to see this country lose all its allies.

So much for the reasons for our limited intervention in Greece. Why, then, approving this action, did I take exception to the language of the President's message?

I took exception to it primarily because of the sweeping nature of the commitments which it implied. The heart of the message and the passage that has subsequently been most frequently quoted was this:

> I believe it must be the policy of the United States to support free peoples who are resisting subjugation by armed minorities or by outside pressures.
> I believe that we must assist free peoples to work out their own destinies in their own way.

This passage, and others as well, placed our aid to Greece in the frame-work of a universal policy rather than in that of a specific decision addressed to a specific set of circumstances. It implied that what we had decided to do in the case of Greece was something we would be prepared to do in the case of any other country, provided only that it was faced with the threat of "subjugation by armed minorities or by outside pres-sures."

It seemed to me highly uncertain that we would invariably find it in our interests or within our means to extend assistance to countries that found themselves in this extremity. The mere fact of their being in such a plight was only one of the criteria that had to be taken into account in determining our action. The establishment of the existence of such a threat was only the beginning, not the end, of the process of decision. I listed, in my presentation to the War College, three specific consider-ations that had supported our decision to extend assistance to Greece:

> A. The problem at hand is one within our economic, technical, and financial capabilities.
> B. If we did not take such action, the resulting situation might rebound very decidedly to the advantage of our political adversaries.
> C. If, on the other hand, we do take the action in question, there is good reason to hope that the favorable consequences will carry far beyond the limits of Greece itself.

These considerations, I pointed out, did not necessarily apply to all other regions. I doubted, for example, that any of them would fully apply in the case of China: the first most definitely would not. But if this was the case, then why use language that suggested that all that was required was proof of the existence of a threat of "subjugation by armed minorities or by outside pressure"—that this was the sole criterion of our response?

Were I reacting today to the Truman Doctrine message, I would certainly have added to this list of specific requirements the willingness and ability of the threatened people to pick up and bear resolutely the overwhelming portion of the responsibility and effort in their own de-fense against both direct and indirect aggression—not just to sit back and hedge against the possibility that resistance might not be effective and leave the burden of the struggle to us. I would also take exception to the repeated suggestions, in the text of that message, that what we were concerned to defend in Greece was the democratic quality of the coun-try's institutions. We would find it necessary to give aid, over the ensuing years, to a number of regimes which could hardly qualify for it on the basis of their democratic character. It was unwise to suggest that this, too, was an essential criterion. But these omissions, the recognition of which does indeed reflect the promptings of hindsight, only reinforce the validity of the objections to the language of the message that suggested themselves at the time.

I was not alone in my awareness of the danger that the sweeping language of the message might be subject to misinterpretation. Mr. Acheson was himself at pains to try to dispel among the members of the Congress the impression that what the President had said represented some sort of a blank check. The fact that we were prepared on principle to extend aid in such situations did not mean, he explained in his testimony before the Senate Committee on Foreign Relations on March 24, 1947, that our action in other instances would always be the same as in Greece. "Any requests of foreign countries for aid," he said in his opening statement,

> will have to be considered according to the circumstances in each individual case. In another case we would have to study whether the country in question really needs assistance, whether its request is consistent with American foreign policy, whether the request for assistance is sincere, and whether assistance by the United States would be effective in meeting the problems of that country. It cannot be assumed, therefore, that this government would necessarily undertake measures in any other country identical or even closely similar to those proposed for Greece and Turkey.

Nevertheless, the misapprehension already conveyed was, as I see it, never entirely corrected. Throughout the ensuing two decades the conduct of our foreign policy would continue to be bedeviled by people in our own government as well as in other governments who could not free themselves from the belief that all another country had to do, in order to qualify for American aid, was to demonstrate the existence of a Communist threat. Since almost no country was without a Communist minority, this assumption carried very far. And as time went on, the firmness of understanding for these distinctions on the part of our own public and governmental establishment appeared to grow weaker rather than stronger. In the 1960s so absolute would be the value attached, even by people within the government, to the mere existence of a Communist threat, that such a threat would be viewed as calling, in the case of Southeast Asia, for an American response on a tremendous scale, without serious regard even to those main criteria that most of us in 1947 would have thought it natural and essential to apply.

On many occasions, both before and after this Greek-Turkish epi-
sode, I have been struck by the congenital aversion of Americans to
taking specific decisions on specific problems, and by their persistent urge
to seek universal formulae or doctrines in which to clothe and justify
particular actions. We obviously dislike to discriminate. We like to find
some general governing norm to which, in each instance, appeal can be
taken, so that individual decisions may be made not on their particular
merits but automatically, depending on whether the circumstances do or
do not seem to fit the norm. We like, by the same token, to attribute a
universal significance to decisions we have already found it necessary, for
limited and parochial reasons, to take. It was not enough for us, when
circumstances forced us into World War I, to hold in view the specific
reasons for our entry: our war effort had to be clothed in the form of an
effort to make the *world* (nothing less) "safe for democracy." It was not
enough for us, in World War II, that the Japanese attacked us at Pearl
Harbor and that both Japanese and German governments declared war
on us: we did not feel comfortable until we had wrapped our military
effort in the wholly universalistic—and largely meaningless—generalities
of the Atlantic Charter. Something of this same compulsion became
apparent in the postwar period in the tendency of many Americans to
divide the world neatly into Communist and "free world" components,
to avoid recognition of specific differences among countries on either
side, and to search for general formulas to govern our relations with the
one or the other. I think, in this connection, of the periodic wrangling
in Congress, in connection with the annual aid bills, over the question
whether most-favored-nation treatment should be extended, or various
forms of aid be granted, to "Communist" countries or to countries
"forming part of the Communist conspiracy" or whatever general language one chose to employ—the idea being always to define a category
of states and to compel the executive to behave in a uniform way with
relation to all of them. Seldom does it seem to have occurred to many
congressional figures that the best thing to do would be to let the President, or the Secretary of State, use his head.

To this day I am uncertain as to the origins of this persistent
American urge to the universalization or generalization of decision. I
suspect it to be a reflection of the extent to which we are a people given
to government by laws rather than by executive discretion. Laws, too,
are general norms, and Congress, accustomed to limiting executive discretion through the establishment of such norms in the internal field,
obviously feels more comfortable when its powers with relation to for-

eign policy can be exercised in a similar way. Unable to control executive decisions on a day-to-day basis, many Congressmen and Senators feel, I suspect, a need for general determinations defining the latitude within which those decisions may be taken.

Whatever the origins of this tendency, it is an unfortunate one. It confuses public understanding of international issues more than it clarifies it. It shackles and distorts the process of decision-taking. It causes questions to be decided on the basis of criteria only partially relevant or not relevant at all. It tends to exclude at many points the discrimination of judgment and the prudence of language requisite to the successful conduct of the affairs of a great power.

Among the many papers prepared in the winter of 1946–1947, there was one that was written not for delivery as a lecture and not for publication but merely for the private edification of Secretary of the Navy James Forrestal. Ever since the receipt in Washington of the long telegram of February 22, 1946, Mr. Forrestal had taken a lively personal interest in my work. It was, I suspect, due to his influence that I was assigned to the War College and later chosen by General Marshall to head the Planning Staff.

During the period of my service at the War College—in December 1946, to be exact—Mr. Forrestal sent me a paper on the subject of Marxism and Soviet power, prepared by a member of his immediate entourage, and asked me to comment on it. This I found hard to do. It was a good paper. With parts of it I could agree; other parts were simply not put the way I would have put them. The whole subject was one too close to my own experience and interests for me to discuss it in terms of someone else's language. I sent the paper back to him with the observation that rather than commenting I would prefer, if he agreed, to address myself to the same subject in my own words. This, he replied, he would like me to do.

The result was that on January 31, 1947, I sent to him, for his private and personal edification, a paper discussing the nature of Soviet power as a problem in policy for the United States. It was a literary extrapolation of the thoughts which had been maturing in my mind, and which I had been expressing in private communications and speeches, for at least two years into the past. Even the term "containment" which appeared in the course of the argument was, as we have just observed, not new.

Mr. Forrestal read the paper. He acknowledged it, on February 17, with the words: "It is extremely well-done and I am going to suggest to the Secretary[1] that he read it."

Now I had as it happened, spoken informally, early in January, at the Council of Foreign Relations, in New York, on the same general subject. The editor of the council's magazine *Foreign Affairs,* Mr. Hamilton Fish Armstrong (a great editor and, incidentally, one with whom this association was to be the beginning of a long and close friendship), asked me whether I did not have something in writing, along the lines of what I had said to the council, that could be published in the magazine. I had no text of what I had said on that occasion, but I thought of the paper I had prepared for Mr. Forrestal. In early March, therefore, I sought and obtained Mr. Forrestal's assurance that he had no objection to its publication. I then submitted it (March 13) to the Committee on Unofficial Publication, of the Department of State, for the usual official clearance. In doing so, I explained that it was the intention that it should be published anonymously. The committee pondered it at leisure, found in it nothing particularly remarkable or dangerous from the government's standpoint, and issued, on April 8, permission for its publication in the manner indicated. I then crossed out my own name in the signature of the article, replaced it with an "X" to assure the anonymity, sent it on to Mr. Armstrong, and thought no more about it. I knew that it would be some weeks before it would appear. I did not know how my position would be changed in the course of those weeks, or how this would affect the interpretations that would be placed upon the article when it was published.

In late June, as I recall it, the article appeared in the July issue of *Foreign Affairs,* under the title: "The Sources of Soviet Conduct." Its appearance was followed shortly (July 8) by that of a piece in the *New York Times* from the pen of the well-known and experienced Washington columnist Mr. Arthur Krock, hinting at the official origin of the article and pointing to the importance that attached to it by virtue of that fact. He, I later learned, had been shown the article by Mr. Forrestal at a time when it was no more than a private paper lying around in Mr. Forrestal's office. His keen journalistic eye had at once recognized it when it appeared in print; and he had put two and two together.

It was not long, after the appearance of Mr. Krock's piece, before the authorship of the article became common knowledge. Others began to write about it, to connect it with the Truman Doctrine and Marshall Plan, to speculate on its significance. It soon became the center of a veritable whirlpool of publicity. *Life* and *Reader's Digest* reprinted long excerpts from it. The term "containment" was picked up and elevated, by common agreement of the press, to the status of a "doctrine," which was then identified with the foreign policy of the administration. In this way there was established—before our eyes, so to speak—one of those indestructible myths that are the bane of the historian.

Feeling like one who has inadvertently loosened a large boulder from the top of a cliff and now helplessly witnesses its path of destruction in the valley below, shuddering and wincing at each successive glimpse of disaster, I absorbed the bombardment of press comment that now set in. I had not meant to do anything of this sort. General Marshall, too, was shocked. It was a firm principle, for him, that "planners don't talk." The last thing he had expected was to see the name of the head of his new Planning Staff bandied about in the press as the author of a programmatical article—or an article hailed as programmatical—on the greatest of our problems of foreign policy. He called me in, drew my attention to this anomaly, peered at me over his glasses with raised eyebrows (eyebrows before whose raising, I may say, better men than I had quailed), and waited for an answer. I explained the origins of the article, and pointed out that it had been duly cleared for publication by the competent official committee. This satisfied him. He was, as I have already observed, an orderly man, accustomed to require and to respect a plain delineation of responsibility. If the article had been cleared in this manner, the responsibility was not mine. He never mentioned the matter again, nor did he hold it officially against me. But it was long, I suspect, before he recovered from his astonishment over the strange ways of the department he now headed.

Measured against the interpretations that were at once attached to it, and have continued to a considerable extent to surround it ever since, the article that appeared in *Foreign Affairs,* in June 1947, suffered, unquestionably, from serious deficiencies. Some of these I might have corrected at the time by more careful editing and greater forethought, had I had any idea of the way it was to be received. But I cannot lay these failures exclusively to the innocent and unsuspecting manner in which the article was written. Certain of the public reactions were ones I would not, in any event, have foreseen.

A serious deficiency of the article was the failure to mention the satellite area of Eastern Europe—the failure to discuss Soviet power, that is, *in terms of* its involvement in this area. Anyone reading the article would have thought—and would have had every reason to think—that I was talking only about Russia proper; that the weaknesses of the Soviet system to which I was drawing attention were ones that had their existence only within the national boundaries of the Soviet state; that the geographic extension that had been given to the power of the Soviet leaders, by virtue of the recent advances of Soviet armies into Eastern Europe and the political exploitation of those advances for Communist purposes, were irrelevant to the weaknesses of which I was speaking. Obviously, in mentioning the uncertainties of the Soviet situation—such things as the weariness and poor morale among the population, the fragility of the constitutional arrangements within the party, etc.—I would have had a far stronger case had I added the characteristic embarrasments of imperialism which the Soviet leaders had now taken upon themselves with their conquest of Eastern Europe, and the unlikelihood that Moscow would be permanently successful in holding this great area in subjection.

To this day, I am not sure of the reason for this omission. It had something to do, I suspect, with what I felt to be Mr. Forrestal's needs at the time when I prepared the original paper for him. I have a vague recollection of feeling that to go into the problems of the satellite area would be to open up a wholly new subject, confuse the thesis I was developing, and carry the paper beyond its intended scope. Whatever the reason, it was certainly not that I underrated the difficulties with which the Soviet leaders were faced in their attempt to exercise political dominion over Eastern Europe. It has been noted above, in Chapter 9, that even as early as V-E Day, two years before, I had expressed the view that the Russians were overextended in this area. Without Western support, I had written at that time

> Russia would probably not be able to maintain its hold successfully for any length of time over all the territory over which it has today staked out a claim ... The lines would have to be withdrawn somewhat.

Similarly, in the long telegram I had sent to Washington from Moscow, in February 1946, I had pointed out that the Soviet internal system

> will now be subjected, by virtue of recent territorial expansions, to a series of additional strains which once proved a severe tax on Tsardom.

Had I included these appreciations in the X-Article, and added to the description of the internal weaknesses of Soviet power a mention of the strains of Moscow's new external involvement in Eastern Europe, I would have had a far stronger case for challenging the permanency of the imposing and forbidding facade which Stalin's Russia presented to the outside world in those immediate postwar years.

A second serious deficiency of the X-Article—perhaps the most serious of all—was the failure to make clear that what I was talking about when I mentioned the containment of Soviet power was not the containment by military means of a military threat, but the political containment of a political threat. Certain of the language used—such as "a long-term, patient but firm and vigilant containment of Russian expansive tendencies" or "the adroit and vigilant application of counterforce at a series of constantly shifting geographical and political points" —was at best ambiguous, and lent itself to misinterpretation in this respect.

A third great deficiency, intimately connected with the one just mentioned, was the failure to distinguish between various geographic areas, and to make clear that the "containment" of which I was speaking was not something that I thought we could, necessarily, do everywhere successfully, or even needed to do everywhere successfully, in order to serve the purpose I had in mind. Actually, as noted in connection with the Truman Doctrine above, I distinguished clearly in my own mind between areas that I thought vital to our security and ones that did not seem to me to fall into this category. My objection to the Truman Doctrine message revolved largely around its failure to draw this distinction. Repeatedly, at that time and in ensuing years, I expressed in talks and lectures the views that there were only five regions of the world— the United States, the United Kingdom, the Rhine valley with adjacent industrial areas, the Soviet Union, and Japan—where the sinews of modern military strength could be produced in quantity; I pointed out that only one of these was under Communist control; and I defined the main task of containment, accordingly, as one of seeing to it that none of the remaining ones fell under such control. Why this was not made clear in the X-Article is, again, a mystery. I suppose I thought that such considerations were subsumed under the reference to the need for confronting the Russians with unalterable counterforce *"at every point where they show signs of encroaching upon the interests of a peaceful world."*

So egregious were these errors that I must confess to responsibility for the greatest and most unfortunate of the misunderstandings to which they led. This was the one created in the mind of Mr. Walter Lippmann. It found its expression in the series of twelve pieces attacking the X-Article (later published in book form as *The Cold War, A Study in U.S. Foreign Policy,* New York: Harper and Brothers, 1947) which he published in his newspaper column in the late summer and autumn of 1947. As I read these articles over today (and they are well worth the effort), I find the misunderstanding almost tragic in its dimensions. Mr. Lippmann, in the first place, mistook me for the author of precisely those features of the Truman Doctrine which I had most vigorously opposed —an assumption to which, I must say, I had led squarely with my chin in the careless and indiscriminate language of the X-Article. He held up, as a deserved correction to these presumed aberrations on my part, precisely those features of General Marshall's approach, and those passages of the Harvard speech, for which I had a primary responsibility. He interpreted the concept of containment in just the military sense I had not meant to give it. And on the basis of these misimpressions he proceeded to set forth, as an alternative to what I had led him to think my views were, a concept of American policy so similar to that which I was to hold and to advance in coming years that one could only assume I was subconsciously inspired by that statement of it—as perhaps, in part, I was. He urged a concentration on the vital countries of Europe; he urged a policy directed toward a mutual withdrawal of Soviet and American (also British) forces from Europe; he pointed with farsighted penetration to the dangers involved in any attempt to make of a truncated Western Germany an ally in an anti-Soviet coalition. All these points would figure prominently in my own later writings. He saw them, for the most part, long before I did. I accept the blame for misleading him. My only consolation is that I succeeded in provoking from him so excellent and penetrating a treatise.

Nevertheless, the experience was a painful one. It was doubly painful by reason of the great respect I bore him. I can still recall the feeling of bewilderment and frustration with which—helpless now to reply publicly because of my official position—I read these columns as they appeared and found held against me so many views with which I profoundly agreed. A few months later (April 1948), lying under treatment for ulcers on the sixteenth floor of the Naval Hospital in Bethesda, very bleak in spirit from the attendant fasting and made bleaker still by the whistling of the cold spring wind in the windows of that lofty pinnacle, I wrote a long letter to Mr. Lippmann, protesting the misinterpretation of my thoughts which his articles, as it seemed to me, implied. I never sent it to him. It was probably best that I didn't. The letter had a plaintive and overdramatic tone, reflecting the discomfort of flesh and spirit in which it was written. I took a more cruel but less serious revenge a year or two later when I ran into him on a parlor car of the Pennsylvania Railroad, and wore him relentlessly down with a monologue on these same subjects that lasted most of the way from Washington to New York.

But the terms of the unsent letter still hold, as I see them, a certain interest as expressions of the way the Lippmann columns then affected me.

I began, of course, with a peal of anguish over the confusion about the Truman Doctrine and the Marshall Plan. To be held as the author of the former, and to have the latter held up to me as the mature correction of my youthful folly, hurt more than anything else.

I also naturally went to great lengths to disclaim the view, imputed by me by implication in Mr. Lippmann's columns, that containment was a matter of stationing military forces around the Soviet borders and preventing any outbreak of Soviet military aggressiveness. I protested, as I was to do on so many other occasions over the course of the ensuing eighteen years, against the implication that the Russians were aspiring to invade the other areas and that the task of American policy was to prevent them from doing so. "The Russians don't want," I insisted,

> to invade anyone. It is not in their tradition. They tried it once in Finland and got their fingers burned. They don't want war of any kind. Above all, they don't want the open responsibility that official invasion brings with it. They far prefer to do the job politically with stooge forces. Note well: when I say politically, that does not mean without violence. But it means that the violence is nominally *domestic,* not *international,* violence. It is, if you will, a police violence . . . not a military violence.
>
> The policy of containment related to the effort to encourage other peoples to resist this type of violence and to defend the *internal* integrity of their countries.

I tried, then, to explain (I could have done it better) that the article was in reality a plea—addressed as much to our despairing liberals as to our hotheaded right-wingers—for acceptance of the belief that, ugly as was the problem of Soviet power, war was not inevitable, nor was it a suitable answer; that the absence of war did not mean that we would lose the struggle; that there was a middle ground of political resistance on which we could stand with reasonable prospect of success. We were, in fact, already standing on that ground quite successfully. And I went ahead to point proudly (and rather unfairly, for after all, Lippmann had approved and praised the rationale of the Marshall Plan in his articles) to what had already been accomplished. I cite this passage here, not as a correction to Mr. Lippmann, to whose arguments it was not really an answer, but as a sort of epilogue to the discussion of both Marshall Plan and X-Article.

Something over a year has now gone by since General Marshall took over his present job. I would ask you to think back on the state of the world, as he faced it last spring. At that time, it was almost impossible to see how Europe could be saved. We were still caught in the fateful confusion between the "one-world" and the "two-world" concepts. The economic plight of the continent was rapidly revealing itself as far worse than anyone had dreamed, and was steadily deteriorating. Congress was in an ugly frame of mind, convinced that all foreign aid was "operation rathole." The Communists were at the throat of France. A pall of fear, of bewilderment, of discouragement, hung over the continent and paralyzed all constructive activity. Molotov sat adamant at the Moscow council table, because he saw no reason to pay us a price for things which he thought were bound to drop into his lap, like ripe fruits, through the natural course of events.

Compare that with today? Europe is admittedly not over the hump. But no fruits have dropped [into Molotov's lap]. We know what is West and what is East. Moscow was itself compelled to make that unpleasant delineation. Recovery is progressing rapidly in the West. New hope exists. People see the possibility of a better future. The Communist position in France has been deeply shaken. The Western nations have found a common political language. They are learning to lean on each other, and to help each other. Those who fancied they were neutral are beginning to realize that they are on our side. A year ago only that which was Communist had firmness and structure. Today the non-Communist world is gaining daily in rigidity and in the power of resistance. Admittedly, the issue hangs on Italy; but it hangs, in reality, on Italy alone. A year ago it hung on all of Europe and on us.

You may say: this was not the doing of US policy makers; it was others who worked this miracle.

Certainly, we did not do it alone; and I have no intention of attempting to apportion merit. But you must leave us some pride in our own legerdemain. In international affairs, the proof of the pudding is always in the eating. If the development of the past year had been in the opposite direction—if there had been a deterioration of our position as great as the actual improvement—there is not one of you who would not have placed the blame squarely on the failure of American statesmanship. Must it always, then, be "heads you win; tails I lose" for the US Government?

In the years that have passed since that time, the myth of the "doctrine of containment" has never fully lost its spell. On innumerable occasions, I have been asked to explain it, to say whether I thought it had been a success, to explain how it applied to China, to state a view as to whether it was still relevant in later situations, etc. It has been interpreted by others in a variety of ways. Pro-Soviet writers have portrayed it as the cloak for aggressive designs on the Soviet Union. Rightwing critics have assailed it precisely for its lack of aggressiveness: for its passivity, for its failure to promise anything like "victory." Serious commentators have maintained that it was all very well in 1947 but that it lost its rationale with the Korean War, or with Stalin's death, or with the decline of bipolarity.

It is hard for me to respond to all these criticisms. What I said in the X-Article was not intended as a doctrine. I am afraid that when I think about foreign policy, I do not think in terms of doctrines. I think in terms of principles.

In writing the X-Article, I had in mind a long series of what seemed to me to be concessions that we had made, during the course of the war and just after it, to Russian expansionist tendencies—concessions made in the hope and belief that they would promote collaboration between our government and the Soviet government in the postwar period. I had also in mind the fact that many people, seeing that these concessions had been unsuccessful and that we had been unable to agree with the Soviet leaders on the postwar order of Europe and Asia, were falling into despair and jumping to the panicky conclusion that this spelled the inevitability of an eventual war between the Soviet Union and the United States.

It was this last conclusion that I was attempting, in the X-Article, to dispute. I thought I knew as much as anyone in the United States about the ugliness of the problem that Stalin's Russia presented to us. I had no need to accept instruction on this point from anybody. But I saw no necessity of a Soviet-American war, nor anything to be gained by one, then or at any time. There was, I thought, another way of handling this problem—a way that offered reasonable prospects of success, at least in the sense of avoiding a new world disaster and leaving the Western community of nations no worse off than it then was. This was simply to cease at that point making fatuous unilateral concessions to the Kremlin, to do what we could to inspire and support resistance elsewhere to its efforts to expand the area of its dominant political influence, and to wait for the internal weaknesses of Soviet power, combined with frustration in the external field, to moderate Soviet ambitions and behavior. The Soviet leaders, formidable as they were, were not supermen. Like all rulers of all great countries, they had their internal contradictions and dilemmas to deal with. Stand up to them, I urged, manfully but not aggressively, and give the hand of time a chance to work.

This is all that the X-Article was meant to convey. I did not suppose, in saying all this, that the situation flowing immediately from the manner in which hostilities ended in 1945 would endure forever. It was my assumption that if and when the Soviet leaders had been brought to a point where they would talk reasonably about some of the problems flowing from the outcome of the war, we would obviously wish to pursue this possibility and to see what could be done about restoring a more normal state of affairs. I shared to the full, in particular, Walter Lippmann's view of the importance of achieving, someday, the retirement of Soviet military power from Eastern Europe, although I did not then attach quite the same political importance to such a retirement as he did. (In this he was more right than I was.)

No one was more conscious than I was of the dangers of a permanent division of the European continent. The purpose of "containment" as then conceived was not to perpetuate the status quo to which the military operations and political arrangements of World War II had led; it was to tide us over a difficult time and bring us to a point where we could discuss effectively with the Russians the drawbacks and dangers this status quo involved, and to arrange with them for its peaceful replacement by a better and sounder one.

And if the policy of containment could be said in later years to have failed, it was not a failure in the sense that it proved impossible to prevent the Russians from making mortally dangerous encroachments "upon the interests of a peaceful world" (for it did prevent that); nor was it a failure in the sense that the mellowing of Soviet power, which Walter Lippmann took me so severely to task for predicting, failed to set in (it did set in). The failure consisted in the fact that our own government, finding it difficult to understand a political threat as such and to deal with it in other than military terms, and grievously misled, in particular, by its own faulty interpretations of the significance of the Korean War, failed to take advantage of the opportunities for useful political discussion when, in later years, such opportunities began to open up, and exerted itself, in its military preoccupations, to seal and to perpetuate the very division of Europe which it should have been concerned to remove. It was not "containment" that failed; it was the intended follow-up that never occurred.

When I used the term "Soviet power" in the X-Article, I had in view, of course, the system of power organized, dominated, and inspired by Joseph Stalin. This was a monolithic power structure, reaching through the network of highly disciplined Communist parties into practically every country in the world. In these circumstances, any success of a local Communist party, any advance of Communist power anywhere, had to be regarded as an extension in reality of the political orbit, or at least the dominant influence, of the Kremlin. Precisely because Stalin maintained so jealous, so humiliating a control over foreign Communists, all of the latter had, at that time, to be regarded as the vehicles of his will, not their own. His was the only center of authority in the Communist world; and it was a vigilant, exacting, and imperious headquarters, prepared to brook no opposition.

Tito's break with Moscow, in 1948, was the first overt breach in the monolithic unity of the Moscow-dominated Communist bloc. For long, it remained the only one. It did not affect immediately and importantly the situation elsewhere in the Communist world. But when, in the period between 1957 and 1962, the differences between the Chinese and Russian Communist parties, having lain latent in earlier years, broke to the surface and assumed the form of a major conflict between the two regimes, the situation in the world Communist movement became basically different. Other Communist parties, primarily those outside Eastern Europe but partly the Eastern European ones as well, had now two poles—three, if Belgrade was included—to choose among. This very freedom of choice not only made possible for them a large degree of independence; in many instances it forced that independence upon them. Neither of the two major centers of Communist power was now in a position to try to impose upon them a complete disciplinary control, for fear of pushing them into the arms of the other. They, on the other hand, reluctant for the most part to take the risks of total identification with one or the other, had little choice but to maneuver, to think and act for themselves, to accept, in short, the responsibilities of independence. If, at the end of the 1940s, no Communist party (except the Yugoslav one) could be considered anything else than an instrument of Soviet power, by the end of the 1950s none (unless it be the Bulgarian and the Czech) could be considered to be such an instrument at all.

This development changed basically the assumptions underlying the concept of containment, as expressed in the X-Article. Seen from the standpoint upon which that article rested, the Chinese-Soviet conflict was in itself the greatest single measure of containment that could be conceived. It not only invalidated the original concept of containment, it disposed in large measure of the very problem to which it was addressed.

Efforts to enlist the original concept of containment with relation to situations that postdate the Chinese-Soviet conflict, particularly when they are described in terms that refer to some vague "communism" in general and do not specify what particular communism is envisaged, are therefore wholly misconceived. There is today no such thing as "communism" in the sense that there was in 1947; there are only a number of national regimes which cloak themselves in the verbal trappings of radical Marxism and follow domestic policies influenced to one degree or another by Marxist concepts.

If, then, I was the author in 1947 of a "doctrine" of containment, it was a doctrine that lost much of its rationale with the death of Stalin and with the development of the Soviet-Chinese conflict. I emphatically deny the paternity of any efforts to invoke that doctrine today in situations to which it has, and can have, no proper relevance.

NOTE

1. Presumably, the Secretary of State.

7

Will the Real Mr. "X" Please Stand Up?
LLOYD C. GARDNER

"If, then, I was the author in 1947 of a 'doctrine' of containment," Kennan admits, "it was a doctrine that lost much of its rationale with the death of Stalin and with the development of the Soviet-Chinese conflict."[1] Like the effort to limit his responsibility for containment geographically, Kennan's desire to halt it chronologically was only a quiet voice raised against Cold War crusaders on the march to provide that unanswerable force he had once called for. In the months after he completed his *Memoirs,* Kennan's wish for an end to containment conflicted with his outrage upon the Soviet invasion of Czechoslovakia, causing him to reassert the impossibility of détente. "I have never understood this talk about détente," Kennan told a newspaper reporter in August 1968. The United States should send 100,000 troops to West Germany immediately, he said, and inform the Russians that they would not be removed until Czechoslovakia was evacuated. "Although speaking in scholarly terms," the *New York Times* report of September 22, 1968, concluded, "Mr. Kennan did not conceal his emotions when he discussed the Soviet-led invasion of Czechoslovakia." In this interview, as in the "X" article, it is not easy to tell where Kennan's moral censure of the Soviet system and its conspiratorial diplomacy leave off, and where his "realistic" views of American foreign policy begin.

"In writing the X-article," Kennan says in his *Memoirs,* "I had in mind a long series of what seemed to me to be concessions, that we had made, during the course of the war and just after it, to Russian expansionist tendencies—concessions made in the hope and belief that they would promote collaboration between our government and the Soviet government in the postwar period." Perceiving that others now saw the failure of this policy, Kennan argues that he was concerned that Americans not jump to the panicky conclusion that war between the two super-powers was inevitable.[2] Like Bullitt and Forrestal, he was dis-

From Lloyd C. Gardner, *Architects of Illusion: Men and Ideas in American Foreign Policy, 1941–1949.* Chicago, Quadrangle Books, 1970, pp. 284-286, 288-297, 298-300. Reprinted by permission of Quadrangle Books. Copyright 1970, by Lloyd C. Gardner.

mayed by Roosevelt's faith in personal diplomacy; and he saw the proposed United Nations as a product of the longstanding American dream of projecting onto the world at large its national consensus and belief in juridical settlements of international disputes.

In George Frost Kennan the Presbyterian elder wrestled with the Bismarckian geopolitician: that struggle produced the "X" article. The moralist was on top when Kennan spoke of disassociating America from the Soviet Union on the occasion of the Warsaw uprising in August 1944, when Stalin refused to permit the Western Allies to come to the aid of the Polish underground against the Nazis. The impact upon Americans in the Soviet Union cannot be gauged from this distance, but in Kennan's case it produced a revulsion at American complicity in Russia's dark undertakings not only in Poland but in other countries. American and British signatures on the Russian-dictated armistice agreements for Rumania and Hungary were black marks on the West's cause, and they made a mockery of the Atlantic Charter and all the rest of it: "We in the West had a perfect right to divest ourselves of responsibility for further Soviet military operations conducted in the spirit of, and with the implications of, the Soviet denial of support for the Warsaw uprising."[3]

But as another "realist," William Hardy McNeill, once suggested, the morality in Polish-Russian relations was never so one-sided as all that. The uprising in Warsaw, he wrote, had all the elements of Greek tragedy about it. But how could Kennan define the Western reaction to that grim occurrence as a "concession" to Soviet expansionist tendencies? Certainly it was not a military concession, for Kennan himself assumed that the United States could not have effectively challenged the Soviets in Eastern Europe without risking an unacceptable confrontation with the Red Army. To disassociate the West from Russia publicly while the war against Germany was still going on—and another war yet to be finished in Asia—would have been a quixotic gesture. It would not have helped the Poles, and could have made their condition even worse. Russian suspicions of a separate peace in the West, followed by an Allied effort to drive to the East, could have produced an even more frantic effort on Stalin's part to secure Eastern Europe. Such a policy would have permitted moralism to dominate national interest with a vengeance. . . .

Much of what Kennan wrote in 1947 had been in his mind since the 1930's. With Russia's great victory over Germany in May 1945, Kennan foresaw no Kremlin attempt to advance communism in the West through the machanized units of the Red Army. Instead, he said in a cable to the State Department, it was possible that Communist parties in Western countries would take advantage of Soviet-American conflicts to further their own cause. "Behind Russia's stubborn expansion," he wrote,

> lies only the age-old sense of insecurity of a sedentary people reared on an exposed plain in the neighborhood of fierce nomadic peoples. Will this urge, now become a permanent feature of Russian psychology, provide the basis for a successful expansion of Russia into new areas of east and west? And if initially successful, will it know where to stop? Will it not be inexorably carried forward, by its very nature, in a struggle to reach the whole—to attain complete mastery of the shores of the Atlantic and the Pacific?

Since the Soviets regarded conflict as inevitable, they counted on a masochistic element in American policy to increase communist power in Europe: "They observe with gratification that in this way a great people can be led, like an ever-hopeful suitor, to perform one act of ingratiation after the other without ever reaching the goal which would satisfy its ardor and allay its generosity."

> Should the western world, contrary to all normal expectations, muster up the political manliness to deny to Russia either moral or material support for the consolidation of Russian power throughout eastern and central Europe, Russia would probably not be able to maintain its hold successfully for any length of time over all the territory over which it has today staked a claim. In this case, the lines would have to be withdrawn somewhat. But if this occurred, the nuisance value of Soviet power in the western countries and in the world at large would be exploited to the full. The agents of Soviet power might have to abandon certain districts where they now hold sway; but they would, to use Trotski's vivid phrase, "slam the door so that all Europe would shake." Every difficulty that could conceivably be created for the western democracies by communist parties and communist claques would be used in this baring of the fangs; and the world would have cause to remember Molotov's warning at San Francisco that if the conference did not give Russia peace and security on her own terms, she would seek and find it elsewhere.
>
> But no one in Moscow believes that the western world, once confronted with the life-size wolf of Soviet displeasure standing at the door and threatening to blow the house in, would be able to stand firm. And it is on this disbelief that Soviet global policy is based.[4]

Kennan's images were never as subtle as his arguments; even in 1945 he introduced his arguments in favor of a policy of containment and patience with visions of Soviet power inexorably moving toward America's Atlantic and Pacific shores. Moreover, he badly misread the political atmosphere in Washington if he thought that Truman intended to play the role of Russia's ever-hopeful suitor. Such images only promoted the very oversimplification of the Russian problem that Kennan deplored in retrospect in his *Memoirs*. "My recollection," Louis Halle has recently said, "remains that the predominant worry in Washington, as the war approached its end, was over the deadly struggle to contain the Soviet Union that could already be foreseen."[5]

The "X" article had come to be written as a result of Forrestal's request that Kennan comment on another paper, Edward F. Willett's "Dialectical Materialism and Russian Objectives." Willett, a former Smith College professor then in the Navy Department, had been asked by Forrestal to do this paper in an attempt to answer "the" question. Willett's paper was far more ambiguous and ideologically oriented than anything Kennan had ever produced. The key sentence was: "We have to deal on the one hand with the seeming *certainty* of war if Marxian Communism prevails, and on the other hand with the *possibility* of avoiding war if Communism does not prevail."[6]

To Willett's all-encompassing statement that war was a certainty if communism "prevailed" (whatever that actually meant), Kennan replied that he had no doubts about America's ability to "contain" the Russians —provided its people managed themselves reasonably well. But he did not agree with Willett's somewhat optimistic assertion that an improvement in living standards in the capitalist countries would automatically negate the internal communist threat. This assertion struck at the very core of Kennan's personal and public philosophy; his reply to it goes a long way toward explaining much of the remaining "mystery" about the "X" article. The Soviet system—as well as the Nazi system—had risen not from the corruptions of man's institutions, but from the deeper corruptions of man himself. Once established, Kennan said, such systems brought out the full capacities for evil within man. Thus, while it was a reasonable conclusion that without Stalin the purges of the 1930's would not have taken place, the final result was not the work of Stalin's personality alone, but of his personality and will as they functioned through a political system dedicated to shutting out the nobler impulses of man. In general, Kennan said, communism seemed to be strongest in nations such as Czechoslovakia and France, where the living standard and degree of cultural advancement were highest, weakest in nations such as Portugal. He doubted whether those members, even of the American labor movement, who served as conscious or unconscious "vehicles for Communist influence" were suffering any material hardships. Communism reflected more subtle and profound maladies than material suffering.

Soviet leaders, Kennan maintained, were no longer committed to improving the living standards of the Russian people. Perhaps they had been so committed at the height of the revolution; now, however, they were concerned with maintaining only a minimum standard so that the people could work efficiently to increase the military-industrial potential of the regime. For communist leaders, power was the main thing. Fortunately there was little evidence that these leaders could extend their power over any area greater than that which they already controlled. Russia simply did not have either the manpower or skill to dominate any greater area—at least unaided.[7]

While Kennan's analyses blended logic and conviction, the mixture varied considerably from paper to paper. Logic predominated in his efforts to describe Stalinist foreign policy tactics—their basic realism and reliance upon Western weaknesses and mistakes; profound conviction filled his pessimistic descriptions of human behavior.[8] In this respect, his response to Willett's paper was especially complex. He wanted, on the one hand, to discourage the notion of the inevitability of war; on the other hand, he was equally anxious to sound a warning against the liberal fallacy that improvement in man's material well-being would bring a solution of his basic problems.

Highly impressed with this critique of Willett's paper, Forrestal asked Kennan to rewrite it along the lines of his suggestions. Kennan replied that because it was difficult to fit oneself into another's attitudes, he would prefer to submit a completely original paper. Thus his approach to the "X" article had three sources: his life-long convictions about human nature; a career-long belief that America had made too many concessions to the Soviets (and others) in the vain hope that a League of Nations would restrain man's inherent traits; and a more recent vexation, widely shared in official Washington, at Henry Wallace's plea for greater "trust" in Soviet-American relations.

Kennan interpreted Wallace's criticisms of the "get-tough" policy as a foolish desire to continue Rooseveltian personal diplomacy and, at Yale University, on October 1, 1946, indirectly criticized him in a lecture on the dangers of misunderstanding Soviet motives and policy. Unhappily, Kennan began, such bids for "trust" in international relations all too often had great appeal "to the Rotarian heart." But the Russian challenge demanded something more from Americans than "a few propitiatory offerings fearfully and hastily tossed in the path of the advancing opposition." It was important to disabuse ourselves completely of such feelings by employing the most dispassionate arguments and logic. Here again, however, Kennan's overreaction to Rooseveltian foreign policy led him to draw militant images for instructional purposes rather than describe the reality of Soviet capabilities. He was chasing Roosevelt's ghost in Henry Wallace.

Kennan went on to say that Wallace apparently thought—as had many vain people before him—that the "golden touch of his particular personality and the warmth of his sympathy for the cause of Russian Communism would modify to some important degree the actions of the Soviet Government." Such a false notion could only be the product of complete ignorance of the conduct of international relations (let alone relations with the Soviets). Wallace was simply flying in the face of the most basic realities of the Russian situation and insulting the ideological firmness of men who had followed the sternest of doctrines, "followed it through extreme danger, through extreme hardship, and through the sacrifice of every other value known to human life." These men would not thank Wallace for slighting their integrity as Marxists, though they might contemptuously take advantage of him.

Some listeners, Kennan said, might find this analysis too ideological. "Never forget that ideology is the only positive feature in a regime which has otherwise brought little but harshness, cruelty and physical misery to the human beings who have fallen within the range of its influence." Ideology was the figleaf of Soviet respectability. Tear it away and all that was left was the last in a series of rulers "who have driven a great people from one military ordeal to another throughout the course of centuries in order to assure the security of their own oppressive regimes."

The destruction of Russia's two great enemies, Germany and Japan, had confronted these men with the horrible possibility that they might be forced to live in a friendly world. "Is it any wonder that they rose up as a body to deny that this precariousness had passed?" The Russians had only themselves to fear and only their backwardness to blame for their insecurity. Appeasement of these fears would not dispel Soviet ideology and could lead only down a path to which there was "no end short of the capitulation of the United States as a great power in the world and as the guardian of its own security."

We can contribute only by a long-term policy of firmness, patience and understanding, designed to keep the Russians confronted with superior strength at every juncture where they might otherwise be inclined to encroach upon the vital interests of a stable and peaceful world, but to do this in so friendly and unprovocative a manner that its basic purposes will not be subject to misinterpretation.[9]

The ratio between logic and conviction was changing, and the imagery had hardened; almost completely bypassed were the specific events which had led to the beginnings of Cold War or to the split in the Truman Cabinet which had produced Wallace's Madison Square Garden speech. It was all psychology and ideology. In this mood Kennan wrote what eventually became the "X" article for Secretary Forrestal.

Among other interruptions as he set to work was a request for a conference from two of Bernard Baruch's aides in the United States delegation to the U.N. Atomic Energy Commission. A meeting was arranged for November 8, 1946. The aides outlined their strategy for bringing the Baruch Plan to a vote before the end of the year, despite the likelihood of the Russians' refusing it. While Kennan approved, he felt the plan should not be regarded as a final step by either side, only an interim position. The Politburo was undoubtedly waiting to see what the United States would do if the Kremlin did not sign up. The proper response after the vote, therefore, was for the United States to begin a series of moves designed to convince the Russians of its serious intent— and of the consequences should they choose to continue their present course. Such moves might include military staff conversations with the British and Canadians, the construction of a new bombproof general staff headquarters somewhere in a remote region, and so forth. "He firmly believes," Baruch's aides reported, "we must keep a constant and firm pressure on the Russians. We must show no sign of weakening whatever in the position we have taken." Despite pessimism, they added, Kennan thought it might ultimately be possible to reach a satisfactory agreement with the Russians on atomic energy controls.[10]

As in the Yale lecture on Wallace's Rotarian-like errors, Kennan placed his real emphasis on American behavior in meeting the Soviet challenge, not on the reality of that challenge itself. In formulating his containment policy, however, it was difficult for him to maintain any balance between reason and principle or political and military tactics. There was simply *no* clear delineation between such internal elements —just as real geographical limitations and boundaries break down when policy is applied. Containment could not be restricted to the five "key" regions, to political tactics, or to nondoctrinaire applications. Argument from moral conviction, especially in the new atomic age, guaranteed the absolutist character of the competition, while discussion of the techniques of this new struggle reciprocally reinforced this absolutism.

The first sentence of the "X" article, completed a few months later, went a long way to justify such a conclusion. Perhaps the nature of Forrestal's specific assignment had been just enough to tip Kennan's balance in favor of principle and military imagery: "The political personality of Soviet power, as we know it today, is the product of ideology and circumstances: ideology inherited by the present Soviet leaders from the movement in which they had their political origin, and circumstances *of the power* which they now have exercised for nearly three decades in Russia." Those circumstances, let us note, were not of Russia's international position in those three decades, but of the power which the Soviet leaders had exercised at home. It was a crucial definition and a crucial distinction. It made Kennan the original popularizer of the so-called "domestic change" thesis as well as the containment thesis. Its supporters have regarded diplomatic adjustment with the Soviets difficult if not impossible until there has been a "domestic change" inside Russia.[11] The persistence of this theme in Kennan's writings even after he had abandoned containment in favor of "disengagement" further illustrates how difficult it was for him to separate his moral judgments from policy recommendations, at least so others could adopt a "realistic" policy. "Can men who can neither eradicate nor deny nor explain the blood that disfigures their own hands be fit leaders of a great country and a great empire today?" he wrote in a 1968 book-review article.[12]

In the "X" article, however, unlike the Yale lecture, Kennan did not insist upon a simple "power" explanation of Soviet behavior, one which had no aim except the perpetuation of cruel rulers. He stressed that the original Bolshevik leaders had not sought absolutism for its own sake; they had believed that they alone knew what was good for society and that they alone would bring it about once their power was absolute. Until that time, however, the happiness and well-being of the Russian people remained far down on the list of operational priorities. The one outstanding characteristic of the Soviet regime was that this process of political consolidation had never been completed according to its satisfaction. The men in the Kremlin had been absorbed with the struggle to make absolute the power they had seized in November 1917. As early as 1924

Stalin had justified retaining the organs of suppression on the grounds that capitalist had encircled the Soviet Union.

Kennan gave no indication in the "X" article that he considered the Stalin-Trotsky struggle after Lenin's death relevant to these problems, nor, more important, did he distinguish between the implications of Stalin's favoring socialism in one country and Trotsky's insistence upon permanent revolution. As for Russian emphasis on the foreign menace, Kennan argued that it was not founded in the realities of international politics, but in the need for explaining the continued dictatorship at home. The foreign menace was a fiction canonized in Soviet philosophy by the excesses committed in its name. It had become anchored in Soviet thought by bonds much greater than those of mere ideology.

But Kennan did not mention America's part in the 1918–1920 intervention against the new Soviet regime, or Western efforts to keep Russia quarantined politically and morally throughout the following decade. As for collective security in the 1930's, Kennan said, there could never have been a time when Moscow regarded its relations with capitalist nations as based upon any mutual interest. Instead, Soviet motives remained implacable behind the changing face of its diplomacy. Whenever that face changed expression, however slight the movement, there would always be foolish Americans eager to rush in and claim that Russian goals had changed—even to take credit for bringing about these marvelous alterations. With this final shot at World War II diplomacy, Kennan moved on to his most famous image, that of the whole Soviet governmental machine moving inexorably along a prescribed path, "like a persistent toy automobile wound up and headed in a given direction, stopping only when it meets with some unanswerable force." But the United States, he concluded, had the power to increase enormously the strains under which Soviet power must operate, and to force upon the Kremlin a far greater degree of moderation and circumspection that it had had to observe in recent years—"and in this way to promote tendencies which must eventually find their outlet in either the break-up or the gradual mellowing of Soviet power. For no mystical, Messianic movement—and particularly not that of the Kremlin—can face frustration indefinitely without eventually adjusting itself in one way or another to the logic of that state of affairs."[13]

No consensus has yet emerged among scholars on the role that ideology played in Soviet foreign policy in the Stalinist era. Because the Russians are not likely to open their archives to Marxist searchers, let alone to anyone else, the nature of the evidence is not going to be very much different in ten or perhaps even in fifty years. "It is clear," writes Marshall Shulman, a former aide to Acheson, in a striking reappraisal of Stalin's foreign policy, "that fundamental differences in the perception of the situation were involved." Russian efforts in 1946 to define their sphere of influence in Eastern Europe may have given the impression that Soviet actions were baldly expansionist. Soviet probes in the Mediterranean, Shulman contends, awakened the West to a realization that until power relationships were defined afresh in both areas, there could be no stabilizing of Soviet-American relations. But the nature of the American response in the Truman Doctrine appeared to confirm, on the other hand, Soviet expectations of capitalist hostility, and stimulated a far greater Soviet militancy against the Marshall Plan as a threat to its hegemony. This response took several forms, but a key one was the effort to turn the French and Italian Communist parties into lines of forceful resistance against their national governments.[14]

By late 1948, Shulman asserts, "it had become apparent that Soviet misreading of events and miscalculations had resulted in a trend massively adverse to Soviet interests. Yugoslavia had been estranged, the Western zones of Germany were on the way toward unification, the militancy of French and Italian Communists had only served to contribute to the further cohesion and mobilization of the Western alliance. In the following years, the Soviet leadership sought to undo these consequences by intermittent gestures toward a reduction in the atmosphere of tension.[15]

Shulman's analysis explicitly refutes both the notion that ideology or the urge to power determined Soviet policy, and the later amendment to that thesis—that Stalin's paranoia was largely responsible for Russian actions in international affairs. The belief that Soviet policy in Eastern Europe was only the prelude to further expansion, perhaps following internal breakdowns in the West, came easily to those who by instinct and definition of national interest distrusted a spheres-of-influence approach to world peace. As Kennan now belatedly recognizes, the "X" article did not enlighten those who shared this belief. It only excited them.

If, as now seems reasonable given Kennan's explanations in his *Memoirs* and his penetrating critiques of the liberal world-view in *American Diplomacy, 1900–1950,* he had set out only to instruct American policy-makers, not to start a crusade, he did himself and his purposes a grave disservice in the "X" article. Always standing behind "Mr. X" was Forrestal, the man who had given him the time and opportunity to perform a special function for the American policy-making community. A profoundly moral man whose revulsion at the excesses and inhumanities carried out in the name of social justice overrode nearly all his other feelings and ultimately led him into equally profound disagreement with his nation's foreign policies in the 1960's, Kennan watched with increasing dismay as the "X" article assumed the attributes and separate life of an anonymous spokesman for American foreign policy, one whose pen sounded the call to arms in the early morning of the Cold War.

NOTES

1. George F. Kennan, *Memoirs, 1925–1950,* Boston, 1967, p. 367.

2. *Ibid.,* p. 365.

3. *Ibid.,* pp. 210-211.

4. "Memorandum by the Counselor of Embassy in the Soviet Union," undated, Department of State, *Foreign Relations, 1945,* V, 853-860.

5. Louis Halle, *Cold War as History,* New York, 1967, p. 39.

6. Arnold Rogow, *James Forrestal,* New York, 1963, pp. 151-153.

7. Kennan to Forrestal, October 7, 1946, James Forrestal mss; on Stalin and the purges, see Kennan's review of Robert Conquest, *The Great Terror,* New York, 1968, in *New York Times Book Review,* October 27, 1968, pp. 2-3.

8. John T. Connor to Kennan, October 29, 1946; Kennan to Connor, October 30, 1946, Forrestal mss.

9. Quotations from a copy of the lecture in Forrestal mss.

10. Franklin A. Lindsay to Staff, November 12, 1946, Bernard Baruch mss.

11. On domestic change thesis, see Coral Bell, *Negotiation from Strength,* New York, 1963, especially Chap. 1.

12. *New York Times Book Review,* October 27, 1968, pp. 2-3.

13. Quotations from "The Sources of Soviet Conduct," in *American Diplomacy, 1900–1950,* Chicago, 1951, pp. 89-106.

14. *Stalin's Foreign Policy Reappraised,* Cambridge, Mass., 1963, pp. 13-17.

15. *Ibid.,* p. 29; quotation from Marshall D. Shulman, *Beyond the Cold War,* New Haven, Conn., 1966, pp. 8-9.

8

What Kind of Containment?

EDUARD M. MARK

Recent years have seen a searching reevaluation of American Cold War diplomacy. Interpretations of the origins of the Cold War have been contradictory, but there has been near unanimity among critics of American policy that American statesmen came increasingly throughout the early Cold War period to emphasize the military implications of the Soviet-American confrontation, thereby aggravating already troubled relations. Authoritative support for this critique has been found in the recently published *Memoirs* of George F. Kennan. In this work Kennan deals at some length with the policy of containment that was perhaps his chief theoretical contribution both to the development of American foreign policy and to public understanding of that policy. Kennan's explanation has left some with the impression that his calls for the containment of a supposedly expansionist Soviet Union represented a "political" alternative to postwar policies. This essay will argue that Kennan's version of containment, far from representing such an alternative, in fact foreshadowed later American military involvement throughout the world.

In the years 1946 and 1947, when Kennan first proposed containment, there was no general fear in Washington that the Soviet Union would attempt a military invasion of Western Europe. Since containment was conceived as a response to Soviet policy, there is little point in dividing the policy-makers of those years into the respective advocates of "political" or "military" containment. Of decided significance to later developments, however, were the competing interpretations of Soviet motives. One influential school of thought held that Soviet behavior could be understood as the practical correlate of Marxist-Leninist ideology. This ideology came increasingly to be viewed as a kind of secular millenarianism, which, it was supposed, enjoined a ruthless expansionism. Kennan figured prominently among these "realists," as they styled themselves, and was perhaps their most articulate spokesman.

Original essay. Printed by permission of the author. Copyright 1972 by Eduard M. Mark.

This view contrasted markedly with that of those few who, like Henry Wallace, thought that the Soviet Union, whatever its unpleasant eccentricities, was essentially another powerful nation-state with the accustomed and legitimate concerns of such powers.

Kennan's views were unequivocable. In the famous "X" article, Kennan asserted that "the political personality of Soviet Power as we know it is the product of ideology and circumstances. ..." Marxist ideology rendered the Soviets unremittingly expansionist and implacably hostile to the Western powers. The circumstances of maintaining a tyrannical rule over a hostile or indifferent population reinforced the ideologically derived hostility, for a mainstay of that rule was the perpetual appeal to the threatening figure of the encircling capitalist bogeyman. Kennan dismissed Soviet expressions of concern about the policies of the Western nations as products of the self-conscious "necessity of explaining away the maintenance of dictatorial rule at home." He employed the famous metaphor of the wind-up toy to describe Soviet expansionism, which, in mindless obedience to an ideology of world revolution, advanced until it met "with some unanswerable force." Barring a radical change in the character of Soviet society, a true detente was out of the question because "there can never be on Moscow's side any sincere assumption of a community of aims between the Soviet Union and powers which are regarded as capitalist."

Kennan's argument for containment foreshadowed in two ways the unimaginative reliance upon military force he later deplored for its effect on American policy toward Europe. The ideological interpretation of Soviet policy, imputing as it did to the Soviets a calculating but ultimately reckless fanaticism, made credible for some the fear that a war-ravaged Soviet Union might embark on overt aggression. More directly, with consequences he could not foresee, Kennan's argument for containment assumed the need and the willingness to use whatever kind and degree of force deemed necessary to meet the Soviet challenge. Kennan's later opposition to a trans-Atlantic defense pact, and a tendency by scholars to discuss containment only in a European context, have obscured the broader implications of containment.

The publication of Kennan's *Memoirs* in 1967 seemed to dispel much of the controversy about the nature of the containment policy that Kennan had proposed in the "X" article. Those observers who had seen the influence of Kennan's thought in the early preoccupation of American policy-makers with the military implications of the Soviet-American confrontation found in the *Memoirs* Kennan's contention that he had advocated not "the containment by military means of a military threat," but the "political containment of a political threat." Kennan contrasts his intentions, which found, he writes, a lamentably imperfect expression in the "X" article, with the decidedly military interpretation which Walter Lippmann gave to containment in the *New York Herald Tribune,* and later reprinted as *The Cold War* (1947). Lippmann wrote under the impression that the author of the "X" article anticipated Russian invasions of neighboring states, and supposed, therefore, that containment was essentially a military strategy requiring the stationing of deterrent forces at strategic points around the Soviet Union.

Kennan concedes in his *Memoirs* that a suggestive ambiguity in the language of the "X" article lent itself to such an interpretation. He regrets his failure to define more carefully either the means of containment or the nature of the threat that was to be contained, and finds Lippmann's consequent misunderstanding "almost tragic in its dimensions." He further points out that Lippmann was similarly misled by the failure of the "X" article to delimit the geographical scope of the policy. Kennan writes that the political containment he proposed was not "something I thought we could, or even needed to do everywhere. . . ." It was his design that the containment policy be applied selectively in defense of those yet un-Communized areas of the world where the "sinews of modern military strength could be produced in quantity": the United States itself, the United Kingdom, Japan, and the Rhine Valley with associated industrial areas.

Kennan's belated clarification, particularly the distinction between the political containment he actually proposed and the military or quasi-military interpretations that have frequently been given to containment, has met with general acceptance, if the reviews of the *Memoirs* may be taken as a fair indication.[1] This is somewhat surprising, for "political" and "military" are not, as Kennan's use of the words suggests, mutually exclusive terms. All military policies are ultimately political, and the most strictly political of policies are frequently premised upon military considerations. The Marshall Plan, of which Kennan approved and for which he was partially responsible, is a case in point. All hopes for a viable European defense pact were clearly contingent upon the economic recovery of the region. Of the Marshall Plan and NATO, President Truman said: "The military assistance program and the European recovery program are part and parcel of the same policy. There is the closest relationship between economic recovery and military defense." Kennan himself thought that a declaration by the United States of its determination to defend Western Europe would contribute to the sense of confidence which had to exist if Europe was to make successful use of the opportunity afforded by the Marshall Plan.[2]

As though not unaware of the imprecision of his simplistic contrast of military with political policies, Kennan defines political containment in his *Memoirs* by introducing an excerpt from a letter which he wrote —but did not send—to Lippmann in the spring of 1948. In this abortive attempt to rectify Lippmann's misunderstanding of the containment policy, Kennan wrote that Lippmann had misconstrued both the policy itself and the threat which it was to contain because

> the Russians don't want to invade anyone. . . . They don't want war of any kind. Above all, they don't want the open responsibility that official invasion brings with it. They far prefer to do the job politically with stooge forces. Note well: when I say politically, that does not mean without violence. But it means that the violence is nominally *domestic,* not *international,* violence. It is, if you will, a police violence . . . not a military violence.
>
> The policy of containment related to the effort to encourage other peoples to resist this type of violence and to defend the internal integrity of their countries.

In the excerpted passage of his letter to Lippmann, Kennan defines "military" and "political" in an arbitrary and idiosyncratic manner. He applies the adjective "military" only to international violence, the overt aggression of the armed forces of one sovereign state against another; violence which occurs within one state without the overt participation of a second state Kennan calls "political." When the words "military" and "political" are used together in intentionally contrasting senses, it is commonly assumed that one mode of action entails violence and the other does not, for military action is political action characterized by the use or threat of that violence. Kennan capitalizes upon the connotative distinctions of ordinary usage when he asserts without qualification that he advocated a "political" rather than a "military" containment. His denotative use of the words (as established in the excerpt) disregards this distinction, so that, while the contrasting connotations are employed in one place for rhetorical effect, the denotations of the words found elsewhere are overlapped so that both entail violence. Kennan distinguishes between political and military actions not by the character of the actions themselves, but by the origin of the violence accompanying them and the kind of forces involved.

There are at least two difficulties with Kennan's explanation. The nature of the distinction which he makes between "political" and "military" actions, ignoring as it does the character of the actions, is such as to make all distinctions between the actions virtually irrelevant. His explanation, moreover, taken on its own terms, does not in fact imply, as Kennan clearly intended it should, that a "political" response is the natural response to a "political" threat. The irrelevancy of the distinction upon which he bases his definitions is perhaps best shown by the use to which his definition of political containment might be put. An uncharitable critic of Kennan might observe, without serious injustice to Kennan's definition, that the intervention of the United States in Vietnam was, before the commitment of American forces in other than advisory capacities, an example of "political" containment. That is to say, the South Vietnamese government was challenged by "stooge forces," whose actions might be characterized as "nominally domestic violence." The United States sought with its aid and advisors to do no more than to "encourage" the Vietnamese to "resist this kind of violence and to defend the internal integrity of their country." Kennan's "political" violence, moreover, implies, in his own terms, a "military" containment. A government attacked by irregular "stooge forces" would surely respond with its conventional "military" forces rather than with "political" *franctireurs.* The violence of this response, further, in so far as it served and was made possible by the containment policy of the United States, would be international in origin. This probable response to a "political" threat is, in the spirit of Kennan's definitions, more accurately termed "military" than "political" action.

In context, Kennan's explanation of "political" containment seems at first clear, because it is contrasted with Lippmann's rather straightforward military interpretation. Despite the fact that they are distinguished by many prescient insights, Lippmann's columns on the containment policy betray the hasty circumstances of their composition. Lippmann made no allowance for ambiguous situations such as civil wars in which "nominally domestic" insurgents might serve, or seem to serve, the interests of foreign powers. Accordingly, he construed both the Russian threat and the containment policy in the simplest possible fashion: Russian invasion, and the consequent attempt to repulse the invasion by either the armed forces of the United States or of client states. Kennan can convincingly disassociate himself from this interpretation because from the first days of the Cold War he had never seriously considered the possibility that Russia would invade any of her neighbors.[3] This, however, was in 1947 not the point of distinction one might suppose. Even so great an alarmist as James Forrestal did not believe during this period that the Russians would attempt to invade Western Europe. Forrestal, who was of course interested in establishing how likely such an event was, recorded in his diary his own opinion on the subject, and the opinions of a number of prominent persons in or close to the administration, none of them conspicuously well disposed to the Soviet Union. General Clay, General Eisenhower, and Ambassador Harriman are all quoted as discounting the likelihood of such an invasion.[4]

The difficulties so far noted with the rather tardy clarification of the containment policy found in Kennan's *Memoirs* are essentially semantic. A comparison, however, of the explanation found in the *Memoirs* with various writings of Kennan's from the period when he was a spokesman for containment suggests other difficulties of a more substantial kind.

It is certainly curious that, appalled as he was at Lippmann's rendering of his article, Kennan should have taken no effective action to counter so serious and so public a misunderstanding. Kennan contented himself with a private action—and that abortive—half a year after the publication of Lippmann's columns—the unsent letter to Lippmann. Kennan did not address himself publicly to Lippmann's critique. He does, to be sure, claim in his *Memoirs* that the official position which he then held prevented his answering Lippmann publicly. It might be observed, however, that his official position was perhaps all the more reason for some sort of public correction of Lippmann. Since the "X" article had been widely interpreted as an official policy statement, Kennan's silence was in effect a potentially serious misrepresentation of government policy.[5] Although the discipline which the State Department imposes upon the expression of personal views by its diplomats probably limited his alternatives, Kennan was not without the means of correcting the interpretation of containment which Lippmann had launched. During the same period, Kennan wrote with some regularity for the *Department of State Bulletin;* in none of his articles did he attempt to clarify the proposals of the "X" article. This failure cannot be attributed to the desire of a senior official to preserve the anonymity with which he had advanced controversial views. Immediately after the appearance of the "X" article in *Foreign Affairs,* Kennan's authorship was revealed by the columnist Arthur Krock, who had seen the article in manuscript form bearing Kennan's signature, in the office of Secretary of the Navy Forrestal.

Indeed, far from clarifying the proposals of the "X" article, in a
1950 article in the *Department of State Bulletin*, "Is War With Russia
Inevitable?" Kennan once more argued for containment, without clearing up any of the ambiguities he claims to have regretted in the "X"
article. He was no more specific about the means of effecting containment, nor did he distinguish between areas of great or lesser importance.
The United States, he wrote, "must continue the policy of throwing its
weight into the balance wherever there are relatively good chances that
it will be effective in preventing the further expansion of the power of
international communism."[6]

How was the United States to throw its "weight into the balance,"
and against what kind of threat? Kennan did not say. And where? Not
in those regions of vital importance because of their potential for manu-
facturing military hardware, but wherever containment might prove
successful—quite a different consideration. Far from downgrading the
importance of military considerations for foreign policy, Kennan wrote
that the very object of foreign policy, the security of the United States,
depended upon military considerations: "Our security rests in remembering that the fiber of political resistance among our allies to Moscow
Communist pressure will be deeply affected by the extent to which they
continue to feel themselves secure in the military sense."[7]

Kennan concluded the 1950 article with four recommendations.
Two of the four—the only two sufficiently concrete to be incorporated
in a foreign policy—stress the importance of military strength.[8] The
previous year he had concluded an analysis of the world situation with
a similar emphasis on the importance of the military:

> So long as things remain this way, there can be no normal peace, and world
> stability will have to depend upon a number of factors which otherwise
> would not have to bear so large a part of the burden. Prominent among
> these factors is the maintenance of a powerful and impressive military
> establishment, commensurate with the great responsibilities we are forced
> to assume in the life of the world community.[9]

And in 1951, no longer in the State Department, Kennan reprinted the
"X" article, without comment and without change, as the first appendix
to his influential book, *American Diplomacy, 1900–1950.*

In the *Memoirs,* Kennan discusses certain examples of his opposition to the growing militarization of American foreign policy in the late
forties. These instances of opposition are, by implication, the proof of the
"political" nature of the policies he advanced. They have generally been

accepted as such. Kennan opposed both the extension of military aid to Turkey under the Truman Doctrine and the direct participation of the United States in a defense pact for Western Europe. He thought that both steps represented an unwarranted militarization of the confrontation with the Soviet Union. The Soviets, in his view, presented no military threat to Turkey; the Turks, he writes, "had nothing to fear but fear. . . ." Kennan thought that the original Brussels Plan for an exclusively European defense pact was a reasonable measure, and he conceded the desirability of a unilateral American declaration to defend Europe. He believed such a declaration would provide the sense of security which Western Europe needed if it was to make successful use of the Marshall Plan. Kennan was, however, opposed to a reciprocal pact between the Western European nations and the United States on the grounds that it would serve only to draw attention to the weakest aspect of the American situation in Europe, the military.[10]

In both instances, Kennan's opposition to the militarization of foreign policy was predicated upon a circumstance peculiar to Europe: the unlikelihood of overt Russian aggression against that area. In his article, "Is War With Russia Inevitable?", Kennan attempted to dispel despairing talk about the inevitability of a third world war. "Current Stalinist doctrine does not demand war," he wrote, "and there is nothing in Stalinist doctrine which would make it necessarily the responsibility of the armed forces of the Soviet Union to overthrow capitalism everywhere." On the contrary, the ideological certainty of the Russian Communists that capitalism was moribund made them reluctant to expose themselves to the risks of the kind of large-scale war which would result from overt armed aggression. They were strongly reinforced in this attitude, Kennan continued, by solicitude for their industrial accomplishments and by their desire to repair the great devastation wrought by the war. He offered no assurances about Communist armies other than the Russian, about violent domestic subversion, or about those situations where aggression would be unlikely to have injurious consequences for the Soviet Union. His opposition to the militarization of certain features of American policy toward Europe, rooted as it was in an analysis of the local European situation, cannot be taken as a very certain commentary on the containment policy as it was to be implemented in other areas of the world.

Kennan writes in his *Memoirs* that through an oversight he neglected in the "X" article to limit explicitly the intended scope of containment to a relatively small number of vital areas. The very logic of the containment policy, however, does not allow for such distinctions save perhaps those which doubts about the feasibility of specific ventures might suggest. Kennan envisioned two possible goals for the containment policy, the curbing of Soviet aggressiveness or the destruction of the Soviet state:

> ... The United States has it in its power to increase enormously the strains under which Soviet policy must operate, to force upon the Kremlin a far greater degree of circumspection than it has had to observe in recent years, and in this way to promote tendencies which must eventually find their outlet in either the break-up or the gradual mellowing of Soviet power.

Either or both of these eventualities were to be occasioned by the unremitting frustration of aggressive Soviet policy by "unalterable counterforce at every point where they show signs of encroaching upon the interests of a peaceful and stable world." Such a policy, Kennan argued, would aggravate certain weaknesses in the Soviet system. In so far as the success of the containment policy depended upon the constant frustration of Soviet expansionism, the policy had an end independent of, and indeed transcending, the importance of specific geographical areas. If this goal of constant frustration was to be achieved, the containment policy could not be applied selectively. The policy's sphere of concern would be, as Kennan put it in "Is War With Russia Inevitable?", "wherever there are relatively good chances that it will be effective in preventing the further expansion of the power of international communism." This pragmatic concern with the chances of success did, however, distinguish Kennan's argument for containment from the seemingly unqualified universal commitment of the President's "Truman Doctrine" speech, to which Kennan took strong and immediate exception.[11]

In the early postwar years, Kennan was primarily concerned with Europe, and there are relatively few references in his published writings to areas outside (or not immediately adjacent to) Europe. It does appear, however, that he did distinguish between the prospects confronting the United States in two areas. In "Is War With Russia Inevitable?," his assurances, such as they were, were limited to Europe and to those areas where the Soviet Union would be confronted with a general conflict if it disturbed the status quo. In the same article, he took note of a Communist threat to the non-European areas of the world, and of the importance of those areas to the United States. He depicted the consequences of Communist domination of them in the most serious terms:

> If the Russian Communists should succeed, by means short of war, in bringing progressively under their influence the remaining non-Communist countries of Europe and Asia, our security would be more subtly (but

perhaps just as dangerously) undermined than by an atomic attack on our own territory. For the world balance of power would then be turned, at least temporarily, against us.[12]

In the influential "long telegram" of February 22, 1946, Kennan had predicted that the Communists would be especially aggressive in the non-European areas of the world: "On unofficial plane particularly violent efforts will be made to weaken power and influence of Western powers [on] colonial, backward, or dependent peoples. On this level, no holds will be barred."[13]

Further indication of Kennan's perception of the Communist threat is to be found in his opinions about the Korean War. Both at the time of the war and subsequently, he thought that the Soviet Union had ordered the attack upon South Korea. He did not doubt the need for American intervention in that conflict. He writes in his *Memoirs* that

> ... it was entirely clear to me from the start that we would have to react with all necessary force to repel this attack and expel the North Korean forces from the southern end of the peninsula. I took this position unequivocally on that first day and in all the discussions that followed over the ensuing days and weeks. ...[14]

Kennan wrote at the time that the war had not been the result of special circumstances. It was a natural and even predictable consequence of Soviet policy:

> It is true that the Kremlin unleashed its Korean puppets against the South Korean Republic. But there is nothing in this fact which is out of accord with the pattern of Soviet behaviour we have known for three decades. At no time has there been any reason to suppose that they would not do this sort of thing, if circumstances seemed propitious. The assertion was made in a magazine article three years ago that the main concern of Soviet power was to "make sure that it filled every nook and cranny available to it in the basin of world power." There was no objective reason to assume that the Soviet leaders would leave the Korean nook unfilled if they thought they had a chance of filling it at relatively little risk to themselves and saw time running out on them.[15]

Kennan had repeatedly denied that war in Europe was likely. He had based his hopes for continued peace in that continent upon Soviet awareness that aggression there would risk a destructive conflict with the United States. In other areas, however, where the interests and prestige of the United States were not so heavily committed, the Soviets could sponsor the aggression of their "puppets" at "relatively little risk to themselves"—as in Korea, where the confrontation was a "nominally domestic" one between contending political factions, the very kind of "political" threat he had described in 1948 in his letter to Lippmann.

Kennan had not merely anticipated such limited non-European conflicts before the outbreak of the Korean War, but had apparently suggested a means of coping with them. In the summer of 1949, the Defense Department gave a series of briefings for Kennan and Paul Nitze, then a newly appointed member of Kennan's Policy Planning Staff. At the first of these briefings, Kennan and Nitze debated the sufficiency of the defense budget. Nitze argued that a general conflict with the Soviet Union was a distinct possibility, and that current defense expenditures were insufficient to insure adequate preparation for such a contingency. Kennan disagreed, maintaining that the United States was more properly concerned with preparing for limited contests, and that current levels of expenditure were in fact sufficient for that purpose, provided that an appropriate tactical doctrine was developed. Kennan reportedly urged the creation of rapidly deployable task forces for dealing with limited conflicts.[16] His proposal reflected concern with the military implications of containment outside Europe. American forces, supported by numerous allies, were already present in Europe, and any conflict there would have been of the kind Kennan thought unlikely. The task force concept, moreover, suggests a broad area of concern, and considerable uncertainty about where in that area the forces would have to be used.

In summary, Kennan insists in his *Memoirs* that he advocated a "political" containment within definite geographical limitations. But the unusually broad and imprecise conception of political action behind Kennan's assertion did not preclude means that would normally be considered military. Kennan contemplated in 1949 the organization of military forces specifically tailored to wage the limited conflicts he had foreseen. In 1950, he certainly advocated the use of American troops in Korea to counter much the kind of "political" threat he had explained in the unsent letter to Lippmann two years earlier. Similarly, Kennan's advocacy of American intervention in Korea, an underdeveloped agricultural nation without significant natural resources, seems to belie the concern expressed in the *Memoirs* for a small number of vital areas where the "sinews of modern military strength could be produced in quantity." Whether or not Kennan conceived the intervention in Korea as a manifestation of the containment policy, his advocacy of intervention was consistent with the logic of that policy, which, as explained in the "X" article, sought the constant frustration of Soviet expansionist efforts, an end very different in conception from the kind of strong-point defense described in the *Memoirs.*

The reasons for the ambiguity of the "X" article are to be found in the expressed purpose of the containment policy itself, rather than in an uncharacteristic lapse from literary precision by so eminently accomplished a writer as Kennan. If the containment policy was to achieve its end of encouraging through more or less constant frustration those "tendencies which must eventually find their outlet in either the break-up or the gradual mellowing of Soviet power," it was not possible to state with any degree of certainty either the means of the containment policy or the places where it would be applied. Theoretically, the policy left the initiative with the Soviets. It was theirs to choose both the nature and the place of the contest. Once they had done so, the only option left to the United States was to respond, if circumstances seemed to warrant the hope that the Soviet effort could be contained.

This being the case, the otherwise inexplicable mystery of why Kennan chose not to reply publicly to Lippmann's influential "misunderstanding" seems resolved. Kennan probably did not reply because Lippmann had not in fact been so terribly wrong in his interpretation of the containment policy. Lippmann had, of course, incorrectly attributed to Mr. "X" a fear of overt military aggression by the Soviet Union. Lippmann had also emphasized the military side of a policy which of necessity encompassed both political and military means (in the ordinary sense of the words), but he had not, as Kennan's *Memoirs* suggests, construed the containment policy itself in some sense altogether contrary to Kennan's intentions. And Lippmann was quite correct in his assumption that, if the logic of the policy were implicitly followed, the United States was bound to intervene wherever the Soviets themselves, or those whom we deemed their representatives, manifested the expansionist tendencies noted in the "X" article. Kennan, in short, could neither disallow the use of force, nor severely circumscribe the purview of containment, without forsaking the whole of the policy.

Kennan's early appeals for the policy of containment gave eloquent expression to many of the intellectual motifs that were to characterize the American response to the Cold War: the ideological definition of the struggle, the belief in the expansionist nature of Soviet Communism and its responsibility for most of the world's revolutionary ferment, the overriding concern with the domestic subversion of foreign nations, and the assumption that the United States had both the need and the right to intervene in some fashion wherever it perceived its interests challenged by what it took to be Soviet expansionism. Neither Kennan's pragmatic reservations about military alliances, nor his insistence on the "political" nature of the Russian threat to Europe, are fundamentally at variance with this intellectual framework.

NOTES

1. Max Frankel reviewed Kennan's *Memoirs* and wrote that Kennan shows that, although the "X" article left the "impression that he was advocating military containment of a military threat," in reality "he had always spoken of political containment of a political threat and was shortly to become opposed to the 'overmilitarization' of the cold war. . . ." ("A Scholarly Diplomat," *New York Times Book Review,* October 29, 1967, p. 1). Richard H. Rovere wrote that "Kennan had always felt that it was a mistake to think of 'containment' in military terms. . . ." ("The Loneliness of the Long-Distance Runner," *The New Yorker,* XLIII [November 11, 1967], p. 242.) Herbert Feis similarly accepted the distinction ("A Perplexing Memoir," *Virginia Quarterly Review,* XLIV [Winter, 1968], 135-140), as did Ronald Steel in his review ("Man Without a Country," *The New York Review of Books,* IX [January 4, 1967]).

2. *Public Papers of the Presidents of the United States, Harry S. Truman, 1949* (Washington, 1964), pp. 433-434. Kennan's remark occurs in connection with his discussion of his opposition to American membership in NATO. Kennan, *Memoirs* (Boston, 1967), p. 407.

3. Although not without qualification. In a despatch from Moscow in 1946, he wrote that while "overt Soviet aggression" against Turkey was unlikely, "with respect to Iraq, situation is not so clear. Here there is some evidence which points toward a Sov inspired and Sov armed Kurdish action to seize Mosul district with Sov forces in background prepared to back up insurgents in favorable circumstances and perhaps to come in after them, ostensibly at Kurd request." Department of State, *Foreign Relations of the United States, 1946,* VII, *The Near East and Africa* (Washington, 1969), p. 363.

4. Walter Millis, Ed., *The Forrestal Diaries* (New York, 1951), pp. 171, 182, 195, 212.

5. According to Louis J. Halle, himself a member of Kennan's Policy Planning Staff, the "X" article was, in effect, a policy statement. The "X" article was published anonymously because, Halle writes, "since this article represented the newly formulated position of the United States Government, it would have been self-defeating to put it forward as the thought of one man, even if the discipline of the career service had not limited the public expression of personal views by its members. . . . It represented, in the broadest terms, the formulated policy of

the United States for the postwar world. ...." Louis J. Halle, *The Cold War as History* (New York, 1967), p. 107.

6.   George F. Kennan, "Is War With Russia Inevitable?" *Department of State Bulletin,* XXII (February 20, 1950), p. 270.

7.   *Ibid.,* p. 271.

8.   Kennan recommended that the United States maintain a strong military posture to deter Soviet aggression. He also recommended that the United States provide a sense of military security for its allies, the desirability of which was noted in the quotation above. The last two recommendations were essentially moral exhortations. National unity must be maintained in the face of the Soviet threat, and the country must remain true to the best aspects of its heritage, continuing to act in a "spirit of justice and good will," viewing itself and others "with a sense of proportion and Christian humility." *Ibid.,* pp. 271, 303.

9.   George F. Kennan, "The International Situation," *Department of State Bulletin,* XXI (September 5, 1949), p. 324.

10.   Kennan, *Memoirs,* pp. 406-409. Kennan also writes that he "had little confidence in the value of written treaties of alliance generally," and "nothing but amused contempt for the legalisms and generalities of verbiage" over which those drafting the treaty labored—an attitude of Kennan's familiar to those who have read his *American Diplomacy, 1900–1950* (Chicago, 1951).

11.   Joseph M. Jones, *The Fifteen Weeks* (New York, 1964), pp. 154-155.

12.   Kennan, "Is War With Russia Inevitable?" p. 270.

13.   Department of State, *Foreign Relations of the United States, 1946,* VI, *Eastern Europe; Soviet Union* (Washington, 1969), p. 705.

14.   Kennan, *Memoirs,* p. 486.

15.   George F. Kennan, "Let Peace Not Die of Neglect," *New York Times Magazine,* February 25, 1951, p. 41.

16.   Warner R. Schilling, Paul Y. Hammond, and Glenn H. Snyder, *Strategy, Politics and Defense Budgets* (New York, 1962), p. 287.

Part Three

CONTAINMENT OR DISENGAGEMENT IN THE 1950s: THE ISSUE IN EUROPE

Introduction

CONTAINMENT OR DISENGAGEMENT IN THE 1950s: THE ISSUE IN EUROPE

Walter Lippmann and John Foster Dulles, in their criticisms of containment, argued for the removal of Soviet influence in Eastern Europe. Lippmann of the two offered the more specific plan; Eastern Europe could be liberated only if Soviet security fears were reduced by the removal of foreign troops from Western Europe. Then, and only then, could Russia feel secure in withdrawing its occupying forces from Eastern Europe. In the mid-1950s, after Stalin's death in 1953 and an apparent thaw in the Cold War, a number of prominent European leaders focused directly on the question of reducing military weapons and troops in Europe. Prime Minister Anthony Eden of Britain spoke for a disarmed zone in Europe in 1955, and in 1957, Adam Rapacki, Polish Foreign Minister, advocated a "nuclear free zone" comprising Poland, Czechoslovakia, and Germany. In November, 1957, Soviet Premier Nikita Khrushchev called for a summit meeting to discuss "ruling war out as a means of dealing with international issues." Washington demonstrated little enthusiasm for such ideas, and openly rejected the Rapacki Plan, indeed suggesting that the United States might give nuclear weapons to West Germany in order to counterbalance alleged Soviet military superiority on the continent.

A number of events stimulated these "disengagement" proposals. Stalin's death and Khrushchev's vehement denunciation of the dictator and espousal of "peaceful coexistence" in 1956 suggested that a less belligerent Soviet foreign policy had developed. Indeed, the peace settlement over Austria in 1955, and the subsequent withdrawal by the United States and Russia from that country, were encouraging. Many world leaders were optimistic about further agreements, but were alarmed because other events seemed calculated to heat up the Cold War. In

1956, the Soviets crushed the Hungarian Revolution, and Britain and France attacked Egypt over the Suez Canal controversy. To some observers the failure of the Hungarian uprising indicated that the only way of relieving Soviet pressure on Eastern Europe was the removal of Soviet troops from the area, which could be realized by a mutual withdrawal of American and British troops from West Germany. Yet West Germany had entered NATO in 1955 and continued to expand militarily. Optimists appealed for immediate negotiations before fears on both sides created new hostilities and further militarization. The dramatic launching of Sputnik in October, 1957, convinced the optimists that talks had to begin quickly, before America responded with an accelerated emphasis on missile development and weaponry.

George F. Kennan had been thinking along these lines, and he counted himself among the cautious optimists. He had spent most of the early years of the 1950s as a member of the prestigious Institute for Advanced Study, housed at Princeton University. From there he lectured and wrote a number of articles and books on Soviet-American relations. From November 14 to December 19, 1957, when diplomats were debating the Rapacki Plan, the rearmament of Germany, the strengthening of NATO, Sputnik, and the heavy Soviet hand in Eastern Europe, Kennan opportunely delivered six eloquent (if sometimes vague) lectures over BBC radio. Broadcast from London, the Reith Lectures were heard by millions in Europe and reprinted in a number of newspapers and magazines. The father of containment, read the headlines, seemed to be abandoning his offspring in favor of "disengagement."

Kennan called for a unified, nonaligned Germany, the withdrawal of foreign troops from the "heart of the Continent" (Eastern Europe and Germany), and restrictions on the deployment of atomic weapons in that area. These suggestions were not original with Kennan; once again, however, Kennan popularized existing ideas and found himself catapulted to the center of a noisy diplomatic debate. Kennan also commented in his lectures that since 1947, Russia had enjoyed impressive economic growth and suffered internal political turmoil. But, unlike 1947, Kennan was less willing to judge Russia: "Their world is not our world." America, he said, should concentrate its attention not on Russia's internal developments, but rather on the "external behavior" of Soviet leaders. Nor should the United States meddle in the "non-European world." Nations of that part of the world should be left to themselves to develop in their own way; foreign aid, complained Kennan, did more harm than good. Finally, he was critical of strengthening

NATO, because what was needed in 1957–1958 was diplomacy, not a "military fixation."

Implied in Kennan's speeches was a belief that the United States had overcommitted itself through global containment. But Kennan had not abandoned the containment of Soviet expansion. Rather he was in essence advocating disengagement as a way of liberating Eastern Europe and defusing any potential Soviet expansion. The Kennan of 1957, as a comparison of the "X" article and his Reith lectures suggest, had been changed by developments in the Soviet-American confrontation and his realization that unlimited containment stultified diplomacy itself. The question was: Had other American diplomats adjusted their ideas to meet the new realities?

A flurry of speeches, serial articles in such opinion magazines as *The New Republic* and *Foreign Affairs,* and heated retorts from Truman and former Secretary of State Dean Acheson were part of the excited debate which erupted after Kennan's Reith lectures. Truman complained that Kennan had never been a "policy maker," and an irritated Acheson charged that Kennan "has never, in my judgment, grasped the realities of power relationships, but takes a rather mystical attitude toward them." It appeared that the "realists" were attacking the "realist."

Beyond these jabs, which reflected debate within the Democratic Party between Kennan and Acheson, among others, came more searching analysis. Opponents of disengagement feared that Russia remained a military threat to Western Europe. Therefore, American troops should continue in West Germany as a deterrent, and NATO should not be weakened. Others protested that Soviet *political* control of Eastern Europe would not end with the removal of Soviet *military* control. What if the people of Eastern Europe attempted to throw off the Communist regimes? Critics predicted the return of Soviet soldiers and subversion of disengagement's benefits. Some asked: Would the Germans themselves accept disengagement and a reduced role in European affairs? With the Chancellor of West Germany, Konrad Adenauer, in vocal opposition to disengagement, and in fact calling for more West German military growth, this question seemed to be answered in the negative. Professor Hans Morgenthau, a German émigré and distinguished political scientist, was cautious about uniting his homeland. Would not, he asked, a united Germany eventually become a new and threatening German empire? And would not Russia prefer a divided Germany, partially restrained by the United States, to a strong one?

But Kennan also received enthusiastic support. British Labour Party and German Social Democratic Party leaders applauded him for endorsing ideas they had already espoused. Senator John F. Kennedy, later to name Kennan Ambassador to Yugoslavia, wrote Kennan personally in early 1958 commending his lectures for their "brilliance and stimulation" and reproving Acheson for his "personal criticisms" of Kennan. And Walter Lippmann, recalling his own pleas in the 1940s, defended Kennan and disengagement in an *Atlantic Monthly* lead article: "The road which Mr. Kennan pointed out is the only alternative which has some promise of leading to the reunification of Germany and to the national independence of the East European states." Lippmann criticized those people who accepted the mistaken premise that Russia would eventually weaken and that America simply had to build superior power and wait.

Dean Acheson delivered the most stinging and unremitting critique. James Reston, chief Washington correspondent for the *New York Times,* observed the Kennan-Acheson tussle: "Next to the Lincoln Memorial in moonlight the sight of Mr. Dean G. Acheson blowing his top is without doubt the most impressive view in the capital." In April, 1958, Acheson used the pages of *Foreign Affairs* to rebut the proponents of disengagement. He first ridiculed Kennan for his vagueness and imprecision, then he dismissed disengagement as "new isolationism," a "futile —and lethal—attempt to crawl back into the cocoon of history," the 1930s. America would be asked next to withdraw from the Far East. He displayed an utter lack of faith in the Soviet Union, which might, he feared, reintroduce troops in Eastern Europe, threaten Western Europe, and sign an anti-American defense pact with the new Germany. Acheson did not let up. In 1958, he continued the debate in his *Power and Diplomacy,* and in 1963, in the Brien McMahon Lecture at the University of Connecticut, he poked fun after having quoted Kennan: "The Delphic oracle made quite a reputation by utterances of this sort, even though its customers often got the wrong steer with disastrous results. The oracle is now a ruin."

Opponents of disengagement were especially suspicious and distrustful of the Soviet Union, despite the assurances of disengagers that Russia in the mid-1950s was not the Russia of Stalin. German-born Henry A. Kissinger, a teacher at Harvard University, and later President Richard Nixon's chief foreign policy adviser, believed strongly that a substantial defense line in Europe had to be maintained against a potentially aggressive Russia. Alarmed by Dulles' emphasis on massive nuclear retaliation, Kissinger advocated, in his *Nuclear Weapons and Foreign Policy* (1957), a mobile, tactical missile system tied to flexible fighting units so that conventional wars would not initiate nuclear annihilation. Kennan had argued against such a military formula for NATO, and Kissinger replied frankly in *Foreign Affairs,* asserting that Russia was more interested in military superiority than in a relaxation of the Cold War.

Unlike Acheson and Kissinger, Kennan now trusted Russia and insisted that, despite the risks, disengagement was a viable alternative to the potentially explosive Cold War confrontation. How would the West know what Russia thought without at least negotiating? In his reply to critics, Kennan once again used the pages of *Foreign Affairs* (January, 1959). He spoke of new "realities" in Europe—"realities" which the rigid Acheson and Kissinger would not recognize. Why? Walter Lippmann gave an answer in the fall of 1959 when he said that they are "like old soldiers trying to relive the battles in which they won their fame and glory. . . . Their preoccupation with their own past history is preventing them from dealing with the new phase of the Cold War." Kennan and Lippmann, deeply divided in 1947, were vigorously battling as compatriots a decade later against Cold Warriors who clung to the memories of the 1940s and who had, therefore, seemed to abandon diplomacy in favor of military might.

9

Demilitarizing the Cold War

GEORGE F. KENNAN

The time has come, it seems to me, for a fresh examination of the main issues which lie between the Soviet Union and the West. It is barely possible we might now find that an approach to a settlement—or at least to a more endurable situation—is not so hopeless as it has long seemed to be.

These issues fall into two categories:

(1) The basic ones, by which I mean disagreements over such things as frontiers and the political control of territory.

(2) The secondary ones flowing from the military rivalry which has grown up between NATO and the Soviet bloc.

The basic issues of genuine gravity arose directly from the manner in which World War II was allowed to come to an end. The authority of a United German government was then expunged within Germany itself and throughout large areas of Eastern Europe; and the armies of the Soviet Union and the Western Democracies met in the middle of this territory and took control of it, before there was any adequate agreement on its future permanent status.

This was, of course, the combined result of the unconditional surrender policy, which relieved the Germans of all responsibility for the future status of this area, and the failure of the Allied government to arrive at any realistic understandings among themselves about it while the war was on. Since it has not been possible to reach such under-

George F. Kennan, "A Chance to Withdraw Our Troops in Europe," *Harper's,* CCXVI (February 1958), 34-41. Based on Reith Lectures. Reprinted by permission of the author.

standings subsequently, except in the case of Austria, the provisorium flowing from these circumstances has endured. It is this that we are faced with today.

The difficulty obviously breaks down into two parts: the satellite area and Germany.

In the past three or four years, the Moscow leaders have made an attempt to undo some of the harm that Stalin had done in the satellites with his policies of ruthless political oppression and economic exploitation. The first effect of this relaxation—shown in the disorders in Eastern Germany and Poland and later in Hungary—was not to reconcile people to the fact of Soviet rule but rather to reveal the real depths of their restlessness and the extent to which the postwar arrangements had outworn whatever usefulness they might once have had. The Soviet leaders, startled and alarmed by these revelations, have now seen no alternative, in the interests of their own political and military security, but to reimpose sharp limits to the movement for greater independence in these countries, and to rely for the enforcement of these restrictions on the naked use or presence of their own troops.

The result has been, as we all know, the creation of an extremely precarious situation—unsatisfactory from everyone's standpoint. The state of the satellite area today, and particularly of Poland, is neither fish nor fowl, neither complete Stalinist domination nor real independence. Things cannot be expected to remain this way for long. There must either be further violent efforts by people in that area to take things into their own hands and to achieve independence by their own means, or there must be the beginning of some process of real adjustment to the fact of Soviet domination.

In the first of these contingencies, we in the West could easily be placed once more before the dilemma which faced us last year at the time of the Hungarian uprising; and anyone who has the faintest concern for the stability of the world must fervently pray that this will not happen.

As for the second alternative, which at this moment seems to be the more likely of the two, it seems no less appalling. If things go on as they are today, there will simply have to be some sort of adjustment on the part of the peoples of Eastern Europe, even if it is one that takes the form of general despair, apathy, demoralization, and the deepest sort of disillusionment with the West. The failure of the recent popular uprisings to shake the Soviet military domination has now produced a state of bitter and dangerous despondency throughout large parts of Eastern Europe.

If the taste or even the hope for independence once dies out in the hearts of these peoples, then there will be no recovering it; then Moscow's victory will be complete.

I can conceive of no escape from this dilemma that would not involve the early departure of Soviet troops from the satellite countries. Only when the troops are gone will there be possibilities for the evolution of these nations toward institutions and social systems most suited to their needs; and what these institutions and systems might then be, is something about which I think we in the West can afford to be very relaxed. If Socialism is what these people want and need, so be it; but let it by all means be their own choice.

It is plain that there can be no Soviet military withdrawal from Eastern Europe unless this entire area can in some way be removed as an object in the military rivalry of the Great Powers. But this at once involves the German problem because it implies the withdrawal of Soviet forces from Eastern Germany, and—so long as American and other Western forces remain in Western Germany—the Russians must view their problem in Eastern Europe in direct relation to the over-all military equation between Russia and the West. Any solution of the problem of the satellite area is thus dependent on a solution of the German problem itself.

This being the case, I think we cannot scrutinize too closely or too frequently in the light of the developing situation both in Europe and in the world at large, the position the Western governments have taken on Germany.

The West has insisted, and with very good reason, that the modalities of German unification, as a domestic program, must flow from the will of the German people, expressed in free elections. But the West has gone farther than that. It has also insisted that no restrictions whatsoever must be placed in advance on the freedom of a future all-German government to determine its own international orientation and to incur military obligations to other states. Specifically, the Western governments have insisted that such an all-German government must be entirely free to continue to adhere to the NATO Pact, as the German Federal Republic does today; and it is taken everywhere as a foregone conclusion that an all-German government would do just that.

If a future united Germany should choose to adhere to NATO, what would happen then to the garrisons of the various allied powers now stationed on German soil? The Western position says nothing specific about this. But while British, French, and American forces would presumably remain in Germany under the framework of the NATO system, one must assume that those of the Soviet Union would be expected to depart. If this is so, then Moscow is really being asked to abandon—as part of an agreement on German unification—the military and political bastion in Central Europe which it won by its military effort from 1941 to 1945, and to do this without any compensatory withdrawal of American armed power from the heart of the Continent.

This is something the Soviet government is most unlikely to accept, if only for reasons of what it will regard as its own political security at home and abroad. It will be hard enough, even in the best of circumstances, for Moscow ever to extract itself from its present abnormal involvements in Eastern Europe without this having repercussions on its political system. It cannot, realistically, be asked—if agreement is wanted—to take this step in any manner that would seriously jeopardize its prestige. The mere fact of Soviet withdrawal, without any compensatory withdrawal on the Western side, would create the general impression of a defeat for Soviet policy in Eastern and Central Europe.

The Soviet leaders will therefore see in these present Western proposals a demand for something in the nature of an unconditional surrender of the Soviet interest in the German question generally; and if they ever should be so weak as to have no choice but to quit Germany on these terms, it would scarcely take an agreement with the Western Powers to enable them to do so. So long, therefore, as it remains the Western position that the hands of a future all-German government must not be in any way tied, I see little hope for any removal of the division of Germany at all—nor, by the same token, of the removal of the division of Europe.

There are those in our Western camp, I know, who find in this state of affairs no great cause for alarm. A divided Germany seems, for the moment, to be less of a problem to them than was the united Germany of recent memory. They regard the continued presence of American forces in Germany as an indispensable pledge of American military interest in the Continent, and they tremble at the thought that this pledge should ever be absent. It is agreeable to them that America, by assuming this particular burden and bearing it indefinitely, should relieve Western Europe of the necessity of coming to grips itself with the German question.

This view is understandable in its way. There was a time, in the immediate postwar period, when it was largely justified. But there is danger in permitting it to harden into a permanent attitude. It expects too much, and for too long a time, of the United States, which is not a European power. It does less than justice to the strength and the abilities of the Europeans themselves. It leaves unsolved the extremely precarious and unsound arrangements which now govern the status of Berlin—the least disturbance of which could easily produce a new world crisis. It takes no account of the present dangerous situation in the satellite area. It renders permanent what was meant to be temporary. It assigns half of Europe, by implication, to the Russians.

Let me stress particularly this question of Berlin. There is a stubborn tendency in England and the U. S. to forget the Berlin situation so long as it gives us no trouble and to assume that everything will somehow work out for the best. May I point out that the Western position in Berlin is by no means a sound or safe one; and it is being rendered daily more uncertain by the ominous tendency of the Soviet government to thrust forward the East German regime as its spokesman in these matters. Moscow's purpose in this maneuver is obviously to divest itself of responsibility for the future development of the Berlin situation. It hopes by this means to place itself in a position where it can remain serenely aloof while the East German regime proceeds to make the Western position in the city an impossible one. This is a sure portent of trouble.

It would, of course, be wholly wrong to suggest that it is only the uncertainty of the Western position about the future of the garrisons in Germany that stands in the way of a settlement. I have no doubt that any acceptable arrangement for German unification would be an extremely difficult thing to achieve in any case. It took ten years to negotiate a similar settlement for Austria. The negotiation of a German settlement might also take years, in the best of circumstances. But I think we are justified in assuming that it is this question of the indefinite retention of the American and other Western garrisons on German soil which lies at the heart of the difficulty; and until greater clarity is achieved about this point, there can be no proper beginning.

It will at once be held against what I have said that Moscow itself does not today want German unification on any terms. Perhaps so. Certainly in recent months there have been no signs of enthusiasm in Moscow for any settlement of this sort. But how much of this lack of enthusiasm is resignation in the face of the Western position, we do not know. Until we stop pushing the Kremlin against a closed door, we shall never learn whether it would be prepared to go through an open one.

We must also bear in mind that things change from time to time in Moscow, just as they do here in the West. If the disposition to conclude a German settlement does not exist today in Moscow, our positions should at least be such as to give promise of agreement when and if this attitude changes.

Finally, the question is not just whether Moscow, as people say, "wants" German unification. It is a question of whether Moscow could afford to stand in the way of it if there were a real possibility for a general evacuation of Europe. Gomulka not long ago promised the Polish people that the day the Americans leave Germany, he will take up with the Soviet government the question of the departure of the Soviet forces from Poland. And it is quite clear that as Poland goes, in this respect, so goes the rest of the satellite area. Khrushchev has not specifically demurred at Gomulka's position; on the contrary, he has, in fact, even murmured things himself, from time to time, about a possible mutual withdrawal of forces, although he has intimated that the price of a Soviet withdrawal might be somewhat higher than what Gomulka implied.

In any case, the interest of the satellite governments in a general evacuation of Germany is perfectly clear. If, therefore, a more promising Western position would not assure agreement at this time, it would at least serve to put a greater strain on Moscow's position, and to shift clearly and definitely to the Soviet side the onus of delaying a reasonable European settlement.

Are there, then, points at which the Western position could safely be improved? It is hard for an outsider to answer to such a question in this rapidly-moving time. I can only say that there are two features of our present thinking which, in my opinion, might well undergo particular re-examination.

I wonder, in the first place, whether it is actually politic and realistic to insist that a future all-German government must be entirely free to determine Germany's military orientation and obligations, and that the victor powers of the recent war must not in any way prejudice that freedom by any agreement among themselves. This is outwardly a very appealing position. It gratifies the Western attachment to the principle of national self-expression. It is, for obvious reasons, a position no German politician can lightly oppose. But is it sound, and is it constructive?

A peace treaty has not yet been concluded. The powers of the victors have not yet formally lapsed in Germany. Might it not just be that the only politically feasible road to unification and independence for Germany should lie precisely through her acceptance of certain restraints on freedom to shape her future military position in Europe? And, if so, is it not just a bit quixotic to cling, in the name of the principle of German freedom and independence, to a position which implies the sacrifice of all freedom and all independence for many millions of East Germans, for an indefinite time? No useful purpose is going to be served by the quest for perfect solutions. The unlocking of the European tangle is not to be achieved except at some sort of a price. Is there not—in this insistence that the hands of a future German government must not be in any way tied—an evasion of the real responsibility of the victor powers?

The second element of Western thinking that might well stand further examination is the common assumption that the Western powers would be placed at a hopeless military disadvantage if there were to be any mutual withdrawal.

It is, of course, impossible to discuss this question in specific terms unless one knows just what sort of withdrawal is envisaged—from where and to where, and by whom and when. Here, as is frequently forgotten, there are many possible combinations; and I am not at all sure that all of these have really been seriously explored.

But beyond this, I have the impression that our calculations continue to rest on certain questionable assumptions and habits of thought:

1) an overrating of the likelihood of a Soviet effort to invade Western Europe;

2) an exaggeration of the value of the satellite armies as possible instruments of a Soviet offensive policy;

3) a failure to take into account all the implications of the ballistic missile; and

4) a serious underestimation of the advantages to Western security to be derived from a Soviet military withdrawal.

One of the arguments most frequently heard in opposition to the introduction of any greater flexibility into the Western position in Germany is that "you can't trust the Germans." It is therefore better, people say, that Germany should be held divided and in part dependent on the West, than that the Germans should once again be permitted independence of action as a nation.

I cannot share this opinion. Germany is in a state of great transition, and one can easily find, within its changing scene, anything one seeks. It is true that many of the older generation are not likely ever to recover entirely from the trauma of the past; they tend to be twisted people in one way or another, which does not necessarily mean that they are still Nazis. But I have seen, as an academic lecturer, whose own education took place partly in Germany, a bit of the younger Germany; and I am convinced that these young people—troubled, bewildered, unsupported at this time by any firm tradition from their own national past—will not fail to respond to any Western appeal that carries the ring of real vision, of conviction, and of seriousness of purpose. The younger generation of

Germans are more threatened today by the inroads of a pervasive, cynical materialism than they are by any extreme nationalistic tendencies; and it is precisely here, in combating this materialism, that we in the West have given them, I fear, little help or inspiration. To stake our future on this younger Germany is admittedly to take a chance—but I can think of no greater risk than the trend toward nuclear war on which we are all now being carried.

If Germany cannot be accorded reasonable confidence in these coming years, then I know of no promising solution to the entire problem of Europe. If we are going to make so negative and so hopeless an assumption, let us be terribly, terribly sure that our judgment is drawn not from the memories and emotions of the past but from sober attention to present realities.

These observations naturally bring up the military aspect of our conflict with Soviet power. Never in history have nations been faced with a danger greater than that which now confronts us in the form of the atomic weapons race. Except in instances where there was a possibility of complete genocide, past dangers have generally threatened only the existing generation. Today it is everything which is at stake—the kindliness of our natural environment to the human experience, the genetic composition of the race, the possibilities of health and life for future generations.

Not only is this danger terrible, but it is immediate. Efforts toward composition of major political differences between the Russians and ourselves have been practically abandoned. Belief in the inevitability of war—itself the worst disservice to peace—has grown unchecked. We have a world order marked by extreme instability. In the Middle East alone, for example, we have a situation where any disturbance could now easily involve us all in an all-out war.

To me it is a source of amazement that there are people who still see the escape from this danger in our continued multiplication of the destructiveness and speed of delivery of the major atomic weapons. These people seem unable to wean themselves from the belief that if the Russians gain the slightest edge in the capacity to wreak massive destruction at long range, they will immediately use it—regardless of our capacity for retaliation—whereas, if we can only contrive to get a tiny bit ahead of the Russians, we shall in some way have won; our salvation will be assured; the road will then be paved for a settlement on our own terms. This cast of thought seems to have been much encouraged, in the U. S. at least, by the shock of the launching of the Russian earth satellites.

I scarcely need say that I see no grounds whatsoever in this approach. The hydrogen bomb, admittedly, has a certain sorry value to us today as a deterrent. When I say this, I probably do not mean exactly what many other people mean when they say it. I have never thought that the Soviet government wanted a general world war at any time since 1945, or that it would have been inclined, for any rational political reason, to inaugurate such a war, even had the atomic weapon never been invented. I do not believe, in other words, that it was our possession of the atomic bomb which prevented the Russians from overrunning Europe in 1948 or at any other time. In this I have disagreed with some very important people.

But now that the capacity to inflict this fearful destruction *is* mutual, and now that this premium *has* been placed on the element of surprise, I am prepared to concede that the atomic deterrent has its value as a stabilizing factor until we can evolve some better means of protection. And so long as we are obliged to hold it as a deterrent, we must obviously see to it that it is in every way adequate to that purpose—in destructiveness, in speed of delivery, in security against a sudden preventive blow, and in the alertness of those who control its employment. But I can see no reason why we should indulge ourselves in the belief that the strategic atomic weapon can be anything more than a temporary and regrettable expedient, tiding us over a dangerous moment.

As for these various frantic schemes for defense against atomic attack, I can see no grounds whatsoever for confidence in them. I do not trust the calculations on which they are based. War has always been an uncertain exercise, in which the best-laid plans are frequently confounded. Today the variables and unknowns in these calculations are greater than ever before. I do not believe there is any human mind or group of human minds or any calculating machine anywhere in the world which can predict with accuracy what would happen if these weapons should begin to be used or which could devise realistic defenses against them.

But beyond this, what sort of a life is it to which these devotees of the weapons race would see us condemned? The technological realities of this competition are constantly changing from month to month and from year to year. Are we to flee like haunted creatures from one defensive device to another, each more costly and humiliating than the one before, cowering underground one day, breaking up our cities the next, attempting to surround ourselves with elaborate electronic shields on the third, concerned only to prolong the length of our lives while sacrificing all the values for which it might be worthwhile to live at all? If I thought that this was the best the future held for us, I should be tempted to join those who say, "Let us divest ourselves of this weapon altogether; let us stake our safety on God's grace and our own good consciences and on that measure of common sense and humanity which even our adversaries possess; but then let us at least walk like men, with our heads up, so long as we are permitted to walk at all."

The beginning of understanding rests, in this appalling problem, with the recognition that the weapon of mass destruction is a sterile and hopeless weapon which may for a time serve as an answer of sorts to itself, as an uncertain sort of a shield against utter cataclysm, but which cannot in any way serve the purposes of a constructive and hopeful foreign policy. The true end of political action is, after all, to effect the deeper convictions of men; this the A-bomb cannot do. The suicidal nature of this weapon renders it unsuitable both as a sanction of diplomacy and as the basis of an alliance. There can be no coherent relations between such a weapon and the normal objects of national policy. A defense posture built around a weapon suicidal in its implications can serve in the long run only to paralyze national policy, to undermine alliances, and to drive everyone deeper and deeper into the hopeless exertions of the weapons race.

This fact is in no way affected by the Soviet earth satellite, nor will it be affected if we launch a satellite ourselves.

But even among those who would go along with all that I have just said, there have recently been other tendencies of thought with which I also find myself in respectful but earnest disagreement. I have in mind here, in particular, the belief that the so-called tactical atomic weapon —the atomic weapon designed, that is, to be used at relatively short-range against the armed forces of the adversary, rather than at long range and against his homeland—provides a suitable escape from the sterility of any military doctrine based on the long-range weapon of mass destruction.

Let me explain what I mean. A number of thoughtful people, recognizing the bankruptcy of the hydrogen bomb and the long-range missile as the bases for a defense policy, have pleaded for the simultaneous cultivation of other and more discriminate forms of military strength, and ones that could conceivably be used for some worthwhile limited national objective, and without suicidal effect. Some have advocated a policy of what they call graduated deterrents. Others have chosen to speak of the cultivation of the capacity for the waging of limited war, by which they mean a war limited both in the scope of its objects and in the destructiveness of the weapons to be employed. In both instances what they have had in mind was to find an alternative to the H-bomb as the basis for national defense.

One can, I think, have only sympathy and respect for this trend of thought. It certainly runs in the right direction. Force is, and always will be, an indispensible ingredient in human affairs. A first step away from the horrors of the atom must be the adequate development of agencies of force more flexible, more discriminate, and less suicidal in their effects. Had it been possible to develop such agencies in a form clearly distinguishable from the atomic weapon, this unquestionably would have provided the most natural path of escape from our present dilemma.

Unfortunately, this seems no longer to be an alternative, at least so far as the great nuclear powers are concerned. The so-called tactical atomic weapon is now being introduced into the armed forces of the United States and there is an intention, as I understand it, to introduce it into Britain's. We must assume that the same thing is occurring in the Soviet Union. While many people in our respective governments have become convinced, I am sure, of the need for being able to fight limited as well as total wars, it is largely by the use of the tactical atomic weapon that they propose to fight them. It appears to be their hope that by cultivation of the tactical weapon we can place ourselves in a position to defend the NATO countries successfully without resorting to the long-range strategic one; that our adversaries can also be brought to refrain from employing the hydrogen bomb; that warfare can thus be restricted to whatever the tactical weapon implies; and that in this way the more apocalyptic effects of nuclear warfare may be avoided.

It is this thesis which I cannot accept. That it would prove possible, in the event of an atomic war, to arrive at some tacit and workable understanding with the adversary as to the degree of destructiveness of the weapons that would be used and the sort of target to which they would be directed, seems to me a very slender and wishful hope indeed.

But beyond this, let us bear in mind the probable effects—the effects, particularly, on the people in whose country such a war might be waged —of the use of tactical atomic weapons. There seems to be a cheerful assumption that these weapons are relatively harmless things, to be used solely against the armed forces of the enemy and without serious ulterior disadvantages. But surely this is not so? Even the tactical atomic weapon is destructive to a degree that sickens the imagination. If the experience of this century has taught us anything, it is that the long-term effects of modern war are by no means governed just by the formal outcome of the struggle in terms of victory or defeat. Modern war is not just an instrument of policy. It is an experience in itself. It does things to him who practices it, irrespective of whether he wins or loses. Can we really suppose that poor old Europe, so deeply and insidiously weakened by the ulterior effects of the two previous wars of this century, could stand another and even more horrible ordeal of this nature? And let us ask ourselves in all seriousness how much worth saving is going to be saved if war now rages for the third time in a half-century over the face of Europe, and this time in a form vastly more destructive than anything ever known before.

There is a further danger, and a very imminent one as things now stand; and this is that atomic weapons strategic or tactical or both may be placed in the arsenals of our continental allies.

I cannot overemphasize the fatefulness of such a step. I do not see how it could fail to produce a serious increase in the existing military tension in Europe. It would be bound to raise a grave problem for the Russians in respect of their own military dispositions and their relations with the other Warsaw Pact countries. Moscow is not going to be inclined to entrust its satellites with full control over such weapons. If, therefore, the Western continental countries are to be armed with them, any Russian withdrawal from Central and Eastern Europe may become unthinkable for once and for all, for reasons of sheer military prudence, regardless of what the major Western powers might be prepared to do.

In addition to this, it is perfectly obvious that the larger the number of hands into which the control over atomic weapons is placed, the smaller will be the possibility for their eventual exclusion from national arsenals by international agreement.

I am aware that similar warnings against the introduction of the atomic weapon into the armaments of the continental countries have also recently been part of the stock-in-trade of Soviet diplomacy. But I think we must beware of rejecting ideas just because they happen to coincide with ones put forward on the other side. Moscow says many harmful and foolish things; but it would be wrong to assume that its utterances never happen to accord with the dictates of sobriety and good sense. The Russians are not always wrong, any more than we are always right. Our task, in any case, is to make up our minds independently.

Is there, then, any reasonably hopeful, alternative to the unpromising path along which we are now advancing? I must confess that I see only one. This is precisely the opposite of the attempt to incorporate the tactical atomic weapon into the defense of Western Europe. It is, again, the possibility of separating geographically the forces of the great nuclear powers, of excluding them as direct factors in the future development of political relationships on the continent, and of inducing the Europeans, by the same token, to accept a higher level of responsibility for the defense of the Continent than they have recently borne.

This is still a possibility. We have not yet taken the fatal step. The continental countries have not yet prejudiced their usefulness for the solution of continental problems, as we have ours, by building their defense establishments around the atomic weapon. If they could be induced to refrain from doing this—and if there could be a general withdrawal of American, British, and Russian armed power from the heart of the Continent—there would be at least a chance that Europe's fortunes might be worked out, and the competition between two political philosophies carried forward, in a manner disastrous neither to the respective peoples themselves nor to the cause of world peace.

I am aware that many people will greet this suggestion with skepticism. On the European continent, in particular, people have become so accustomed to the thought that their danger is a purely military one, and that their salvation can be assured only by others, that they rise in alarm at every suggestion that they should find the necessary powers of resistance within themselves. There is an habitual underestimation among these peoples of the native resources of Europe. The Western Europe of today reminds me of the man who has grown accustomed to swimming with water wings and cannot realize that he is capable of swimming without them.

It is plain that in the event of a mutual withdrawal of forces, the continental NATO countries would still require, in addition to the guarantees embodied in the NATO Pact, some sort of continuing local arrangements for their own defense. For this purpose their existing conventional forces, based on the World War II pattern, would be generally inadequate. These conventional forces are designed to meet only the least likely of the possible dangers: that of an outright Soviet military attack in Europe, and then to meet it in the most unpromising manner, which is by attempting to hold it along some specific territorial line.

But this is not the problem. We must get over this obsession that the Russians are yearning to attack and occupy Western Europe. The Soviet threat is a combined military-political threat, with the accent on the political. If the armed forces of the United States and Britain were not present on the Continent, the problem of defense for the continental nations would be primarily one of the internal health and discipline of the respective national societies, and of the manner in which they were organized to prevent conquest by unscrupulous and foreign-inspired minorities. What they need is a strategic doctrine addressed to this reality.

Under such a doctrine, armed forces would indeed be needed; but

I would suggest that as a general rule these forces might better be paramilitary ones, of a territorial-militia type, somewhat on the Swiss example, rather than regular military units on the World War II pattern. Their function should be primarily internal rather than external. It is on the front of police realities, not on regular military battlefields, that the threat of Russian Communism must primarily be met.

The training of such forces ought to be such as to prepare them not only to offer whatever overt resistance might be possible to a foreign invader but also to constitute the core of a civil resistance movement on any territory that might be overrun by the enemy. For this reason they need not, and should not, be burdened with heavy equipment or elaborate supply requirements and this means—and it is no small advantage —that they could be maintained at a fraction of the cost per unit of the present conventional establishments.

I would not wish to suggest any sweeping uniform changes. The situations of no two NATO countries are alike. There are some that will continue to require, for various reasons, other kinds of armed forces as well. I mean merely to suggest that, if there could be a more realistic concept of the problem and the evolution of a strategic doctrine more directly addressed to the Soviet threat as it really is, the continental countries would not be as lacking in the resources or means for their own defense as is commonly assumed.

The primary purpose of the dispositions would be not the defense of the country at the frontier—though naturally one would aim to do whatever could be done in this respect—but rather its defense at every village crossroads. The purpose would be to place the country in a position where it could face the Kremlin and say to it:

"Look here, you may be able to overrun us—if you are unwise enough to attempt it—but you will have a small profit from it; we are in a position to assure that not a single Communist or other person likely to perform your political business will be available to you for this purpose; you will find here no adequate nucleus of a puppet regime; on the contrary, you will be faced with the united and organized hostility of an entire nation; your stay among us will not be a happy one; we will make you pay bitterly for every day of it; and it will be without favorable long-term political prospects."

I think I can give personal assurance that any country which is in a position to say this to Moscow, not in so many words, but in that language of military posture and political behavior which the Russian Communists understand best of all, will have little need of foreign garrisons to assure its immunity from Soviet attack.

10

Disengagement Equals Isolationism
DEAN ACHESON

Mr. Kennan's views are not new to him. They do not spring from a fresh analysis of the current situation. He has held and expressed these views for at least a decade. The effect which they have had currently makes us realize anew that the reception given to the expression of ideas depends upon the mood of the hearers. This reception may have little to do with the truth of the ideas expressed; it has a great deal to do with their power. Mr. Kennan has told people what they want to hear, though not because they want to hear it. What is it that he has said?

The ideas are almost as vague as the style is seductive. The thoughts are expressed as musings, wonderings, questionings, suggestions. But what comes out of it is about this: First, there is the idea of disengagement in Europe. By this is meant mutual withdrawal of American, British and Canadian, as well as Russian, forces from somewhere. This somewhere first appears to be East and West Germany; then the "heart of Europe;" again, the Continent; and sometimes, from the general ethos of the discussion, it appears to be all overseas areas.

The second idea is the neutralization of Germany. The third is that there should be no nuclear weapons in Europe. And the fourth is that throughout Asia and Africa, in what are called the "uncommitted areas," there is little "to be done . . . except to relax;" that "It is perfectly natural that Russia . . . should have her place and her voice there too;" that "our generation in the West" has no "obligation vis-à-vis the underdeveloped parts of the world," and, anyway, there is no "absolute value attached to rapid economic development. Why all the urgency?" If any sound schemes for development are presented, we should support them, "when they arise;" but, only on the condition that they tell us first "how you propose to assure that if we give you this aid it will not be interpreted among your people as a sign of weakness and fear on our part, or of a desire to dominate you." If Asian and African states should find in this grudging, meager and humiliating policy no opportunity to push their

From Dean Acheson, "The Illusion of Disengagement," *Foreign Affairs,* XXXVI (April 1958), 374-381, 382. Reprinted by permission from *Foreign Affairs.* Copyright by Council on Foreign Relations, Inc., New York.

economic development within the non-Communist system, and should turn to Communist methods and Communist help, we should accept their action without concern and with good nature.

One sees at once that these conceptions are the very opposite of those which the West has been following for the past ten years or more. It is an assertion that the struggle naught availeth; that it is dangerous, unwise and unproductive. It is a withdrawal from positive and active leadership in the creation of a workable system of states. It is a conception, blended of monasticism and the diplomacy of earlier centuries, by which the United States would artfully manoeuvre its way between and around forces without attempting to direct or control them.

If we attempt to analyze these suggestions, the problems which they create promptly emerge. First, let us consider the idea that something called disengagement can be brought about by removing American, British, Canadian and Russian troops from some area in Europe. What disengagement does this bring about? Very little, as one sees if one pauses to consider the realities. Compare the confrontation which takes place between the United States and the Soviet Union in Germany with that which occurs along the DEW line—that system of early warning stations which stretches from Alaska, across the Arctic regions and far out into the Atlantic. Here there are daily contacts on a thousand radarscopes, and doubtless the same is true on the other side of the screen. Some of these blips on the radar are actual aircraft; sometimes atmospheric conditions produce them. But they represent a contact which no action in Germany can disengage. There is confrontation in every part of the world where the area of the open and free world system may be reduced by Soviet military, economic or political penetration. No action in Germany will produce disengagement here. The word is a mere conception, which confuses and does not represent any reality.

So, let us turn from it to consider something more capable of delineation. For instance, exactly what is the extent of the mutual withdrawal about which we are asked to negotiate? The answer to this question does not depend upon penetrating the vagueness of Mr. Kennan's language. For there can be little doubt, I believe, that, once a withdrawal begins, it will be complete, so far as United States, British and Canadian troops are concerned. All the forces, foreign and domestic, will combine to bring this about. As the withdrawal makes the military position weaker, our forces will be less desired wherever they may remain. If withdrawal is represented as advantageous for Germans, it would seem equally advantageous to Frenchmen. Icelanders, Moroccans, Saudi Arabians and the rest would quickly follow. And once the idea caught hold,

Americans would, of course, join in the general demand. The *New Statesman* shows us how the matter is now being presented to a small section of British opinion and how it could bemuse a still larger one in that country:

> Yet the missile agreement is one of the most extraordinary and complete surrenders of sovereignty ever to be made by one country for the exclusive benefit of another. For the missiles are not intended to defend Britain; on the contrary, they decisively increase its vulnerability. Their prime purpose is to reduce the likelihood of a Soviet ICBM onslaught on America during the crucial three-year period which must elapse before America possesses ICBMs herself. The sole beneficiary will be America.[1]

We should not deceive ourselves. After disengagement, we would soon find ourselves discussing complete withdrawal from all European areas and, very possibly, from bases in the Far East and Near East as well. Indeed, Mr. Khrushchev has twice served warning, once in Berlin in 1957 and again in January of 1958, that the sort of withdrawal which he is talking about is withdrawal from all overseas bases. This would cut the striking power of the free world by at least a half, and, perhaps, until our missile program accelerates, by much more.

We must think of what we purchase for this vast price. What would Russian withdrawal from Germany or the heart of Europe amount to? Is it possible to believe that the Soviet Government, whatever it may say or whatever agreement it may sign, would, or could, contemplate withdrawing its forces behind, say, the River Bug, and keeping them there? And, by forces, I mean effective Russian physical power, by whatever name called. It is hard to see, after the events in Poland and Hungary, whatever the Russian Government might wish, how it could possibly undertake so hazardous a course. For, if its physical force were permanently removed from Eastern Europe, who can believe that even one of the Communist régimes would survive? Therefore, wherever Soviet forces might be garrisoned, the expectation and threat of their return must continue to be ever present (at most it would require from 12 to 18 hours) if Russia is to maintain the power which it has insisted upon as recently as the Hungarian uprising.

At this point in our discussion we must examine the conception of the neutralization of Germany; and then bring together the consequences of withdrawal and neutralization. It is necessary, we are told, that Germany should not be allowed to be free to choose its own course after unification. It must accept limitations upon its military forces and its military alignment. In other words, its national life will be conducted under far greater limitations than those in which other sovereign people live. The possibility that any such situation could endure seems to me quite fantastic.

Whatever Germans might initially think they would be willing to do, there is no precedent in history for, nor does there seem to me to be any possibility of, the successful insulation of a large and vital country situated, as Germany is, between two power systems and with ambitions and purposes of its own. Constant strain would undermine the sanctions of neutralization. The final result would be determined by the relative strength of the pressures from the two sides. As I have already suggested, the pressure would all be from the Russian side. For, there would be no Power in Europe capable of opposing Russian will after the departure of the United States from the Continent and the acceptance of a broad missile-free area. Then it would not be long, I fear, before there would be an accommodation of some sort or another between an abandoned Germany and the great Power to the East. Under this accommodation, a sort of new Ribbentrop-Molotov agreement, the rest of the free world would be faced with what has twice been so intolerable as to provoke world war—the unification of the European land mass (this time the Eurasian land mass) under a Power hostile to national independence and individual freedom.

But, without this withdrawal of forces and the neutralization of Germany, Mr. Kennan sees "little hope for any removal of the division of Germany at all—nor, by the same token, of the removal of the division of Europe." Naturally enough, these words have found a strong echo in Germany. But it is a fading one, as Germans ponder the conditions which would flow from unification by withdrawal and neutralization, and see the end of the best hopes of the German people. Two weak states —East and West Germany—jockeying for position in a sort of no-man's land, could raise the East-West "tensions" to a point compared to which anything we have yet experienced would seem mild indeed. In all this West Berlin would, of course, be the first victim. It would be a wholly inadequate judgment upon those whose naïveté and weakness produced this result that they should share the guilt of those Western politicians whose preaching of "liberation" encouraged the uprisings in East Berlin and Hungary, and, like them, should sit in supine impotence while more gallant men suffered. The best hope for German unification I shall mention shortly.

Turning to Eastern Europe, Mr. Kennan sees those countries, without the withdrawal of Russian troops, caught between the dilemma of constant revolutions, bloodily suppressed, and the acknowledgment of

Soviet domination. This view seems to me founded on nothing but its assertion. I cannot for the life of me see how the movement toward a greater degree of national identity in Eastern Europe is furthered by removing from the Continent the only Power capable of opposing the Soviet Union.

Nor do I see that the facts bear out Mr. Kennan's gloomy predictions. For instance, if the experience of 1956 had produced only the development in Poland or if the Hungarians had acted with as much restraint, it would have been plain to all that the attraction of the power of the West, of the possibilities which its system opens to all, was proving very strong indeed—stronger even than the secret police and Soviet occupation troops. The fact that in Hungary the reaction was pushed to the point where the Russians felt it necessary to suppress it with force proves only that it was handled unwisely.

So, as we think about the matter, we must wonder whether there is anything we can purchase "one-half so precious as the goods" we sell. We are told not to worry about this; that, even though it seems quite unlikely that the Russians would carry out any withdrawal, nevertheless, it is good propaganda to make the offer and cause them to refuse it. This seems to me profoundly false. In the first place, it treats international negotiations as though all the figures on the chessboard were made of wood or ivory; whereas, in fact, we are dealing with living people, subject to all the emotions of mankind. If I were a European and had to live through two or three years of American negotiations about withdrawing from the Continent, I think that very early in the game I would discount America's remaining and would prepare to face a new situation. Furthermore, to believe that the Russians can be put in the position of refusing to evacuate Europe underrates their skill in negotiation. They would simply, as they have already done, continue to raise the price. And it would be we and not they who would do the refusing.

The evils of a timid and defeatist policy of retreat are far deeper than its ineptness as a move in the propaganda battle. It would abandon the efforts of a decade, which are bringing closer to realization the hopes of Western Europe, of Germany, and of Eastern Europe as well. From the low point of 1946–1947 the economic, social and political health and strength of Western Europe—of which West Germany has become an integral and vital part—have grown greatly. Their pull on Eastern Europe continues to mount. To continue this the American connection is essential. The success of the movement toward unity in the west of

Europe is no longer in doubt. Only the rate of progress is undecided. The Coal and Steel Community, Euratom, the Common Market have been accepted. A common currency and political community are on the way. All of this is threatened by the call to retreat. It will not do to say that a united Germany, made militarily impotent and neutralized, can play an effective part in bringing to fruition a united and vigorous European community. The slightest puff of reality blows this wishful fancy away. The jockeyings and tensions of the two parts of Germany, the unopposable threat of Russian power, the bribes which can be dangled before Germany by the Soviet Union in the form of boundary rectifications and economic opportunities—these alone are enough to put an end to hope of a united and strong Europe, invigorated by Germany.

For those who believe that Eastern Europe would welcome American and Russian troop withdrawals as the beginning of liberation, I suggest a quiet sampling of candid Polish opinion. I venture to predict that what they would find is a horror at being abandoned by the West and left between the Soviet Union and a Germany similarly abandoned, to which the offer of another partition of Poland might be irresistible.

But, if one looks at the other side of the medal, what a different face it bears! A strong, united Europe could have the men and the resources —along with British and United States contingents—to deal by conventional forces with invasion by conventional forces, particularly as the Eastern European satellites are becoming a danger, and not an asset, to Soviet military power. This, if pressed, gives real mutuality of benefit to a negotiated reduction in forces. It makes possible, too, a time when nuclear forces would no longer have to be relied on as a substitute for conventional forces, and with it a real opportunity to negotiate this threat further and further into the background.

Finally, a thriving Western Europe would continue its irresistible pull upon East Germany and Eastern Europe. This would, in turn, have its effect upon the demands of the Russian people on their government. With a rise in the standards of living in the Soviet Union, and as some broader participation in the direction of affairs was made essential by their very magnitude and complexity, the Russian need for the forced communization and iron control of Eastern Europe would diminish. Then negotiations looking toward a united Germany, under honorable and healing conditions, and toward the return of real national identity to the countries of Eastern Europe, while preserving also the interests of the Russian people in their own security and welfare, could for the first time be meaningful and show the buds of hope. This has been the goal of Western policy for the past decade.

It would be self-delusion to close our eyes to the difficulties which lie before us along this road. Some we have created ourselves. Our military strategy, with its sole reliance on massive retaliation, and a budgetary policy which has neglected even that, have caused us a loss of relative military power and of prestige. Some of our political policies have weakened our alliances. Our allies, too, are having their troubles. In what are perhaps the two closest of them, we could wish (as they undoubtedly do, too) that both the present and the immediate future held greater promise for the development of strength and popular attitudes more attuned to reality. We all share together the common problem of devising a military policy for NATO which will avoid making the proposed defense seem as fearsome as the potential enemy's threat, and which will be a real deterrent because it is a credible one.

I have suggested elsewhere that this is possible. Briefly, the way is to create a situation in fact which equals the political purpose of the North Atlantic Treaty—that is, a situation where in order for the Soviet Union to attack, or coerce, Europe it would have to attack, or coerce, the United States as well. This, if we all use a fair degree of intelligence about our defenses, the Soviet Union could be deterred from doing. What is required is a short-range effort which does not preclude a sustained effort toward a wiser long-range goal. The short-range effort would be to provide NATO with such effective nuclear power that the Soviet Union could not have its way without destroying that power; and an attempt to destroy it would be impractical apart from a simultaneous attempt to disable the United States, which could be made too dangerous. The longer-range purpose would be to develop adequate conventional forces in Europe, with British and American participation, to make mutually desirable a real reduction and equalization of both Soviet and NATO forces and a controlled elimination of nuclear material for military use.

I quite understand that all of this is difficult. But I believe also that "the mode by which the inevitable comes to pass is effort." . . .

May I conclude by repeating that the new isolationism which we have been discussing, and the reception it has received, is gravely disturbing, not only because it is utterly fallacious, but because the harder course which it calls on us to forego has been so successful. If one compares the non-Communist segments of the world today with what they were 12 years ago, one sees enormous progress. If one compares, as we have tried to do here, the pull of a vigorous free system, held together by the joint efforts of at least some of its members to provide military security, economic power and political leadership, one sees how strong it is and what effect it has had. If one considers the changes which have already occurred within the Soviet Union, one can see the time approaching when adjustments in Eastern Europe are possible, when military forces can be reduced, and when the menace of nuclear destruction will be greatly diminished, if not removed. Surely, there are dangers, and great dangers, but with good sense we can live through these. We will not make them less by weakening ourselves, destroying the confidence of our allies, and refusing to help those people who are willing to work to some extent, at least within the system which we and our allies, together, have created and can make ever more vigorous and appealing.

NOTE

1. "Britain's Suicide Pact," *New Statesman: The Week-end Review,* January 4, 1958, p. 1.

11

Can the United States Trust Russia?

HENRY A. KISSINGER

It is easy to sympathize with the motives behind the "disengagement theory." As long as two large military establishments face each other in the center of Europe, so the argument goes, the danger of an incident that might spark a conflagration is ever present. Another argument maintains that the establishment of a neutral belt is the quid pro quo which might bring about a withdrawal of Soviet forces from the satellite states and thus permit a more normal evolution of the Communist regimes there. Disengagement is desirable, according to this theory, because NATO as now constituted is not capable of stopping a full-scale Soviet attack, and thus increases tensions without providing security. Finally, disengagement is said to be essential as a means of reassuring the Soviet Union about the sincerity of Western intentions.

The immediate difficulty with these arguments is that they run counter to the entire experience of the postwar period. Where Western and Communist forces face each other directly incidents have been rare and the few that have occurred (such as the Berlin blockade) have not benefited the Soviet Union; the risks are so enormous that both sides generally go to great lengths to forestall clashes wherever they can control events. By contrast, Soviet encroachments have almost always occurred where resistance seemed feeble or impossible. The only case of overt Communist aggression, after all, followed an American attempt to "disengage" itself in Korea and would probably not have occurred otherwise. And the arguments that NATO is both dispensable and a threat to Soviet security are clearly inconsistent with each other. No level of NATO military strength now in prospect will be able to fight an offensive war against the Soviet Union.

We must also take account of the possibility that the Soviet Union is more interested in negotiating about disengagement than in achieving it. Once negotiations were entered upon, it is more than likely that the

From Henry A. Kissinger, "Missiles and the Western Alliance," *Foreign Affairs*, XXXVI (April 1958), 394-396. Reprinted by permission from *Foreign Affairs*. Copyright by Council on Foreign Relations, Inc., New York.

expectation of disengagement would effectively demoralize NATO planning and undermine any military effort on the Continent. And we can be virtually certain that there will be endless evasions and delays so that the Soviet Union might well achieve one of its prime objectives by default —the dismantling of NATO without any concessions on its part.

That the Soviet Union is more concerned with achieving strategic preponderance than in reducing tensions is shown by the only proposal for disengagement that the Soviet Union has put forward—the Rapacki plan for a zone in Central Europe from which nuclear weapons would be banned. Acceptance of the Rapacki plan would not remove the Soviet nuclear threat from Central Europe, for even short-range Soviet missiles can reach much of Western Europe from Soviet territory. Because our whole strategy is dependent on nuclear weapons, it *would* lead to the withdrawal of *all* American forces from Central Europe. And the precedent having once been established, tremendous pressures would be mounted to exclude nuclear weapons from all of Europe including Great Britain. Since there is no prospect of arresting a Soviet advance without nuclear weapons, a non-nuclear zone in Central Europe would not only create a vacuum in which Soviet conventional strength would predominate but would destroy the balance of forces on which Western Europe's security depends. For ultimately NATO would be so weakened that withdrawal of the American military establishment from the Continent would be almost certain.

This situation would not be changed fundamentally by a simultaneous withdrawal of American and Soviet forces from the center of Europe and the creation of a "neutral belt." Soviet forces would withdraw only 600 miles, within easy missile range of Central Europe, while American forces, for the reasons outlined above, would cross the Atlantic. And would the Soviet Union feel less menaced by a neutral armed Germany than a Germany integrated in the Western Alliance and restrained by the collective interests of the NATO countries? Germany unaligned may be forced by domestic pressures to push its claims to the Eastern territories to the limit. Alternatively, an *un*armed neutral Germany would increase tensions by creating a vacuum at the very point at which the great Powers are competing most bitterly.

Instead of adding to stability, the consequences of a neutral belt may thus make a tense situation even more explosive. A major purpose of the neutral belt is declared to be to permit a more favorable evolution within the satellite orbit. A withdrawal of Soviet forces may, however, turn a long-smoldering resentment into open revolution. Yet Khrushchev has declared repeatedly that the "socialist achievements" in the satellite orbit are sacrosanct, that the Soviet Union would always lend "timely assistance to a fraternal socialist state"[1]—in short, that the U.S.S.R. stands prepared to suppress any upheaval that threatens local Communist régimes. Indeed, neutralization may actually prevent liberalization in the satellite countries, for only with Russian troops can the Soviet rulers feel confident of controlling the situation. The presence of Soviet forces provides assurance that change will not go beyond tolerable limits. If Russian troops are withdrawn, on the other hand, the Soviet leaders may calculate that they must resist *any* change however small, lest it set in motion a series of events they are no longer able to control.

Thus disengagement invites a variety of new dangers while reducing the forces to meet them. It is not a safe but a daring policy, and it makes sense only if we are ready to prevent the crushing of satellite revolutions. Otherwise it will assure only a temporary withdrawal of Soviet forces from Central Europe, with every likelihood of their return after the American military establishment on the Continent has been dismantled and Europe has been rendered defenseless. A policy of disengagement which has no answer, political or military, to the problem of upheavals in the Soviet satellite orbit, or to the return of Soviet forces under another pretext, is likely to bring about the very conditions it seeks to avoid. Its results will be either a demonstration of Western impotence and irresolution or all-out war.

NOTE

1. Interview with James Reston, *The New York Times,* October 10, 1957.

12

Facing Reality: Disengagement Defended

GEORGE F. KENNAN

One of the first arguments with which one is met is the flat assertion that "the Russians don't want any agreement on Germany;" therefore there is nothing to be gained by any reexamination of the Western position in an effort to see whether it could not be brought closer to meeting Russian requirements. The evidence usually cited to support this statement is that the Soviet Government has shown no serious interest in any of the Western proposals of recent years. This, one is told, plainly reflects the fact that the Soviet Government could not afford to remove its troops from any of the areas in which they are at present stationed in Eastern or Central Europe because that would lead to immediate revolt against the Communist régimes there and, accordingly, to a general collapse of Soviet prestige and influence in those areas. The events of 1953 in Eastern Germany and of 1956 in Hungary and Poland are cited as evidence for this assumption.

No one would question the seriousness of the problem which has recently faced Moscow in the political attitudes of the peoples of these three countries, or the unfortunate bearing of all this on the prospects for a removal of Europe's present division. But none of the three examples just cited warrants the sweeping conclusion that at no time in the foreseeable future, and in no circumstances, could Soviet forces ever be withdrawn from these areas without drawing down upon Moscow's head wholly unacceptable consequences. There is, first, the fact that Moscow has unquestionably consolidated its political position in all of these areas since the sensational events of 1953 and 1956. But beyond this it must be remembered that each of these crises arose against the background of the membership of Western Germany in NATO, of the presence of American forces in Germany, and of the absence of any over-all European security framework to include states which might detach them-

From George F. Kennan, "Disengagement Revisited," *Foreign Affairs,* XXXVII (January 1959), 189-202, 206-208, 210. Reprinted by permission from *Foreign Affairs.* Copyright by Council on Foreign Relations, Inc., New York.

selves from the Soviet military and political orbit. The sharpness of the challenge which was presented to Soviet interests by all three situations was heightened by the fact that any Soviet withdrawal in the face of the respective pressures would have had the nature of a forced unilateral retreat unattended by any comparable concessions, or indeed by any concessions at all, on the Western side. Not only would a yielding to pressures of this sort have been immediately humiliating, but there was the further danger, against which Moscow had no visible protection, that territories thus released from participation in the Warsaw Pact might end up by joining the Atlantic Alliance, thus effecting a major alteration in the world balance of power.

Surely there could conceivably be forms of readjustment in the lines of military responsibility in Europe, and a re-definition of the zones in which foreign troops might be stationed, which would not necessarily involve all these same dangers and disadvantages from the standpoint of Soviet political interests. Any mutual withdrawal would have implications quite different from a unilateral one. Beyond that, there are various possibilities for gradual, or partial, withdrawal which would present less danger of political embarrassment to Moscow than would a sudden and sweeping one. Obviously, any reduction or relocation or retirement of the Soviet garrisons in Central and Eastern Europe which had an element of gradualness, which was carried out as part of a general international agreement and which was accompanied—as this would surely be—by a major relaxation of political tensions generally, would have political connotations entirely different from those that would attend a Soviet retirement forced by defiant local revolt and without assurance that territories evacuated might not end up in military alliance with the United States.

Let us not forget that thoughtful people in Eastern Europe, both of Communist and of non-Communist persuasion, would have an interest in assuring the success of any scheme that held real prospects for changing, if only slowly and gradually, the abnormal situation that has prevailed there in recent years. The problem is to provide these people with an alternative somewhere between the extremes of a continued slavish and hopeless subordination to Soviet power and a sharp, defiant break with the "socialist camp." They themselves are fully aware of this problem and willing to help where they can. It was not by accident that the Rapacki plan originated in Warsaw; and one may well ask whether it was wise or necessary that this initiative should be so cavalierly rejected as it was in the Western chanceries.

The question is not whether the Soviet Government could afford to get out of Eastern Europe tomorrow. The question is whether the various constructive impulses and initiatives which attempt to meet this problem must always be so gruffly and timidly received by the major Western governments—whether there, too, one could not welcome, and join in, the search for solutions less dangerous and less obviously unacceptable to Soviet interests than the simple unilateral Soviet retirement from Eastern Europe which the present Western position appears to demand.

It is said that Moscow can never permit the peoples of this area to abandon the "achievements of socialism." To this one can only reply by asking whether it is necessary for the question to be put that way. If the experiences of recent years have proved anything in the realm of economic and political theory, it is that ownership of the means of production is a far less important question than the Marxists have considered it to be, and represents a feature of national economy in which the differences between "socialism" and "capitalism" are of steadily diminishing significance. It would not really be so drastic a transition today from the institutions of contemporary Poland to those of the more extreme examples of the Western welfare state. The West can afford to be relatively relaxed about the name by which the social and economic institutions of the East European peoples are described. What is immediately important is that development of national life there should not be impeded by abnormal military strictures, that the very real dangers of the Berlin situation be in some way removed, and that some progress should become possible in the creation of the prerequisites of a true European community. That these prospects would be improved if at least the military deadlock in Central Europe could be loosened seems obvious.

Ranged alongside those who dispute the political feasibility of a relaxation of the Soviet military hold on Eastern Europe—and yet in curious contradiction to them—are those who question its value from the standpoint of Western interests.

In part, the question is raised on straight military grounds. Little importance is apparently attached by the protagonists of this view to the significance of Eastern Germany as an area of deployment and possible point of departure for Soviet forces in the heart of Europe. For them, a Soviet retirement of a mere 550 miles seems small compensation for such concessions as the Western powers might be expected to make in return and particularly for the general American withdrawal from Europe which many of them insist on regarding as the only possible alternative.

They see Soviet forces accomplishing with ease, in the space of a few hours (12 to 18, if we accept Mr. Dean Acheson's figure), the re-passage of the area from which they might have been withdrawn. They perceive no political factors that might inhibit the Soviet Government from suddenly making such a move. From this, they argue that the political effects of a Soviet withdrawal would also be unsubstantial: the continued proximity of Soviet armed forces and the attendant fear of their imminent return would paralyze independent policy in the Eastern European countries; and in the absence of a compensatory proximity of American forces, or of any American guarantee of the independence of these countries, Soviet domination would be, if anything, more real and more binding than it is today.

In the shaping of this view, the experience of Hungary seems to have played a prominent part. Many commentators, in assessing the significance of the Hungarian uprising, seem unaware that Soviet forces were already in Hungary, on a treaty basis, when the Hungarian uprising began. Nor does it seem to have occurred to many of them that the continued presence of United States forces in Western Germany, or the lack of any assurance that a Hungary released from the Warsaw Pact would not promptly join the Atlantic one, could have had any influence on Soviet policy in the Hungarian crisis. The Soviet action is portrayed as a simple act of aggression. From this it is adduced that any country from which Soviet forces might in future be withdrawn either would continue, out of sheer fear of possible Soviet repression, to endeavor anxiously to conform to Soviet desires in the shaping of its domestic life, or, if it failed to do so, would at once become the victim of a new Soviet military intervention.

The strictly military facets of this view will be mentioned in another context. But a word may be said here about its political connotations. It rests, clearly, on the assumption that publicly-assumed contractual obligation has no inhibiting effect whatsoever on Soviet policy, and that, accordingly, the Soviet Government would be quite capable of conducting an initial withdrawal from Central and Eastern Europe only as a ruse of sorts, designed to get the United States to leave the continent, after which it would feel wholly free to violate its own part of the bargain at will.

This view fails to take into account the real political situation of the Soviet Government and the checks and balances that do operate to limit its freedom of action. It is simply not true that the Soviet Government is not obliged to take any account of world opinion or domestic opinion, or to pay any debt whatsoever, in the formulation of its policies, to the outward appearance of consistency and fidelity to obligation. The degree to which it has made the cause of "peace" and "noninterference" the basis of its propaganda, internally and externally, already represents a form of commitment to opinion within the Communist orbit and throughout the non-European world more serious than is generally recognized in the West. This is not to say that public opinion of this sort represents a force which could permanently inhibit Soviet policy in any vital matter; but it is a factor which cannot be wholly ignored or too abruptly and cavalierly treated by Soviet policy-makers at any given point. It is also important to remember that now, in contrast to previous decades, Soviet power operates within the framework of a genuine alliance. The other members of that alliance are not exactly the spineless, anxious slaves of Russian whim that some of us like to picture them as being. Moscow, for various reasons, cannot habitually play fast and loose with their interests without jeopardizing the unity and strength of the Communist bloc.

This being the case, it is quite wrong to suppose that a Soviet withdrawal from the satellite area, pursuant to solemn international agreement, would not represent a serious political commitment on the part of the Soviet Government. Moscow could of course throw all these inhibitions aside and do, flagrantly, all the things that the opponents of disengagement fear; but it could do so only once and only for the highest stakes: in the contingency, that is, of general war. If it is anything less than a general war which Western policy has in mind, if the game is still conceived as one of relative advantage in a limited political competition, then sober analysis must recognize that any general agreement entered into by the Russians involving mutual concessions with respect to Central and Eastern Europe would constitute a serious political move, having the widest sort of political implications. It would create a new situation which even Moscow itself could hardly expect to reverse except by the most drastic of means, and hence would not be lightly entered into.

If this is, or should be visible, to people in the West, it will be no less visible to people in Eastern Europe, whose difficult situation demands of them a harsh realism of outlook and the courage to take reasonable chances in the interests of its alleviation. It is all very well to say that these countries, appalled at the thought of the proximity of Soviet power, and at the absence of American forces from Germany, would fall over themselves to discover Soviet pleasure and to make themselves the instruments of it, whether Russia actually re-invaded them or not. But experience simply fails to bear this out. The Finns have existed for years in a state of complete vulnerability to Soviet power and without the faintest reason to expect that anyone in the West would come to their assistance if the Russians put real pressure on them. This has not prevented them from leading an acceptable national existence and from cultivating institutions and practices wholly different from those of the Soviet Union. The Jugoslavs did not ask whether they had Atlantic Pact support when they made their break with Moscow. If the Poles have shown confidence and imagination in developing their own "path to socialism," a path which, again, departs materially from the Soviet example, it is certainly not an American guarantee which has given them this courage. The Turks did not wait for the formation of the North Atlantic Alliance before showing stoutness in the face of Soviet demands. In vain one seeks, in the Austrian scene, the evidences of that panicky running-for-cover before internal Communist pressures which critics of the concept of disengagement have portrayed as the inevitable result of leaving parts of Europe without the protection of American garrisons or of membership in NATO.

The reluctance of some Americans to believe that others could conceivably survive without immediate American military protection has its element of justification in the sense that the general maintenance of American strength is required for the preservation of a world balance in which the restraints now operating on Soviet policy can continue to have full validity. But to assume from this that no independence of national life can survive in the neighborhood of Soviet power without specific American guarantees or the immediate proximity of American garrisons is to ignore all the political imponderables and to succumb to that over-militarization of thought about the cold war in the face of which no peaceful solutions of world differences are even thinkable. Not only do many of us underrate the courage and ingenuity which others are capable of manifesting in the protection of their national independence; but we forget that there are those who would rather risk this effort independently than commit their fortunes entirely to the protection of a Western alliance which appears to be increasingly inspired by an acceptance of the inevitability of major war.

The fear is often expressed that a Soviet violation of a general agreement on disengagement would come in a manner so gradual as to place the Western powers before the choice of resorting to major war over a relatively insignificant issue or accepting a piecemeal Soviet infiltration of the area from which Soviet forces might have been withdrawn. But is it beyond the resources of human ingenuity to take account of this problem in any new negotiation? What is at stake here is, after all, not political infiltration—the Eastern European countries bordering on the Soviet Union already have régimes acceptable to Moscow. What is at stake here is the possible return of units of the Soviet armed forces: a relatively definite and ascertainable circumstance. Is there any reason in principle why an agreement on disengagement could not have, built into it, its own sanctions for the event of violation: sanctions by virtue of which any infringement of this nature would give the other party clearly specified and automatic rights of reëntry? If what we are talking about is a gradual and piecemeal reintroduction of Soviet armed units (in itself not a very likely contingency), there would be plenty of time for the Western powers to avail themselves of such a right.

Among those who are most apprehensive about any discussion of the problem of disengagement are those whose minds are riveted less on the danger of a permanent Soviet control of Eastern Europe than on the dangers of a possible re-assertion of the power of a united Germany in European affairs. It would be wrong to underestimate the number of people, on both sides of the Iron Curtain, and particularly in some of the smaller European countries, who would actually prefer the divided Europe and divided Germany of today to an undivided Europe from which the forces of the great non-European powers would have departed and in which a united Germany, not bound by exclusive and formal ties with the West, could again play the rôle of a great power. There are even those in Western Europe who, in preference to this latter alternative, would be prepared to accept Soviet hegemony over the entire continent.

It is not the purpose here to reproach people for these feelings, to question the validity of the trauma from which they proceed, or to deny the magnitude of the uncertainties that would be produced by any alteration of the present status. Who is to measure the monstrosity of what took place between 1938 and 1945?

In principle, the thesis of German partition was not without its force and its logic. The German problem, in its present dimension, began with the achievement of German unification in 1870. The fearful European wars of this century have been the expression of the failure to find—and perhaps even the impossibility of finding—any acceptable place in a community of fully sovereign European states for a united Germany likewise fully sovereign. To the writer of these lines it has seemed for many years self-evident that a truly constructive European policy for the postwar period could not have as its goal merely another attempt to fit a sovereign united Germany into a system of smaller European sovereignties whom it was bound to outclass in many vital manifestations of national energy. Germany could conceivably go only one of two ways: backward, by process of partition, to a point where sovereignty would be tolerable because it was not united; or forward, toward membership in a broader and higher system of political loyalties—in some sort of European federation, where unification would be tolerable because it was not truly sovereign. But the first alternative, plainly, was anachronistic, politically impractical and pregnant with possibilities for a reënactment of the unhappy past. In the second lay the hope.

There is, accordingly, no disposition here to challenge the proposition that a constructive future for a united Germany is thinkable only within the framework of a set of international obligations which would draw German energies into channels broader and more worthy than those of the mere realization of competitive national ideals. The questions at issue are only, first, whether the framework to be sought should be an exclusively Western European one, and should embrace only one portion of Germany, or whether it should be a general European one, embracing all of the German people and presumably some of the other peoples of Central and Eastern Europe as well; and, secondly, if it is to be the latter, by what stages one is to proceed in this direction.

If the eastern half of Europe is not to become in permanence a part of the Russian empire, it would seem obvious that the sights of Western policy ought to be set on the wider rather than the more narrow concept. Had they been so oriented, this would not have precluded the development within Western Europe of the immensely valuable and hopeful institutions of a European community, the growth of which we have witnessed in recent years. It would, however, have put us on our guard against developing these institutions in a way to prejudice their eventual extension to the entire continent or their replacement by similar institutions on a continental scale. In particular, we would have been warned against too close an identification of these institutions with military arrangements applicable to only a portion of the continent. If there is ever to be a prospect of unlocking the great political and military cramp by which the life of the continent is now restricted, a way will have to be found to differentiate sharply between the military obligations of individual continental countries to extra-continental powers—the means, that is, by which their security is to be guaranteed, on the one hand, and the arrangements which may exist among them for intimate collaboration and even for the bridging of the barrier of sovereignty in economic and technical fields, on the other. What has worried some of us in recent years is the impression that this distinction has become increasingly blurred in the formulation of Western policies, and that the development of the elements of community within the European family —a process infinitely important in principle to the very prospects for the survival and prosperity of European civilization—is occurring in Western Europe in such a way that only by the hopeless device of general war or in the unlikely event of a total collapse of Russian power could it conceivably be spread to the remainder of the continent.

Even if the validity of these fears be accepted, there is, admittedly, a further problem of phasing. It was possible at one time to suppose that it might not be necessary to regard the definition of Germany's supranational obligations within the European community as an integral part of any initial agreement on German unification and disengagement of Europe; it was possible to suppose that the change from a hopelessly divided to a hopefully united Europe might be carried out in modest, tentative and easy stages, whereby the creation of German unity would precede the final definition of Germany's place and obligations within the European family.

The tenor of the debate that has taken place within the past year on the subject of disengagement, and particularly the earnestness of the fears revealed regarding any German unification that would operate to weaken Germany's present obligations to her Western European neighbors, suggests that this concept of staging may have been wrong. Perhaps it is not realistic to discuss German unification and a possible modification of Germany's relation to the Atlantic Pact without at the same time specifying precisely both the political guarantees and strictures which would affect a united Germany and the supra-national institutions in which she as well as any other affected countries would be embraced. It is possible, in other words, that such problems as the formulation of a general European security pact, the future scope of the institutions of the European community, and probably even the bitter question of Germany's eastern borders, may have to be faced simultaneously with the first steps toward a general disengagement.

One might hope that this would not be so; for if it is, the whole approach to this problem obviously becomes more complex, more delicate, more comprehensive in its implications, more closely related to the general problem of the weapons race and of world security than it would otherwise be; and the principle of gradualness, essential perhaps to any politically feasible solution, is placed in question. But the problem does not thereby become theoretically impossible of solution, nor is its urgency thereby reduced. If this must be the scope of the discussion, so be it. But let the discussion at least proceed.

A large proportion of the doubts and hesitations that have surrounded the question of disengagement has related to the possible military effects of any move in this direction. There is, in the first place, the fear of the effect of any disengagement on the Western ability to resist, by local tactical operations, a Soviet attack on the western part of the continent. Closely connected with this fear is the belief that a removal of the American, British and French garrisons from Western Germany and any alteration in Germany's obligations under the Atlantic Pact would amount to "the dismantling of NATO" and would demoralize the Western community politically in addition to weakening its military posture. Finally there is the argument that any disengagement which would serve to deny to the United States or the NATO command, as the case might be, the possibility of maintaining missile sites on German territory would cripple the Western deterrent power in the face of the Soviet capability in the long-range strategic weapons. The composite effect of these anxieties is to produce a frame of mind which sees any modification of present NATO military policies as possible only when the United States can be sure of matching the Soviet Union in the field of intercontinental ballistic missiles and when the Soviet Government agrees to a program of conventional disarmament which would make it no longer possible for it to overshadow the NATO group by its scale of conventional armaments.

None of these considerations is without force or substance. Precisely for this reason it is perhaps well, before looking critically at them, to bear in mind that the cultivation of the ideal military posture will always be in conflict with any serious effort to ease international political tensions. There is no conceivable agreement with the Soviet Union, even in the field of disarmament itself and all the more so in any field involving territorial questions, which would not involve concessions in the military field and the acceptance of new risks disagreeable and shocking to Western military planners. The ideal military posture is simply the enemy of every political *détente* or compromise; and whoever is not prepared to make sacrifices and to accept risks in the military field should not lay claim to any serious desire to see world problems settled by any means short of war.

The fears relating to the effect of a possible disengagement on the balance of conventional weapons in Europe are predicated, as a rule, on that same depreciation of the value of a possible Soviet withdrawal from Eastern Germany which was mentioned above. Of course, if no appreciable military value is to be attached to the question of the area of peacetime deployment of the Soviet armies in Europe—if, that is, it is to be regarded as a matter of indifference whether Soviet forces are stationed in Eastern Germany or whether their western limit is to be 500 miles further east—then, obviously, any compensatory move made by the Western powers, whether it be a reduction or relocation of their present garrisons in Germany, or a complete withdrawal to the United States, appears as an inordinate price to pay. The civilian obviously lacks the authority to debate this point, but he may perhaps be forgiven if he ventures to suppose that *some* importance must attach to this factor, and that, in particular, it must make *some* difference whether Soviet forces start, in a possible military encounter, from behind the Polish-Soviet border or from a line 30 miles from Hamburg and 100 miles from the Rhine. The predictions of an effortless return of the Soviet army over this entire distance in a matter of a few hours carry singularly little conviction to one whose memories of governmental discussions inform him that in the world of military planning it always is only the enemy's forces who are capable of such staggering feats: one's own military authorities invariably have a hundred solid reasons why nothing of the sort would be possible if it were *their* forces who had to do it. Is it too much to suppose that Soviet statesmen are sometimes confronted with similar reactions?

For the actual effect of a possible disengagement on the balance of conventional forces, let us glance briefly at what is now occurring and what is likely to be the situation within a few years. If present trends continue unchecked, the present program of German rearmament will culminate in the achievement by the year 1961 of the present goal of 12 German divisions. When this goal has been reached—in fact, long before —the German army will be by far the strongest component of NATO strength generally on the continent and a much more important factor than the Western garrisons now stationed on German territory. When this occurs (and its occurrence, let us remember, is now less than two years off), Germany will have a ground strength which would be fully able to assume the rôle fulfilled in the past by the Western garrisons: namely, of assuring that any military encroachment by the Russians would, to stand chances of success, have to assume dimensions which would make a general war unavoidable. The question will then present itself to Western military planners as follows: Is the retention of the foreign garrisons in Western Germany, themselves no longer the essential element in Germany's local protection, of greater value than the strategic advantage to be obtained by the removal of the Soviet divisions now in Eastern Germany to a point several hundred miles further east? It is hard to believe that the answer, from the German standpoint, could be an affirmative one; and it is hard to see that even NATO as a whole would be militarily weakened by the change, grievous as might be the political effects of a withdrawal that came about in this manner.

So far, therefore, as the prospects of disengagement relate to the balance in conventional armament, it is difficult to see the justification for the charge that this would amount to a "dismantling" of Western strength. Even if a future united Germany were not to be a member of the NATO group, she would presumably continue to have an interest in her own survival; the ground force she would be maintaining would still be greater in conventional weapons than that which NATO has been maintaining in Western Germany in recent years; this force would presumably be no less resolutely attached to the idea of the defense of Western German territory than have been the NATO forces of the recent period; and the danger of surprise attack, as well as the strength of the possible Soviet punch in Central Europe, would have been appreciably weakened by the geographic relocation of the Soviet forces.

It is, therefore, primarily in the matter of the missile sites, if anywhere, that the real military sacrifice involved in a possible disengagement must, from the NATO standpoint, be seen. But is this really so grievous a sacrifice? Western Germany is not the only place where such missiles can be stationed or from which they can be launched. To judge from the Rapacki proposal, which mentioned only Poland, Czechoslovakia and Germany, an abstention from the installation of missile sites in Western Germany would not necessarily affect the possibility of their being retained elsewhere in Europe, on the territory of other NATO countries. Beyond this there is the fact that as the development of the I.C.B.M. proceeds and as the use of the submarine as a floating missile site is perfected, the need for missile sites in Western Europe will presumably decline.

Many Western minds have come to be dominated so exclusively by military considerations that they are inclined to dismiss the possibility or the utility of any political agreements with the Russians in the absence of some general agreement in the field of disarmament, and particularly one which would reduce the Soviet conventional forces to levels compa-

rable with those maintained by the NATO group. If this view is author-
itatively adhered to, it is a poor augury for the future.

It is not likely that the Russians are going to agree at this juncture
to any major diminution in the power of their ground establishment.
Least of all are they likely to consent to equate it with the relatively small
establishments of the Western countries, some of whom have permitted
the maintenance of ground forces to become so expensive and so cumber-
some that they have tended to price themselves out of the military
competition. The imbalance in ground forces is partly an internal Western question.

There are two things that people in the West might do to correct
the present imbalance in conventional forces. The first would be to have
a hard and unsparing look at the presuppositions for the prevalent view
that the West must always be hopelessly inferior to Russia in this field
and ask itself whether everything possible has really been done to
cheapen the maintenance of ground forces, to eliminate administrative
and logistical luxuries, and to give them maximum real efficiency for the
conditions of modern war. The second would be to explore the possibility
of negotiating concessions not in respect to the total strength of Russian
ground forces but in respect to the geographic area of their deployment.
But this is precisely the possibility that is so emphatically rejected by
those who throw up their hands in horror at the thought of any explora-
tion of possibilities for modifying the present lines of political and military responsibility in Europe. . . .

Those who cherish and cultivate the values of a "little Europe"
deserve our fullest respect. They include some of the finest Europeans.
Their arguments are powerful ones. Perhaps they are even right. But they
cannot expect to eat their cake and have it, too. They must face the fact
that what they are affirming is a Europe divided permanently, and that
in the face of this reality the Russians, whatever their preference, will
have in the long run no choice but to digest and incorporate their half
of Europe as they have digested and incorporated many border areas
before, whether the cost be patient persistence of political discipline
exerted on the respective peoples, or a dispersal of them, or outright
genocide, or a mixture of all three. The present Berlin crisis is itself only
a manifestation—one of the first of many—of this reality. Can the West
really adjust to this process, even assuming the Berlin crisis is in some
way surmounted? A final Russian absorption of Eastern Europe would
obviously have most profound connotations for the entire balance of
political, economical and military power on a world scale. It may even
be questioned whether these results would be consistent with the basic

presuppositions of the North Atlantic alliance itself, which was surely not originally predicated on a belief that the problem was to contain militarily, in permanence, a Soviet empire extending from the Elbe to the Pacific.

Or was it? Perhaps the deepest issue at stake in this whole problem of disengagement resolves around this point. There were those of us who, in the inspiring days of the birth of the Marshall Plan and NATO, conceived that the purpose of the cultivation of Western strength was to place the West in a position where it would some day be able to negotiate the liquidation of the vast misunderstanding represented in the division of the continent. What loomed to us at the end of this road we were entering upon was not the crushing of Soviet power by the force of our actions but compromise—compromise on terms more favorable to ourselves than the conditions of that day would have permitted—compromise that would have given not only to a portion of Europe but to the great body of it the possibility to live. Here lay the connection, which many have found it so hard to discern, between "containment" and "disengagement." And while it did not occur to us that the *substance* of the gains we hoped to see made in Western Europe could ever be regarded as expendable for purpose of negotiation (this would have been patently self-defeating), it also did not occur to us that there was to be, in the institutional and particularly the military devices which we were then creating, anything so sacrosanct that these devices could not one day be modified or exchanged in favor of ones with a wider range of relevance and acceptance.

There were others, we must now conclude, who saw these things quite differently. For them, the purpose of the building of Western strength was not the creation of bargaining power with a view to eventual compromise but the achievement by Western Europe of a political and military posture so powerful and so eloquent that recalcitrance would melt before it and Europe would eventually find its unification automatically on *our* terms, without the necessity of dealing with our major adversaries or making concessions to their interests. In the forceful and moving statement contributed to *Foreign Affairs* some months ago by Mr. Dean Acheson,[1] one finds indeed the word "negotiations" but one is at a loss to discover what content this expression might be expected to have. "The interests of the Russian people in their own security and welfare" are, he says, to be preserved. But surely the Soviet Government cannot be expected to perceive these interests and this security precisely as we do, and they will be unlikely to regard as a fit subject of negotiation a mere retraction of their power in favor of the extension to Eastern Germany and Eastern Europe of the international military, political and economic arrangements now prevailing, under American aegis or encouragement, in the western half of the continent. The rosy prospects which Mr. Acheson and others discern at the end of the present road of Western policy seem to rest in general on the possibility for an extensive breakdown of Soviet power. While this possibility cannot be excluded (anything can happen in a political society whose constitutional foundation is so unfirm and so much in transition as that of Russia today), the probability of any such development is surely far too slight to warrant its entering seriously into the calculations of Western policy. The evolution of Soviet society in the wake of Stalinism is now in progress. It is by no means inconsiderable, nor is it devoid of hopeful elements. But it contains no signs of a total breakdown; it has not yet been such as to modify the irrealism with which Soviet leaders view the outside world; and it has not served to reduce—on the contrary—the general military and diplomatic potential of the Soviet state. . . .

Under the lowering clouds of sputnik, of Quemoy and Iraq, of the glaring disingenuousness of Soviet attitudes in questions of disarmament, and of the vicious distortions that are used to shore up the move on Berlin, it is perhaps too much to ask that men should still find the heart to address themselves to the slender possibilities for political compromise in Europe. But there are some of us who will depart with great reluctance from a belief that the basic elements of reasonable compromise are actually present in the realities of the European situation, however deeply they may be buried behind all the mutual fears and inhibitions and all the confusions of the atomic rivalry. Our concern is not to persuade people that the problem is an easy one, or that the prospects for solution are favorable, or that the concessions necessary to permit agreement have only to be made on the Western side. Our concern is to assure, as a matter of conscience no less than practicality, that in what may be a moment of the utmost gravity in our history and in the history of the world, the position adopted by American statesmanship be such as to test and exhaust every last possibility that may exist for the peaceful resolution of the differences in question.

NOTE

1. "The Illusion of Disengagement," *Foreign Affairs,* April, 1958.

Part Four

CONTAINMENT OR DISENGAGEMENT IN THE 1960s: THE ISSUE IN ASIA

CONTAINMENT OR DISENGAGEMENT IN THE 1960s: THE ISSUE IN ASIA

The reluctance of most American leaders to abandon global containment and a heavy military emphasis was evident not only in Europe in the 1950s, but also in Asia in the 1960s. As anti-colonial rebellions, civil wars, nationalist movements, and guerilla warfare swept over much of Asia, Washington supported and maintained a corrupt conservative Saigon regime demonstrating little interest in improving the lives of the Vietnamese people. The Viet Cong movement in the South, with support from North Vietnam, seemed to American officials to be part of a Communist master plan to subvert governments in developing Asian nations.

But growing numbers of Americans became confused and skeptical. Who exactly was the "enemy" in Vietnam? The Soviet Union? Observers pointed out that Soviet weapons were vital to the "enemy," but that the Soviets were not masterminding a Communist conspiracy. Others more frequently mentioned the People's Republic of China and its endorsement of national liberation movements. Secretary of State Dean Rusk linked China and North Vietnam; the "enemy," then, was "Hanoi-Peking." Still others within the Johnson Administration identified North Vietnam, or the Viet Cong, or Asian Communism as the chief disrupters of peace. At times, all Communists and Communist nations merged as America's foe in Southeast Asia. It was a frustrating set of possibilities. Increasingly, Administration spokesmen settled on China as the main culprit. Policies and images from the historical experiences of the 1940s in Europe were transferred to the confusing turmoil in Asia. Secretary of State Dean Rusk and other officials paraded the Truman Doctrine, especially at its twentieth anniversary in 1967, as justification for significant military involvement in Asia. Vietnam was Greece; China was Russia; containment was containment. Containment had worked in the 1940s against Russian expansion, why would it not work again?

Seasoned diplomats, advisers, and soldiers like Dean Acheson, Dean Rusk, General Maxwell Taylor, Clark Clifford, Robert Murphy, John J. McCloy, W. Averell Harriman, Walt and Eugene Rostow, and McGeorge Bundy, among many others, believed in the early 1960s that containment would work again. Many of them were members of President Lyndon Johnson's influential "Senior Advisory Group on Vietnam." Clark Clifford, an adviser to President Truman and one of the writers of the Truman Doctrine speech, became Secretary of Defense in early 1968. He recently noted, "I am a product of the Cold War. . . . But I think part of our problem in the early nineteen-sixties was that we were looking at Southeast Asia with the same attitudes with which we had viewed Europe in the late nineteen-forties, and we were therefore misevaluating what was taking place there. The world had changed but our thinking had not, at least not as much as it should have."

After assuming office, Clifford began to reevaluate the American presence in Southeast Asia. His Undersecretary of the Air Force, Townsend Hoopes, encouraged Clifford's movement from hawk to dove, and in *The Limits of Intervention* (1969) recorded his reminiscences of the 1968 debate between unreconstructed Cold Warriors and the partially reformed Cold Warriors like himself and Clifford. Hoopes measured the strong link between the 1940s and 1960s and the permanence of the containment doctrine. Counterinsurgency developed as the new weapon of containment, and Walt Rostow and Dean Rusk established themselves as key manipulators of that weapon against what they perceived as China's aggressive thrust through wars of national liberation.

Many of the Cold Warriors like Dean Acheson and Clifford did not dissent from the seemingly endless morass in Vietnam until 1968, when America had over 500,000 soldiers there, had suffered over 30,000 dead, and was spending over $30 billion a year. Yet their belated opposition to the war seemed to be aroused not by a thorough reassessment of global containment, but rather by the discouraging day-to-day reports from Southeast Asia which made it evident that a "victory" in the traditional military sense was impossible and that further disasters, like the Viet Cong's Tet offensive in early 1968, might rip America apart at home.

George F. Kennan, beginning at least as early as 1965, saw not only that Vietnam as a war was hopelessly futile, but also that Washington had reaped the unfortunate consequences of global containment. Kennan noted that Washington was a captive of past Cold War experiences. To disassociate himself from the interventionists and their supposed faulty use of the containment doctrine, Kennan accepted an invitation to speak before the Senate Foreign Relations Committee in February, 1966. The Committee, under the tutelage of Senator J. William Fulbright, was then in an early stage of rebellion against military escalation in Vietnam and looking for respectable allies and critics. Students and faculties had been marching and protesting, but neither the Committee nor Kennan felt comfortable with their frank, determined, and iconoclastic style.

Kennan's testimony once again shot him to the center of a major foreign policy debate. The headlines blared the news: Kennan declared that the traditional containment doctrine was inapplicable to Asia. The former diplomat had always argued against the influence of public opinion in diplomacy (see especially his *American Diplomacy, 1900–1950*, [1951], yet here he was, so upset by Vietnam, that he was attempting to sway public opinion toward a gradual American withdrawal from Vietnam. "I find myself," he remarked, "in many respects sort of a neo-isolationist." By that he meant that the United States should be modest and discriminating in its commitments abroad. He insisted that a military solution in Vietnam was fantasy, that it was an area of secondary interest to the United States, and that the conflict was disrupting American relations with Russia and Japan. Facile analogies with the 1940s, as he and Senator Frank Church agreed in the Committee hearings, did not face the new realities of the 1960s.

Kennan was not alone in his reasoned dissent. Respected scholars like Hans Morgenthau of the University of Chicago, George Kahin of Cornell University, and Mary Wright of Yale University, provided critical analyses of American foreign policy. A China expert at the RAND Corporation in 1967 and now a professor at Cornell University, David P. Mozingo, wrote a particularly cogent study titled "Containment in Asia Reconsidered." Mozingo addressed himself directly to the 1940s analogy and found it wanting. He compared the Europe of that decade with the Asia of the 1960s and concluded that conditions and traditions were quite different. Importantly, America's "problem" in Asia was not Communism or the bogeyman China, but rather the ardent force of nationalism.

The combination of street demonstrations, analysis from scholars like Kennan and Mozingo, and Communist victories in Vietnam had their impact. In 1968, President Lyndon B. Johnson removed himself from the presidential race, halted full-scale bombing of North Vietnam, and invited the North Vietnamese and Viet Cong to the conference table. As the 1960s ended, the "peace talks" in Paris had stalled and the war still raged in Vietnam, although with fewer American casualties.

13

Cold Warriors under Kennedy and Johnson

TOWNSEND HOOPES

What seemed in retrospect to have made large-scale military intervention all but inevitable in 1965 was a fateful combination of the President's uncertainty and sense of insecurity in handling foreign policy, and a prevailing set of assumptions among his close advisers that reinforced his own tendency to think about the external world in the simplistic terms of appeasement versus military resolve. The President seemed, from the beginning to the end, uncomfortable and out of his depth in dealing with foreign policy. His exposure to the subject as a member of relevant House and Senate Committees had been long, but superficial. For reasons which seemed to have their roots deep in his personal history, he lacked the kind of confidence in his own judgments that permitted Truman, Eisenhower, and Kennedy to overrule their principal foreign policy and military advisers on major issues. In matters of war and peace he seemed too much the sentimental patriot, lacking Truman's practical horse sense, Eisenhower's experienced caution, Kennedy's cool grasp of reality. The most exhaustive search of the Johnson record reveals no solid core of philosophical principle or considered approach to foreign policy—indeed no indication that he gave the subject much serious attention before 1964. There is only an erratic rhythm of reaction to those foreign crises that impacted upon the particular elements of domestic politics that had engaged his interest or his ambition. Philip Geyelin, in his perceptive book of mid-1966,[1] said of President Johnson that "by political background, by temperament, by personal preference he was the riverboat

From Townsend Hoopes, *The Limits of Intervention.* New York: David McKay Company, 1969, pp. 7-17, 126-128. Reprinted by permission of David McKay Company, Inc. Copyright 1969 by Townsend Hoopes.

man . . . a swashbuckling master of the political midstream—but only in the crowded, well-travelled familiar inland waterways of domestic politics. He had no taste and scant preparation for the deep waters of foreign policy, for the sudden storms and unpredictable winds that can becalm or batter or blow off course the ocean-going man. He was king of the river and a stranger to the open sea."

The prevailing assumptions among his close advisers were firmly grounded in the Cold War order of things, in the frame of existing pacts and alliances and alignments—above all, in the notion that the "Communist Bloc" remained an essentially cohesive international conspiracy manifesting itself primarily in military and paramilitary assaults against that other comprehensible entity, the "Free World." An important corollary was the belief that an accretion of "communist" influence *anywhere* must redound to the direct benefit of the main power centers in Moscow and Peking, for from this flowed the logic that counterthrusts in kind were everywhere and almost automatically necessary; otherwise a progressive, irreversible, unacceptable erosion of the world power balance could not be averted.

Like everyone else in the United States over forty, the President's advisers were children of the Cold War in the sense that their thinking about world strategy and world politics had been decisively shaped by that phenomenon. Still relatively young and impressionable when they emerged from the wholesale fighting of World War II, they had found that the fruit of victory was a bitter bipolar enmity stretching around the globe, and apparently restrained from the plunge into final holocaust only by a delicate balance of terror. They had lived in this political-military frame of iron for the better part of twenty years, urgently preoccupied with mortal struggle against a formidable Communist structure.

But by 1965 many of the major elements of the Cold War mosaic had undergone drastic transformation or had ceased to exist. There was an effective military balance in the center of Europe—the product of NATO counterpower sustained over twenty years—and it was a stable balance in the sense of being relatively insensitive to changes in the level and composition of forces on either side, within a fairly wide spectrum. The likelihood of deliberate Soviet attack seemed very low because it was understood on both sides that *any* dramatic attempt to alter the military balance could lead rapidly to a probably uncontrollable nuclear war. Moreover, Western Europe behind the NATO shield was no longer the weak and dispirited war refugee of 1946, but strong, prosperous, and almost confident. And on the other side of the line, time was demonstrating that not even the doctrines of Marx and Lenin could render Communism immune to the inherent traps and pitfalls of the historical process —from schism, territorial dispute, the aging process, and the effects of affluence. In combination, these factors were seriously undermining the Soviet position as the ideological fountainhead of doctrine, making a shambles of party discipline in the world movement, and sharply reducing Soviet revolutionary fervor in relation to the underdeveloped world.

The Sino-Soviet rupture was a developing fact of the greatest strategic consequence. From limited beginnings it had progressed, even by 1965, to an apparently irreparable conflict over the fundamentals of ideology and power. It was a split that not only destroyed the vaunted unity of Communist doctrine, but also saved the United States and its allies from having to face the combined and coordinated resources of Russia and China. The leaders in Peking had become the most vehement radical revolutionaries in the world, but their ideological ferocity seemed to strike no profoundly responsive chord in the hearts of other backward nations. Their continuing attempt to project China as the natural ally of the world's impoverished was indeed marked by surprising ineptitude and failure, attributable, I thought, to their ingrained imperialist attitude toward all non-Chinese which alienated Africans and Asians alike. There was also the bald fact that Maoist rule had been such an economic disaster that China could offer neither meaningful economic aid nor convincing advice on how to achieve economic growth.

The loosening of Soviet control in Eastern Europe was a visible reality, reflecting the radiated consequences of de-Stalinization in the USSR, broader economic and cultural relations with the West, and the gradual recovery and reassertion of separate national identities. These developments were not moving Eastern Europe toward democracy or even a repudiation of close ties with the Soviets; and out of a deep concern for their security and a fading commitment to the revolutionary mystique, it was apparent that the Soviets would hang on in Eastern Europe for a long time. Yet their efforts to build a stable, integrated empire had failed. Nationalism had proved stronger than imposed ideology. What Stalin with total power could not do was no longer a serious possibility for his successors. In Professor Brzezinski's striking phrase: "East Europe is where the dream of Communist internationalism lies buried."[2] (This was a judgment not basically affected, but in major respects confirmed, by the 1968 invasion of Czechoslovakia).

In Western Europe and indeed in all the areas of the world beyond the direct reach of Soviet military power, the loss of Soviet control and influence over local Communist parties was an operative political fact. The coming to nationhood of some sixty small and fragile ex-colonies whose vital concerns were economic development, political independence, and racial equality, and who were essentially indifferent to ideological crusades, was creating new centers of political initiative. These developments were diluting the ability of both the Soviet Union and the United States to manage old coalitions and control events.

The Soviet Union itself presented a curious anomaly. Presumably its leaders possessed inherited impulses to serve as a revolutionary vanguard for the world's downtrodden. But they were also masters of a powerful industrial nation, a fact which was reviving pre-Bolshevik imperial aspirations that had long been in hibernation. Just as Stalin pursued a strictly continental foreign policy because he lacked the resources to do otherwise, so Khrushchev began to give Soviet policy a wider orientation as the necessary resources and technology became available. By 1965, the Brezhnev-Kosygin leadership was giving further shape to a political strategy that seemed to commit the Soviet Union to full global competition with the United States. Russia showed evidence of a new determination to become, and perhaps even more to be accepted as, a genuine world power. There was an evident increase of military influence within the Soviet power structure, a fact which led to the disquieting possibility that the next stage of development in an industrialized Communist state might be right-wing military dictatorship—i.e., Fascism. These new developments did not materially reduce the dangers of U.S.-Soviet confrontation, but they did begin to shift the context from that of an emotionally charged ideological struggle to a more classic Great Power rivalry.

Seen in the large, these shifts indicated the gradual breakdown of the Cold War boundary lines, which had been as clear and hard as ice, and promised a proliferation of large and small power centers characterized by rather transient relationships. The world was no longer neatly divided between Free World and Communist Bloc and while these new realities did not greatly diminish the dangers of an inherently precarious century, they did alter the shape and character of problems in ways that strongly suggested the need for new analysis and new responses.

It is of the greatest significance that these new perspectives did not materially alter the judgments of the men closest to President Johnson.

The tenets of the Cold War were bred in the bone. In fairness, it must be said that nothing is more difficult to confront than the need to outgrow conceptions that have had undeniable validity—have been in truth basic reference points for thought and action involving the life of the nation. It is a difficulty that persists even when one is intellectually aware that the familiar conceptions no longer fully square with the facts. As the President's advisers appraised the world situation in 1965, the Russians and the Chinese still seemed to them in full pursuit of bellicose, expansionist policies across the globe, and still quite ready and able to join in the support and manipulation of proxies for purposes inimical to our own.

Five years earlier, the new Kennedy Administration had of course inherited a still untempered Cold War and, on the basis of evidence available in 1960, had little choice but to accept the bequest. In the circumstances, President Kennedy's eloquent Inaugural Address, taken as a whole, was a remarkable effort to break free of the inherited strictures, to lift the vision of his own countrymen and of his adversaries above the ideological trenches. He asked for a new civility, called for detailed proposals to control the nuclear arms race, and pointed valiantly toward "a new world of law, where the strong are just and the weak secure and the peace preserved." The Address was to prove a harbinger of his steady efforts to dilute the moralistic tone of U.S. foreign policy set by Dulles, so that the problems of a world in seething ferment could be seen in truer perspective, through lenses less tinged with ideology, and could thus be approached with greater reasonableness by both sides. But this lofty perspective notwithstanding, the Address was not unnaturally permeated with the sense of bipolar struggle and confrontation across the globe. And it contained that famous unlimited commitment: "Let every nation know, whether it wishes us well or ill, that we shall pay any price, bear any burden, meet any hardship, support any friend, oppose any foe, in order to assure the survival and success of liberty. This much we pledge—and more."

Arthur Schlesinger might subsequently cavil at the inertia of a bureaucracy that still used terms like "Sino-Soviet Bloc" and "International Communism" in studies and staff papers, but the Kennedy Administration's considerable efforts to broaden the spectrum of practical U.S. military response strongly attested to its *own* conviction that the United States did indeed face a hostile, coordinated power bloc bent on world conquest; moreover, that the U.S. must be ready to fight at nearly every level of armed conflict to defend interests that had no apparent geographical limit.

Indeed the Kennedy-McNamara plans to strengthen the U.S. ability to wage limited conventional and counterguerrilla war had been given new urgency by the Khrushchev speech of January 1961, the first month of Kennedy's incumbency. In the course of an eight-hour exposition, which rang with the confidence born of new economic and technical achievement, the Soviet leader described three kinds of conflict: nuclear wars, conventional wars, and national-liberation wars. Nuclear wars, he said, could have no victor because they would end in mutual destruction; and even conventional wars were unacceptably dangerous because, if they came to involve nuclear powers, they might escalate into nuclear wars. National-liberation wars, on the other hand, were a suitable means of advancing the Communist cause, and he announced that such "just wars" would have the unreserved and whole-hearted support of the Soviet Union.

President Kennedy, reportedly alarmed by the prospect that Communist expansionist efforts would now move to a concentration on stimulating protracted subversion and guerrilla warfare throughout the politically fragile and explosive underdeveloped world, appeared to believe that Khrushchev was posing a threat of global dimension. In his first State of the Union message just a few days later, he said: "We must never be lulled into believing that either power [Russia or China] has yielded its ambitions for world domination—ambitions which they forcefully restated only a short time ago. On the contrary, our task is to convince them that aggression and subversion will not be profitable routes to pursue these ends."

He quickly followed this up with a broad effort to impress the meaning of Khrushchev's new challenge upon the whole foreign affairs-military bureaucracy, and to reorient and reorganize it under the stirring, if ambiguous, banner of counterinsurgency. Robert Kennedy, Maxwell Taylor, Walt Rostow, Richard Bissell, and Roger Hilsman were in the vanguard of this effort. The works of Mao Tse-tung and Che Guevera were avidly studied and became established reference points for a new American counterdoctrine; soldiers, diplomats, and economic aid administrators of all ranks were required to take a "counterinsurgency course" before being posted to underdeveloped countries; special warfare centers were established in several parts of the world, and a high level Counter-Insurgency Committee under General Taylor (and later under

Averell Harriman) was created to keep close watch on situations of incipient subversion in every corner of the globe. By early 1962, Hilsman and Rostow had developed a cogent and comprehensive "strategic concept for counterinsurgency" that emphasized the need for central control of all antiguerrilla activities within the country under attack, subordination of military actions to political purposes, and reliance on small-scale counterguerilla units, as opposed to conventional military formations. Predictably, this concept met with determined resistance from the upper echelons of the U.S. military hierarchy—particularly in the Army—and was ironically and most unfortunately never applied in Vietnam.

As [Arthur] Schlesinger admitted, "there was, to be sure, a faddish aspect of this enthusiasm" for the development and application of a counterinsurgency doctrine. In terms of its effect on official attitudes within the U.S. government, a far more serious deficiency was the implicit assumption that henceforth Washington would be predisposed to view an effort to overthrow the existing order *anywhere* as a national-liberation war fomented by and for the benefit of Russia or China. In a revolutionary era characterized by profound discontent throughout the underdeveloped world (and not only there), by an epidemic frustration born of the conflict between intractable conditions and inflated expectations, such an assumption could only lead the United States toward interventions based on quite misperceived assessments. It was perfectly true, for example, that frustrated men professing radical doctrines, including Communism, were behind the revolutionary turmoil in Latin America; and that aided to some extent and in varying degrees by Maoist guerrilla doctrine, Soviet money and Cuban training, Latin American Communists and other radicals were engaged in a wide range of violent, dangerous, and subversive activities. It was far from clear, however, that such activity was controlled, or even seriously influenced, by an outside power; most evidence suggested that the motivation and initiative were largely indigenous. It was equally unclear whether, in the absence of Great Power meddling, such activity presented a situation that the U.S. could reasonably expect to ameliorate by military intervention.

The point is that the Cold War syndrome prevailing in Washington in 1965 represented no break with the Kennedy period. Indeed all of President Johnson's principal foreign policy advisers were Kennedy men. All carried in their veins the implicitly unlimited commitment to global struggle against Revolutionary Communism which had grown out of our total immersion in World War II, and which had been specifically enunciated in the Truman Doctrine of March 1947. None as yet perceived the necessity—or the possibility—of redefining U.S. interests or the U.S. role in the world in ways that would permit the drawing of more careful distinctions between those commitments and interventions that are in fact *vital* to our national security, and those that spring more or less from our deeply held view of what the world "ought" to be and of how it "ought" to be organized—that is, from our reforming zeal and our desire for wish fulfillment. To the President's men in early 1965, there seemed no logical stopping point between isolationism and globalism.

Of the close advisers on Vietnam, Dean Rusk seemed the very embodiment of the embattled Cold Warrior with convictions rooted in the Stalinist period. An intelligent man, he could not have been unaware of the trends that were fragmenting the "Communist Bloc" and creating new problems of orientation within each Communist country. But he was careful not to allow these developments to affect his basic judgments. He was, moreover, possessed of a special mania about China and of a knack for arguing by dubious analogy. Not only in public, but in private conversations with colleagues and with President Johnson, Rusk expounded his thesis that Communist China was actively promoting and supporting aggression in Vietnam, that aggression in Vietnam was not different from Hitler's aggression in Europe, that appeasement in Vietnam could have the same consequences as appeasement at Munich. In his always articulate, sometimes eloquent, formulations, Asia seemed to be Europe, China was either Stalinist Russia or Hitler Germany, and SEATO was either NATO or the Grand Alliance of World War II. This insistent drawing on the past as a basis for meeting problems that were radically different, that presented themselves in unlike circumstances, and that involved a quite dissimilar degree of U.S. national interest could hardly fail to make a major contribution to the enormous national confusion regarding the character and meaning of U.S. involvement in the Vietnam War. Rusk thus contributed to the Administration's credibility problem—directly, because his formulations could not withstand the test of even cursory historical analysis; indirectly, because they were apt to be replayed on the President's Texas amplifier. As Philip Geyelin reported it, "The backstage Johnson ... was quite capable of telling one of the Senate's more serious students of foreign affairs that 'if we don't stop the Reds in South Vietnam, tomorrow they will be in Hawaii, and next week they will be in San Francisco.' "[3]

In his State of the Union Message of January 17, [1968] the President said of Vietnam, "it is our will that is being tried not our strength

... the enemy has been defeated in battle after battle." This theory rested on the assumption that the United States, being by far the stronger party, must surely win in the end, provided only that the American people stayed the course. It argued that the North Vietnamese were in fact already beaten, but continued to fight on chiefly because Hanoi perceived weakness of purpose in America. General Wheeler said at this time, "The single most important factor in prolonging the war is Hanoi's calculation that there is a reasonable possibility of change in U.S. policy before the ultimate collapse of the Viet Cong manpower base and infrastructure. ... We are winning the war in Vietnam, but Hanoi is still not ready to give up—the major campaign of the war is being fought here in the United States."

It was mildly astonishing to me that the inner group's assessment could be so consistently wide of the mark, but this fallacy, as so much else, flowed from the Rusk-Rostow view that the war in Vietnam was for Communism a global testing of the liberation-war doctrine, and therefore had to become for the U.S. the war to end all wars of national liberation. Within that context it was vital to disabuse Asian Communists, once and for all, of any notion that the United States was indecisive or unwilling to make a total effort to defeat them, at any time or place. But this view seemed to obscure the truth that was right under our noses. North Vietnam was fighting *primarily* to achieve an unfulfilled national purpose. While it was, to be sure, fully aware of the implications for the wider application of the Mao-Ho-Giap insurgency doctrine, it was fighting not an abstractly ideological war, but a very particular war—in a particular place, characterized by a particular kind of terrain and weather, peopled by a particular breed of men and, above all, conditioned by a particular history. What really drove Ho's sacrificial legions was not the dream of world conquest, nor even the notion of generating a new momentum for Communist advance and triumph throughout Asia. What motivated Hanoi and enabled its leadership to hold 19 million primitive people to endless struggle and sacrifice against odds that were statistically ludicrous was the goal of national independence. That goal, almost gained at the end of World War II, had been callously denied by an absentminded U.S. acquiescence in the return of French military forces and French colonial interests; almost gained again in 1954 after a grim, protracted war of attrition against the French, it had been frustrated once more by John Foster Dulles, SEATO, and the willingness of all the Great Powers, including Russia, to look the other way when Diem refused to hold the promised all-Vietnam elections in 1956; almost won a third time in 1964–65, it had been denied yet again by large-scale U.S. military intervention.

National aspiration was the historical imperative that explained Ho Chi Minh. The international Communist overtones were real enough, but secondary. Maintaining a broad base of support for the war over several decades; instilling the Army cadres with tenacity, ingenuity, and readiness for sacrifice in the face of enormous odds; nurturing resiliency in the face of repeated disappointment; reorganizing the economy and distribution system under the heavy pressure of U.S. bombing—in short, defeating one renowned military power and holding at bay the most powerful nation in the world—these were achievements which, viewed objectively, would cause Ho Chi Minh to go down in history as an extraordinary leader. But they were explainable primarily in terms of nationalism; ideology was a fuel of insufficient octane rating. But if nationalism was the principal driving force, it followed that the war in Vietnam was not a test of wills between two parties—Hanoi and Washington—with equal interests at stake. For North Vietnam it was a fundamental struggle, the priority task that embraced all others, a matter of survival. To the United States, it was far more peripheral, necessarily competing for attention and resources with the other manifold interests and commitments of a global power. Yet this was a fact of life which neither the President nor his inner advisers seemed to understand.

NOTES

1. Philip L. Geyelin, *Lyndon B. Johnson and the World* (New York: Frederick A. Praeger, 1966).

2. Zbigniew Brzezinski, *Alternative to Partition* (New York: McGraw-Hill Book Company, 1965).

3. Geyelin, *Lyndon B. Johnson and the World.*

14

Vietnam and Containment
GEORGE F. KENNAN

The first point I would like to make is that if we were not already involved as we are today in Vietnam, I would know of no reason why we should wish to become so involved, and I could think of several reasons why we should wish not to.

Vietnam is not a region of major military and industrial importance. It is difficult to believe that any decisive developments of the world situation would be determined in normal circumstances by what happens on that territory. If it were not for the considerations of prestige that arise precisely out of our present involvement, even a situation in which South Vietnam was controlled exclusively by the Vietcong, while regrettable, and no doubt morally unwarranted, would not, in my opinion, present dangers great enough to justify our direct military intervention.

Given the situation that exists today in the relations among the leading Communist powers, and by that I have, of course, in mind primarily the Soviet-Chinese conflict, there is every likelihood that a Communist regime in South Vietnam would follow a fairly independent course.

There is no reason to suspect that such a regime would find it either necessary or desirable in present circumstances to function simply as a passive puppet and instrument of Chinese power. And as for the danger that its establishment there would unleash similar tendencies in neighboring countries, this, I think, would depend largely on the manner in which it came into power. In the light of what has recently happened in Indonesia, and on the Indian subcontinent, the danger of the so-called domino effect, that is the effect that would be produced by a limited Communist success in South Vietnam, seems to me to be considerably less than it was when the main decisions were taken that have led to our present involvement.

From U.S. Senate, Committee on Foreign Relations, 89th Congress, 2nd Session, *Supplemental Foreign Assistance Fiscal Year 1966—Vietnam.* Washington: Government Printing Office, 1966, pp. 331-333, 337-338, 350-351, 355-358. Testimony of February 10, 1966.

Let me stress, I do not say that that danger does not exist, I say that it is less than it was a year or two ago when we got into this involvement.

From the long-term standpoint, therefore, and on principle, I think our military involvement in Vietnam has to be recognized as unfortunate, as something we would not choose deliberately, if the choice were ours to make all over again today, and by the same token, I think it should be our Government's aim to liquidate this involvement just as soon as this can be done without inordinate damage to our own prestige or to the stability of conditions in that area.

It is obvious on the other hand that this involvement is today a fact. It creates a new situation. It raises new questions, ulterior to the long-term problem, which have to be taken into account. A precipitate and disorderly withdrawal could represent in present circumstances a disservice to our own interests, and even to world peace, greater than any that might have been involved by our failure to engage ourselves there in the first place.

This is a reality which, if there is to be any peaceful resolution of this conflict, is going to have to be recognized both by the more critical of our friends and by our adversaries.

But at the same time, I have great misgivings about any deliberate expansion of hostilities on our part directed to the achievement of something called victory—if by the use of that term we envisage the complete disappearance of the recalcitrance with which we are now faced, the formal submission by the adversary to our will, and the complete realization of our present stated political aims.

I doubt that these things can be achieved even by the most formidable military successes.

There seems to be an impression about that if we bring sufficient military pressure to bear there will occur at some point something in the nature of a political capitulation on the other side. I think this is a most dangerous assumption. I don't say that it is absolutely impossible, but it is a dangerous assumption in the light of the experience we have had with Communist elements in the past.

The North Vietnamese and the Vietcong have between them a great deal of space and manpower to give up if they have to, and the Chinese can give them more if they need it. Fidelity to the Communist tradition would dictate that if really pressed to extremity on the military level these people should disappear entirely from the open scene and fall back exclusively on an underground political and military existence rather than to accept terms that would be openly humiliating and would represent in their eyes the betrayal of the future political prospects of the cause to which they are dedicated.

Any total rooting out of the Vietcong from the territory of South Vietnam could be achieved, if it could be achieved at all, only at the cost of a degree of damage to civilian life and of civilian suffering generally for which I would not like to see this country responsible.

And to attempt to crush North Vietnamese strength to a point where Hanoi could no longer give any support for Vietcong political activity in the South, would almost certainly, it seems to me, have the effect of bringing in Chinese forces at some point, whether formally or in the guise of volunteers, thus involving us in a military conflict with Communist China on one of the most unfavorable theaters of hostility that we could possibly choose. . . .

The CHAIRMAN. If I may start with one observation which interests me particularly because of your own experience in Yugoslavia where I know you served with great distinction and where in a Communist country you were largely responsible for helping this country establish cordial relations in our own interest. I think, I believe it is on page 2 where you say—

> Given a situation that exists today in the relations among the leading Communist powers there is every likelihood that a Communist regime in South Vietnam would follow a fairly independent political course.

It came to my mind when you stated that, you may have thought of Yugoslavia, a Communist country which is following an independent course of its own, but which is not inimical to our own interests. Is that what you have in mind? If we wisely, I think, approach this problem, it could be created there or could have been created, and still might be created, a situation which would not be to the detriment of our own interests.

Is that what you had in mind?

Mr. KENNAN. Yes. I meant to say with this statement that we must not always assume that any Communist faction that comes into power anywhere in the world will function simply as the spineless executor of the orders of one of the great Communist powers. It is true that in the years that I spent in Yugoslavia, while I certainly did not see eye to eye with its government, while I sometimes resented, and had bitter arguments over, statements made by its leaders concerning our foreign policies, nevertheless it was my conclusion that the present policies of that government, especially the policies it follows in its relations with its neighbors, the neutral policy that it has long followed between East and West in military matters, all this, taken in conjunction with the highly strategic position that it occupies in the Balkans, has operated to our interest, and that we might have been worse off.

Now, I simply want to point to the possibility that these considerations might apply in other cases, too. I realize that such a statement, Mr. Chairman, is easily open to misinterpretation. I would not like to convey the impression that I think it would be fine if the Communists took South Vietnam. I think it would be regrettable. I think that we should do all that we can with due regard to our own security and to our own interests in world peace to prevent it. But I think that we should also be careful not to overrate or to misinterpret the possible implications of it. It is not so that when men call themselves Communists some sort of magic transportation takes place within them which makes them wholly different from other human beings or from what they were before. Feelings of nationalism, ordinary feelings, still affect them to a large extent. I think this reality plays a part in all of Vietnam. I don't think they want domination by the Chinese. I think the fact that there is an alternative to the Chinese within the Communist world in the form of the Soviet Union, and an alternative which incidentally is in a much better position to give them the economic aid they need. I think all this represents a state of affairs which would be very, very carefully and sensitively taken into account by any South Vietnamese Communists: and I merely wished to say, therefore, that while their domination there would not be desirable, it might not be perhaps quite as tragic or as fatal as many of us assume.

The CHAIRMAN. Of course, I don't think many of us are under any illusions that any settlement can be a desirable one in the sense that it is perfection and exactly like we would like it. It is going to be, if any settlement is reached, one that is only tolerable but not satisfactory. Is that not true?

Mr. KENNAN. Absolutely true.

The CHAIRMAN. Among the other comments you made that arouse my interest on page 6, that you are not looking at this purely from a moral standpoint, but from a practical one, of what can be achieved. You call attention to the great differences in the culture and race and language and so on between this area and other areas where we have become involved.

I take it by this you mean that this is simply not a practicable objective in this country. We can't achieve it even with the best of will.

Mr. KENNAN. This is correct. I have a fear that our thinking about this whole problem is still affected by some sort of illusions about invincibility on our part, a feeling that there is no problem in the world which we, if we wanted to devote enough of our resources to it, could not solve.

I disbelieve in this most profoundly. I do not think that we can order the political realities of areas in a great many other parts of the world. So far as I can see we are not being very successful in ordering them on islands very close to our own shores, and I deeply doubt that we can enter into the affairs of people far, far away like this, and by our own efforts primarily determine what sort of political conditions are going to prevail there.

Now, this is separate from my sympathies. I have seen as much as anyone, I daresay, in this room, of people living under communism, and I think I know as well as anyone here does what that means. These people have my sympathy. But as John Quincy Adams says, there are limits to what our duties and our capabilities are, and our first duty is to ourselves, and if we get lost in the attempt to rescue or even to establish in many instances the liberties of others, and particularly of people who have never known them as we know them in this country, who don't even know what the words mean that we use, we can lose our own substance and, I think, we can have very little to show for it when it is all over. . . .

Senator LAUSCHE. Ambassador Kennan, it has been said frequently that you were the designer and architect of the policy of the United States that we cannot suffer the expansion of communism, and, therefore, there must be adopted a plan of containment. Were you a participant in the design of that plan?

Mr. KENNAN. Senator Lausche, I bear a certain amount of guilt for the currency this word "containment" has acquired in this country. I published an article, an anonymous article, in 1947, written actually in 1946, in which this word was used, and the article got much more publicity than I thought it would get. It is true that in this sense I am guilty of the authorship, or at least of the use, of this word with regard to our policy toward the Soviet Union.

Senator LAUSCHE. Right.

Isn't it a fact that when this policy was announced, it was predicated upon the belief that the security of our country required that there be a stoppage of the aggressive advancement of communism into areas of the world other than those in which it was already prevalent?

Mr. KENNAN. Yes, sir. At that time——

Senator LAUSCHE. If that is so, has your view changed then?

Mr. KENNAN. No, the situation has changed. There was at that time——

Senator LAUSCHE. Well, if there has been a change in the situation, has your view changed in that it would now be within, let's say, the general security of our country to permit an expansion of Communist aggression?

Mr. KENNAN. It would certainly not be in our interest to encourage it. But I did not mean to convey, in the article I wrote at that time, the belief that we could necessarily stop communism at every point on the world's surface. There were things I failed to say, I must admit, in that article, which should have been said, and one of them was that certain areas of the world are more important than others; that one had to concentrate on the areas that were vital to us.

But in addition to this, I must point out that at that time there was only one center of Communist power, and it was to this that I was addressing myself.

Today there is more than one, and that makes a great deal of difference.

Senator LAUSCHE. Right.

There is now more than one, and with that I agree. But the nation included now is Red China, and Red China does not believe in peaceful coexistence, but urges the expansion of communism by whatever means are necessary. Do you agree with that?

Mr. KENNAN. I agree with that.

Senator LAUSCHE. The split between Red China and Russia has come about because Khrushchev believed in peaceful coexistence, thinking that by ideological combat, communism would be triumphant, but the Chinese did not subscribe to that theory. Is that correct?

Mr. KENNAN. I think this could stand as an explanation of one of the reasons for the Russian-Chinese conflict, but by no means all of them.

Senator LAUSCHE. All right.

If China is the real aggressor now, doesn't the policy of containment become more demandable than it was when you announced it back 20 years ago?

Mr. KENNAN. Senator Lausche, the policy of containment certainly has relevance to China, but it is a question of what and where and what lies within our resources. If we had been able, without exorbitant cost in American manpower and resources and in the attention of our Government, in the emphasis of our foreign policy, if we had been able to do better in Vietnam I would have been delighted, and I would have thought that the effort was warranted. . . .

Senator CHURCH. Mr. Ambassador, I have been very much impressed by the eloquence and profundity of the testimony you are making
today. I suppose, most of all, I like your courage, particularly in these
days when criticism of American policy is often met with charges of
appeasement or allegations of being soft on communism or sold on
surrender or some such abuse.

Your own record in our diplomatic service alone should demonstrate how strongly you have opposed communism, and how great was
your contribution in devising a prudent policy in Europe designed to
bring an end to Russian aggression there.

My questions won't relate to Vietnam as such. I think that what has
been done there cannot be readily undone. The options now open to the
President are limited, and I am confident that the President is striving
to keep this war confined within manageable limits. He certainly has
indicated his sincere desire to bring about a political settlement that will
restore peace to southeast Asia.

Rather, I would like to question you about some of the underlying
premises which led us into Vietnam in the first place, and which could,
if they remain unchanged, lead us into other guerrilla wars, indeed, into
an endless succession of guerrilla wars in the future.

I think, to get this point clearly made on the record, we should
compare the policies you advocated in Europe with the situation that
confronts us in Asia, which has just thrown off European rule.

Now, isn't it true that in Europe, following the Second World War,
we were faced with a problem of Russian aggression, with the Red army
in occupation and control of much of Eastern Europe?

Mr. KENNAN. This is correct.

Senator CHURCH. And, at that time, Russian aggression and Communist aggression seemed to be synonymous, did they not?

Mr. KENNAN. Exactly.

Senator CHURCH. And isn't it true that the NATO Alliance was
designed to put a stop to Russian aggression, that is to say, the Russian
movement of the Iron Curtain westward across the face of Europe?

Mr. KENNAN. That is absolutely correct, and it was designed especially to protect from further Communist expansion the vitally important industrial areas of the Rhineland and contiguous regions, which are
among the most important in the world.

Senator CHURCH. We felt, did we not, that if the Russian movement
westward across Europe were not stopped, then the balance of power in

the world would shift from our favor to the Russian favor?

Mr. KENNAN. This is absolutely correct.

Senator CHURCH. Now, the NATO defense line didn't stifle communism, that is to say, there are still Communist Parties existing behind the NATO defense line, the largest political party in Italy is Communist, and a very formidable Communist Party exists today in France, isn't that right?

Mr. KENNAN. That is correct.

Senator CHURCH. And the reason that we don't have, behind the NATO defense line, guerrilla wars in Western Europe, or so-called wars of national liberation in Western Europe, is because the economies there have revived, there is internal cohesion, there is strong majority support for democratic institutions in these countries. Isn't that the reason that communism has not come to prevail behind the NATO defense line in Western Europe?

Mr. KENNAN. Absolutely, and if I may add, also the fact that the peoples of these countries were willing to pick up and shoulder the burden of the load. They didn't look to an outside force to do the main job.

Senator CHURCH. In other words, we were able to join with them in a genuine collective defense.

Mr. KENNAN. Correct.

Senator CHURCH. Isn't it also true that when we intervened militarily in Europe, we intervened in a region where we shared with the Europeans a common culture, and a common civilization, and commonly held attitudes against communism?

Mr. KENNAN. This is absolutely right.

Senator CHURCH. Now, I think we have made no mistake so fundamental in American foreign policy than concluding that a design that was suitable for Europe would also be suitable for those regions of the world that have just thrust off European rule. We have failed to take into account how very different the underlying situation is in Asia and in Africa, in the ex-colonial regions of the world.

Would you agree with that?

Mr. KENNAN. I couldn't be more strongly in agreement. At the time when the containment policy with relation to Europe was being thrashed out in a practical way, and that was the time when the Marshall plan was devised, we, in the policy planning staff of the Department of State, who had something to do with the Marshall plan, were pressed repeatedly, and sometimes by people here in Congress, to produce a similar plan for China, and for Asia; and we always resisted this, precisely for the reasons you have given, not because we did not want to see communism contained in Asia, but because we felt that the devices that were effective in Europe would not necessarily be effective here.

Senator CHURCH. May I suggest here that we just briefly review the basic conditions in Asia to contrast them with what we had to work with in Europe?

Isn't it true that in Asia and in Africa we have governments that are very unstable, having just been newly established, that we have popular aspirations for a better life that often outrun, by a considerable distance, the capacity of the new governments to fulfill. We have, in addition, a situation quite different with respect to popular attitudes toward communism, that is to say, would it be your judgment that, in these areas of the world, the people may be less concerned or less fearful or less opposed to communism, as such, than they are to imperialism or colonialism, which they have experienced for two centuries and which, with great sacrifice and ofttimes with great struggle, they have finally overthrown?

Mr. KENNAN. Oh, yes.

The power of these various semantic symbols is entirely different in Asia than it is in Europe. And not only that, but the Europeans have things to lose by communism, by a Communist form of rule, which the Asians are not conscious of having to lose.

Senator CHURCH. They have freedom to lose, do they not, Mr. Ambassador?

Mr. KENNAN. Precisely.

Senator CHURCH. Is there freedom, as we know freedom, in most of the countries of Asia and Africa today?

Mr. KENNAN. There is not. I recall reading only 2 days ago an article by one of our greatest authorities in this country on Chinese culture, in which he pointed out that the Chinese language has only one word which remotely resembles our word freedom, and that conveys the sense of license, of rather turbulent indiscipline.

The CHAIRMAN. Who was that?

Mr. KENNAN. John Fairbanks.

Senator CHURCH. Now, in these countries which are mostly totalitarian, although we always include them in that phrase we use constantly, the "Free World," isn't it true that change, if it is to come at all, will often have to come through violence, that is to say, through revolution, rather than through the process of free elections?

Mr. KENNAN. I'm sure this is inevitable in large parts of the world.

Senator CHURCH. Because most of these countries are simply not democratic enough to allow for peaceful change.

Mr. KENNAN. No.

Senator CHURCH. For a free and unviolent way to achieve change, isn't that so?

Mr. KENNAN. Senator Church, the free elections presuppose a certain state of mind in great masses of people.

We had the same problem again in the Russian intervention. Woodrow Wilson and other people hoped there might be some sort of elections in Russia; and they couldn't understand that this was a country so torn by violence, by terror, by fear, by the miserable experiences of the past, that no Russian would even have trusted another Russian to open the ballots and read them fairly.

Senator CHURCH. Then, Mr. Ambassador, apart from what happens in Vietnam—and you and I both hope that the best possible solution can be achieved there for our country—but apart from what happens in Vietnam, aren't we going to be facing a situation in this vast region of the undeveloped world fairly beset by revolutions for many years to come?

Mr. KENNAN. Yes. By violence of all sorts, I think.

Senator CHURCH. And don't you think, then, that we have to begin to devise a new policy for Asia and Africa?

Mr. KENNAN. Yes.

Senator CHURCH. One not based upon the fixed concepts which were suitable for Europe, but designed to cope with the phenomena of revolution in the newly developing parts of the world?

Mr. KENNAN. I do, indeed.

Senator CHURCH. Do you think we have yet begun to develop that new policy?

Mr. KENNAN. No, I don't; and I think we find ourselves hampered in that by the slogans and the semantic symbols of the past. I wish we could drop all these things and look at these situations realistically. I think we could perhaps devise an approach to these problems, let's say, rather than a policy, which would be much more effective than the sort of talking we have been doing among ourselves in recent years.

Senator CHURCH. My time is up, Mr. Ambassador, but I just merely want to say that I agree with you. I think we are prisoners of the past, that we must break out of this old bondage if we are to fashion a policy that will effectively advance American interests in the volatile ex-colonial regions of the world.

15

The Containment of China
DEAN RUSK

In assessing Peiping's policies and actions, and the problems they present to American foreign policy and to the free peoples of the world, we must ask ourselves certain key questions:

What does Peiping want, and how does it pursue its objectives?

How successful has it been, and how successful is it likely to be in the future?

Is it on a collision course with the United States?

What are the prospects for change in its policies?

What policies should the United States adopt, or work toward, in dealing with Communist China?

First, the Chinese Communist leaders seek to bring China on the world stage as a great power. They hold that China's history, size, and geographic position entitle it to great-power status. They seek to overcome the humiliation of 150 years of economic, cultural, and political domination by outside powers.

Our concern is with the way they are pursuing their quest for power and influence in the world. And it is not only our concern but that of many other countries, including in recent years the Soviet Union.

Peiping is aware that it still lacks many of the attributes of great-power status, and it chafes bitterly under this realization.

The Chinese Communists are determined to rectify this situation. They already have one of the largest armies in the world. They are now developing nuclear weapons and missile delivery systems. They are pouring a disproportionately large proportion of their industrial and scientific effort into military and military-related fields.

What is all this military power for? Some believe it to be for defensive purposes alone:

To erect a token "deterrent" nuclear capability against the United States or the U.S.S.R.;

To demonstrate symbolically that "China must be reckoned with";

To react to an imaginary, almost pathological, notion that the United States and other countries around its borders are seeking an

From Dean Rusk, "United States Policy Toward Communist China," *Department of State Bulletin,* LIV (May 2, 1966), 688-691, 693.

opportunity to invade mainland China and destroy the Peiping regime.

But such weapons need not serve a defensive role. They can be used directly by Peiping to try to intimidate its neighbors, or in efforts to blackmail Asian countries into breaking defense alliances with the United States, or in an attempt to create a nuclear "balance" in Asia in which Peiping's potentially almost unlimited conventional forces might be used with increased effect.

These weapons can ultimately be employed to attack Peiping's Asian neighbors and, in time, even the United States or the Soviet Union. This would be mad and suicidal, as Peiping must know, despite cavalier statements that mainland China can survive nuclear war. Nevertheless, a potential nuclear capability, on top of enormous conventional forces, represents a new factor in the equilibrium of power in Asia that this country and its friends and allies cannot ignore.

Peiping's use of power is closely related to what I believe are its second and third objectives: dominance within Asia and leadership of the Communist world revolution, employing Maoist tactics. Peiping is striving to restore traditional Chinese influence or dominance in South, Southeast, and East Asia. Its concept of influence is exclusive. Foreign Minister Ch'en Yi reportedly told Prince Sihanouk recently that his country's "friendship" with Cambodia would be incompatible with Cambodian ties with the United States. Peiping has tried to alienate North Viet-Nam and North Korea from the Soviet Union. It has had uneven success in such maneuvers. But it has not abandoned this objective. Where Peiping is present, it seeks to exclude all others. And this is not only true in its relations with its neighbors but in the Communist world as well.

Peiping has not refrained from the use of force to pursue its objectives. Following Korea, there were Tibet and the attacks on the offshore islands in the Taiwan Straits. There have been the attacks on India. It is true that, since Korea, Peiping has moved only against weaker foes and has carefully avoided situations which might bring it face to face with the United States. It has probed for weaknesses around its frontier but drawn back when the possibility of a wider conflict loomed.

While the massive and direct use of Chinese Communist troops in overt aggression cannot be ruled out, Peiping's behavior up to now suggests it would approach any such decision with caution.

If the costs and risks of a greater use of force were reduced by, for example, our unilateral withdrawal from the region, Peiping might well feel freer to use its power to intimidate or overwhelm a recalcitrant opponent or to aid directly insurgent forces.

As I have said, the Chinese Communist leaders are dedicated to a fanatical and bellicose Marxist-Leninist-Maoist doctrine of world revolution. Last fall, Lin Piao, the Chinese Communist Minister of Defense, recapitulated in a long article Peiping's strategy of violence for achieving Communist domination of the world. This strategy involves the mobilization of the underdeveloped areas of the world—which the Chinese Communists compare to the "rural areas"—against the industrialized or "urban" areas. It involves the relentless prosecution of what they call "people's wars." The *final* stage of all this violence is to be what they frankly describe as "wars of annihilation."

It is true that this doctrine calls for revolution by the natives of each country. In that sense it may be considered a "do-it-yourself kit." But Peiping is prepared to train and indoctrinate the leaders of these revolutions and to support them with funds, arms, and propaganda, as well as politically. It is even prepared to manufacture these revolutionary movements out of whole cloth.

Peiping has encouraged and assisted—with arms and other means —the aggressions of the North Vietnamese Communists in Laos and against South Viet-Nam. It has publicly declared its support for so-called national liberation forces in Thailand, and there are already terrorist attacks in the remote rural areas of northeast Thailand. There is talk in Peiping that Malaysia is next on the list. The basic tactics of these "wars of liberation" have been set forth by Mao and his disciples, including General Giap, the North Vietnamese Communist Minister of Defense. They progress from the undermining of independent governments and the economic and social fabrics of society by terror and assassination, through guerrilla warfare, to large-scale military action.

Peiping has sought to promote Communist coups and "wars of liberation" against independent governments in Africa and Latin America as well as in Asia.

Some say we should ignore what the Chinese Communist leaders say and judge them only by what they do. It is true that they have been more cautious in action than in words—more cautious in what they do themselves than in what they have urged the Soviet Union to do. Undoubtedly, they recognize that their power is limited. They have shown, in many ways, that they have a healthy respect for the power of the United States.

But it does not follow that we should disregard the intentions and plans for the future which they have proclaimed. To do so would be to repeat the catastrophic miscalculation that so many people made about the amibtions of Hitler—and that many have made at various times in appraising the intentions of the Soviet leaders.

I have noted criticism of the so-called analogy between Hitler and Mao Tse-tung. I am perfectly aware of the important differences between these two and the countries in which they have exercised power. The seizure of Manchuria by Japanese militarists, of Ethiopia by Mussolini, and of the Rhineland, Austria, and Czechoslovakia by Hitler, were laboratory experiments in the anatomy and physiology of aggression. How to deal with the phenomenon of aggression was the principal problem faced in drafting the United Nations Charter, and the answer was: collective action. We do ourselves no service by insisting that each source of aggression or each instance of aggression is unique. My own view is that we have learned a good deal about this phenomenon and its potentiality for leading into catastrophe if the problem is not met in a timely fashion.

The bellicosity of the Chinese Communists has created problems within the Communist world as well as between Peiping and the non-Communist world.

Recently a leading official of a Communist state said to me that the most serious problem in the world today is how to get Peiping to move to a policy of "peaceful coexistence."

At times the Communist Chinese leaders seem to be obsessed with the notion that they are being threatened and encircled. We have told them both publicly and privately, and I believe have demonstrated in our actions in times of crisis and even under grave provocation, that we want no war with Communist China. The President restated this only last month in New York. We do not seek the overthrow by force of the Peiping regime; we do object to its attempt to overthrow other regimes by force.

How much Peiping's "fear" of the United States is genuine and how much it is artificially induced for domestic political purposes only the Chinese Communist leaders themselves know. I am convinced, however, that their desire to expel our influence and activity from the western Pacific and Southeast Asia is not motivated by fears that we are threatening them.

I wish I could believe that Communist China seeks merely a guarantee of friendly states around its borders, as some commentators have suggested. If it was as simple as this, they would have only to abandon their policies which cause their neighbors to seek help from the United States.

The trouble is that Peiping's leaders want neighboring countries to accept subordination to Chinese power. They want them to become political and economic dependencies of Peiping. If the United States can be driven from Asia, this goal will be in their grasp. The "influence," therefore, that Peiping's present leaders seek in Asia is indeed far reaching. . . .

It is of no help in formulating policy to describe Peiping's behavior as neurotic. Its present policies pose grave and immediate problems for the United States and other countries. These must be dealt with now. The weapons and advisers that Peiping exports to promote and assist insurrections in other countries cannot be met by psychoanalysis. At the present time there is a need for a counterweight of real power to Chinese Communist pressures. This has had to be supplied primarily by the United States and our allies.

We should be under no illusion that by yielding to Peiping's bellicose demands today we would in some way ease the path toward peace in Asia. If Peiping reaps success from its current policies, not only its present leaders but those who follow will be emboldened to continue them. This is the path to increased tension and even greater dangers to world peace in the years ahead.

We expect China to become some day a great world power. Communist China is a major Asian power today. In the ordinary course of events, a peaceful China would be expected to have close relations—political, cultural, and economic—with the countries around its borders and with the United States.

It is no part of the policy of the United States to block the peaceful attainment of these objectives.

More than any other Western people, we have had close and warm ties with the Chinese people. We opposed the staking out of spheres of influence in China. We used our share of the Boxer indemnity to establish scholarships for Chinese students in the United States. We welcomed the revolution of Sun Yat Sen. We took the lead in relinquishing Western extraterritorial privileges in China. We refused to recognize the puppet regime established by Japan in Manchuria. And it was our refusal to accept or endorse, even by implication, Japan's imperial conquests and further designs in China that made it impossible for us to achieve a *modus vivendi* with Japan in 1940–41.

We look forward hopefully—and confidently—to a time in the future when the government of mainland China will permit the restoration of the historic ties of friendship between the people of mainland China and ourselves.

What should be the main elements in our policy toward Communist China?

We must take care to do nothing which encourages Peiping—or anyone else—to believe that it can reap gains from its aggressive actions and designs. It is just as essential to "contain" Communist aggression in Asia as it was, and is, to "contain" Communist aggression in Europe.

At the same time, we must continue to make it plain that, if Peiping abandons its belief that force is the best way to resolve disputes and gives up its violent strategy of world revolution, we would welcome an era of good relations.

16
Containment in Asia Reconsidered
DAVID P. MOZINGO

Since the Korean War, United States policies in Asia have gradually developed along the lines of the "containment" doctrine so successfully applied in Europe after 1947. Washington has increasingly seen the problem of Chinese power in Asia in much the same light as that posed by Soviet power in Europe and has behaved as if both threats could be contained by basically the same kinds of responses. In both Asia and Europe, containment measures have reflected a perceived need for complementary interaction between military policies and aid programs in order to prevent aggression by Communist powers and to foster the internal stability of nations in the area. Although difficulties have arisen in seeking the best balance of these components of the containment policy in Europe, most of the essential American objectives in the West have been attained.

For some time, however, it has been apparent, particularly in Southeast Asia, that the application of containment measures in the Far East has not yielded results comparable to those achieved in Europe. While it is widely recognized that this disparity in results reflects special Asian problems not encountered in Europe, there has been a general reluctance to question whether the containment philosophy really addresses the basic sources of the instability in Asia that alarms the United States. It is time to analyze the relative failure of the containment doctrine in Asia by considering both the obvious special difficulties confronting the United States there and the inherent differences between the situation in Asia and that in Europe.

Had the sense of historical perspective exerted a more prominent influence on Asian policy formulation, it is likely that containment's central objective of establishing a hard political and military line between a U.S. and a Chinese sphere of influence would have seemed infeasible from the beginning. In Western Europe, the basis for effective U.S. containment measures was soundly conceived because these measures

David P. Mozingo, "Containment in Asia Reconsidered," *World Politics,* XIX (April 1967), 361-377. Reprinted by permission of Princeton University Press. Copyright 1967 by Princeton University Press.

were applied in defense of communities long-established within the framework of a nation-state system. Moreover, special ties bound the United States to Great Britain and France. By applying the containment doctrine in the West, the United States, for the third time in this century, reaffirmed the strategic principle that had formerly governed Britain's policy toward Europe: No single continental power was to be permitted to conquer or dominate the European nation-state system. Further, the U.S. measures to contain Russia in Europe were strengthened by the historic determination of the Western democracies to preserve their established order and values.

In Asia, the containment doctrine has been applied to an area where a nation-state system is only just beginning to emerge amid unpredictable upheavals of a kind that characterized Europe three centuries earlier. It is only since 1949 that the restoration of a strong, unified China, the withdrawal of the Western colonial powers, and the formation of new independent countries have created the beginnings of a modern nation-state system in Asia.

The question in Asia is not how a traditionally functioning system can be rehabilitated but how a very new system will evolve and mature. The kinds of American technical and economic power that helped to restore the historic vitality of the European system would seem to have, at best, only partial relevance to the Asian situation. It may be doubted whether the kinds of tools and power available to the United States can induce stability in an environment in which most countries are experiencing a profound and rapid transformation of their societies, values, and attitudes. Much of the American experience and structure of values has already shown itself to be not only inapplicable but also not even wanted. The results of the competition between the United States, Russia, and China in Asia thus far seem to indicate that attempts by external powers to shape the emerging Asian system are unlikely to succeed. None of these powers has been able, whether by appeals to ideology or common national interests or by large-scale economic and military aid, to exert enough influence to draw the more important Asian powers into close alignment. In the absence of firm ties and mutual interests of the kind that have bound the United States to Western Europe (and these did not emerge overnight), a policy of containment in Asia must rest on unstable foundations.

The Soviet threat to Europe has been regarded primarily as a military one. Even when the Western part of that continent was most weakened, immediately after World War II, Communist parties were unable to take power in any country by popular consent. Western Europe's economic recovery was rapid. National conflicts were not so severe as to prevent the formation of an alliance. Until very recent times, there was broad agreement among the Western powers about the nature of the Soviet threat and how to meet it. Consequently, it was possible to lay a firm political foundation for the NATO structure.

The political conditions that were indispensable to the creation of security arrangements in Europe are absent in Asia, where very few powers see their security interests in the same way. Except for Taiwan, all of the Asian powers have an enemy or enemies whom their leaders apparently regard as more threatening than China. Japan, for example, still regards Russia as at least as great a threat to her security as China. Moreover, the common threat to South Korea and Japan that developed as a result of the Korean War has yet to result in a real rapprochement between these two countries; but without such an understanding, no "little NATO" in Northeast Asia can be built. For these and other historical, economic, and psychological reasons it is doubtful that any anti-China security arrangement can win Japan's enthusiastic participation. In fact, only the United States and South Korea have indicated interest in an alignment with Taiwan against Peking.

In Southeast Asia, the menace to Thailand, Laos, and South Vietnam comes in the first instance not from China but from a very independent and highly nationalistic regime in Hanoi. North Vietnamese expansion into Southeast Asia also alarms Cambodia, but not as much as her fear of Thai and South Vietnamese aspirations to recover lost territories at Phnom Penh's expense. Prince Sihanouk believes these two historic enemies have aligned themselves with the United States, not so much to contain China or North Vietnam as to secure the arms and tacit backing of the United States for the pursuit of their irredentist claims on Cambodia—hence, his close ties with Peking and deference to Hanoi. Similar fears influence Pakistan, whose government (understandably) believes India is gearing her defenses less to protect the subcontinent from Chinese invasion than to dominate Pakistan. In Rawalpindi's view, New Delhi is using the boundary dispute with Peking to secure U.S. and Soviet aid that will more likely be used against Pakistan. Indonesia, the Philippines, and Malaysia are geographically beyond the reach of Chinese power. They have predominantly the same racial composition. In spite of these favorable conditions, in recent times the relations between the three countries have been strained by harmful rivalries they themselves have generated, not Peking.

Such strife among Asia's non-Communist powers, for which their own governments are responsible, has been far more beneficial to China's aspirations and interests as a great power in the Far East than have any actions she has initiated herself. It is therefore difficult to see how a containment policy directed primarily against China can be truly effective as long as the Far East seethes with conflict between jealously independent rival nationalist regimes whose policies are essentially their own. To a certain extent it would seem that previous U.S. attempts to back one or another potentially anti-Communist state and to promote the growth of its petty military power have not so much deterred or contained the dubious military threat from China as they have sharpened the very national conflicts, internal and external, that undermine local stability and hence frustrate the development of a broader basis for conciliation among the nations in this region. American objectives would perhaps have been better served by policies that emphasized the American role as a "conciliator" in Asia (for example, in the India-Pakistan, Indonesia-Malaysia, or Cambodia-Thailand-Vietnam disputes) than by so much emphasis on building anti-Communist "positions of strength" through military alliances aimed at China. Actually, the United States has the strongest kind of interest in promoting conciliation between all the states of Asia in this century of intense nationalism. This interest includes even such issues as the Sino-Indian boundary dispute. However, it is clear that the incessant conflict and rivalry among Asia's non-Communist states go further to destabilize Asian politics than do the actions taken thus far by the Peking regime.

The existence of intense rivalries among Asia's non-Communist powers, rivalries that result from their own conceptions of national interests and objectives, has produced a response in Asia to the fact of Chinese Communist power that is altogether different from Europe's reaction to the Soviet threat. At no time has there emerged anything like an Asian consensus about how to regard Chinese military or political intentions. It would be difficult to show that any Asian countries capable of independent action have accepted the United States' assessment of China. This judgment is supported by the fact that the United States has been unable to construct, even informally, an alliance structure in the Far East, directed against Peking, which includes the major Asian powers. It is well known that even some allies of the United States, given the balance of power that so heavily favors Russia and the United States, do not regard Peking as a serious military menace to themselves. At the same time, there can be scarcely a government in the Far East today that is not aware of how useful it is, in dealing with the United States, to invent or exaggerate fears of a Chinese bogeyman.

The United States, far removed from Asia and from direct threat by China, stands almost alone in emphasizing the urgent menace of Peking, while most of the countries in the region, who ought to be highly sensitive to any Chinese threat, have taken a more conservative view of their Chinese neighbor's intentions. Even India's bitter hostility to Peking has not produced anything like the devil-theory of China that has grown up in the United States. To sum up, the states of Asia have not agreed on the existence of a common external threat; but such an agreement seems to be an indispensable condition for the success of policies modeled on European-type containment.

It is not only the inherent differences between the political structure of non-Communist Asia and Western Europe that cast doubt on the validity of applying European-type containment doctrines to the Far East. The aims and direction of Chinese Communist policy—indeed, the nature of the Communist challenge in Asia itself—must be evaluated in terms that are largely irrelevant to European experience. Menacing Soviet actions in Europe presented such a clear and present danger to all concerned that they provoked the creation of the NATO alliance. Since the Russian forward pressure came after the Western powers had already acquiesced in considerable territorial and political concessions in Eastern Europe to meet alleged Soviet security interests, there was general agreement in Western Europe that Moscow's intentions were not defensive in nature. The American effort to equate China's intervention in the Korean conflict and her use of force in the Taiwan dispute, in Tibet, and on the Indian boundary with Soviet behavior in Eastern Europe has obviously failed to convince most Asian governments that China has aggressive intentions toward them. This failure suggests why the United States has been unable to crystallize opinion in these countries behind any genuine Asian regional security arrangements to curb a supposed threat of Chinese expansion.

In explaining Chinese action, Pakistan, Burma, Cambodia, Nepal, even Indonesia and our ally Japan, have tended to give more weight to traditional, nationalistic, and defensive motives than to purely "aggressive" Communist revolutionary impulses. This is not to say that these non-Communist Asian countries have been unconcerned about China's actions, her power, or her Communist system. But it is clear that most of these countries rely on their own perception of their Chinese neighbor, and their perception is such that the United States is unlikely to succeed in arousing a high level of Asian fear about China unless Peking behaves in a manner far more threatening to them, collectively and individually, than she has done to date. It is recognized in a number of Asian capitals that China's belligerence is largely a function of her special rivalry with the United States over Taiwan and other issues. Hence these countries have chosen to avoid alignments that would conflict with their own interest in stabilizing relations with Peking. Their aim has been, quite obviously, to avoid inflaming relations with China, and they do not wish to be drawn into the Sino-American quarrel. Asian reactions to the issues raised in Korea, Taiwan, Tibet, India, and Vietnam have been extremely varied and at no time has any of these conflicts produced an Asian front against China similar to that which the Soviet Union brought on herself by her actions in Europe. The disparity of views among the non-Communist Asian powers, and between them and the United States, about China's intentions robs the policy of containment of the basic consensus that was essential to its success in Europe.

China's foreign policy has also helped to undermine the appeal of the containment doctrine in Asia. The basic direction of her foreign policy in Asia since 1954 has been toward seeking an adjustment of contentious issues between herself and such of her neighbors as were not allied with or seemingly under the control of the United States. Thus, for more than a decade, China has worked to normalize relations with Afghanistan, Burma, Pakistan, Cambodia, Ceylon, Nepal, and Indonesia. Peking is outspokenly hostile to all members of the American anti-China bloc. She seeks in various ways, including the threat to support revolutionary elements, to convince their leaders that making common cause with the United States carries certain risks; that it is not possible for any of them to support the United States in opposing China and have friendly relations with Peking at the same time. Even in relation to countries in this category, however, China's actions—as distinguished from her verbal condemnations—have been cautious and restrained. To those Asian governments that decline alignment with the United States, Peking offers such explicit rewards as border settlements, aid, and China's nonsupport of insurrectionary tactics by local revolutionaries. This Chinese stance reflects not only the limitations on Peking's military capabilities for large-scale aggressive actions, but, vastly more important, her recognition that naked and unprovoked aggression against her neighbors would threaten the collapse of her entire diplomacy in Asia. Since the Bandung Conference, China has attempted to compose her relations with any genuinely nonaligned neighbors in order to identify and isolate the United States as the aggressive power and to find common ground with Asian nationalism for the purpose of organizing opposition to the policies of the United States.

Since the mid-1950's, China's diplomatic efforts to prevent her neighbors from being drawn into the American anti-China alignment have consistently enjoyed priority over Peking's commitment to support Communist revolutions. The Chinese position on revolution, which is central to an accurate understanding of her policies in Asia, should not be misunderstood or distorted. China encourages armed "revolutionary" action on the part of Communists or other dissidents in countries where special conditions exist—that is, where the so-called "imperialist" powers have interposed themselves, as in Taiwan, South Korea, Japan, Laos, South Vietnam, and most recently, Thailand (after U.S. Military forces arrived in that country). Ostensibly nonaligned governments, as in India, have also to reckon with Peking's anger when they adopt "anti-China" policies. One listens in vain, however, for the strident Chinese call to "revolution" in any Asian country that is clearly independent of American tutelage and pursues a policy of accommodation with Peking.

Where supporting revolution conflicts with China's hope to wean non-Communist Asian governments away from the United States, revolution is pushed into the background. China has advised in her ideological pronouncements on revolution that local Communist parties, though they should learn from Chairman Mao, must in the final analysis find their own formulas for taking power. In those Asian countries that remain independent of the United States and friendly to China, Peking shuns calling upon the local parties to attempt "adventurist" revolutionary actions that conflict with her own diplomacy. Toward governments in this category, China's basic policy for more than a decade has been to concentrate wherever possible on currying favor with nationalist leaders (some of whom, from the Communist viewpoint, can scarcely be described as "progressive") and to encourage the local party to develop the art of skilled united-front tactics. Local Communists are expected to exploit the various "contradictions" in their own country so as to place themselves in a position to take power when the old incompetent order collapses. Peking encourages local parties to take power by the parliamentary or peaceful path if they can, but she points out that there is no instance in which the bourgeois classes have permitted a Communist party to win power "democratically." Hence, the Chinese argue, it is indispensable that a real Marxist-Leninist party organize for and be prepared to use armed revolutionary struggle. Otherwise the chances are very slim that a Communist party could come to power, much less be strong enough to carry out a dictatorship of the proletariat.

Peking's actual behavior and her ideological theses on revolution reveal that she is prepared to refrain from direct interference in the competition (whether peaceful or violent) between Communist parties and the "bourgeois" classes in Asian countries, so long as the United States also does not directly intervene in these countries' politics.[1] This is the essence of the Chinese version of peaceful coexistence in Asia, formulated more than ten years ago at the Bandung Conference.[2] China has not violated her own ground rules in relation to any independent Asian country, regardless of its social system, except where the United States has come to play a direct role in support of "bourgeois" regimes' competition with local Communist parties. The dispute with Moscow on the meaning of peaceful coexistence has arisen over the issue of what the policy of the Communist powers should be in situations where the United States rushes in to prop up a non-Communist regime that is in danger of losing the competition with its local Communist opponent. China argues that the Communist bloc should try to deter, or by various means oppose, attempts by the United States to use her own power unilaterally to determine the outcome of the competition between the bourgeois elites and the Communist forces. The Chinese leaders' view of their own national interests requires this position, for they regard the United States as bent on organizing all Asia into a belt of client-states opposing Peking. These fears are less disturbing to the Soviet leaders, who have long betrayed noticeable ambivalence about the desirability of fully opposing the United States in Asia if to do so would benefit the interests of the Chinese state.

As her power increases, of course, it is possible that China may abandon her present compromise with independent Asian nationalist regimes and, under the protection of her own nuclear deterrent, energetically attempt to impose Communist regimes on her neighbors. That possibility cannot be dismissed lightly, but it is a course of action fraught with grave risks for Peking. While it is conceivable that China might attempt to invade small neighboring countries or to foment and support revolution in them, it is far less likely that she will feel confident enough to undertake such measures against large Asian powers such as India, Pakistan, Indonesia, and Japan. Some of these nations will be able to move in the nuclear direction at some future time; should Peking, without provocation, take an aggressive attitude toward these countries, she would run the risk of hastening the development of an anti-China nuclear club. Nothing would seem so well calculated to drive non-Communist Asia closer to the United States (or Russia) as an attempt by Peking to coerce her neighbors into unconditional surrender to Chinese demands.

Seen dispassionately, China's policies in Asia are more characteristic of a traditional great power than of a revolutionary renegade. The commitment to revolution plays a special part in Chinese policies, but in aspiring to great-power status, Peking emphasizes such traditional and conventional instruments as diplomacy, economic power, and the presence or threat of force. The demands of the Chinese regime for certain irredentas, spheres of influence, and concessions to its security interests are opposed by the United States and the Soviet Union, each of them much more powerful than China. Peking cannot hope to force concessions from either of these powers by provoking a direct test of strength. But it is quite evident that Communist China does not intend to accept passively a position and influence in the world, particularly in Asia, that she regards as being dictated either by the Soviet Union or by the United States. It is doubtful that any Chinese leadership born in this century would react differently. But the Chinese leaders are not the only ones in Asia and in other areas with aspirations that go beyond the position Russia or America would assign to them. China's call to "revolution" is directed primarily to existing and potential elites in Asia and elsewhere whom she regards as likely to share with her an interest in altering any status quo imposed by U.S. or Soviet policies.

The model she has offered to these potential Communist and nationalist allies, in the hope that their revolutionary efforts will shake U.S. and Soviet domination, is one derived from Chinese Communist revolutionary experience. The Chinese leaders believe that under favorable conditions, well-trained and indoctrinated Communist parties can integrate this model with their own concrete situations and can ultimately take power. The Chinese do not say that revolution can or should be launched everywhere; they actively support unrest only in certain carefully defined revolutionary situations: where "imperialism" (i.e., the United States) is present, and where the prescribed local conditions of success exist. Peking is the master, not the servant, of its revolutionary ideology.

The entire Chinese line on revolution has been fashioned to support the great-power policies Peking pursues in her contest with the United States and the Soviet Union. Where China's leaders have believed their interests in this fundamental struggle could be best served by supporting foreign Communist revolutionary movements, they have done so. But wherever they have believed they could advance in the contest with Moscow and Washington by supporting an odd assortment of friendly nationalist, militarist, or monarchial regimes, they have not hesitated to leave local Communist parties to their own fate. Had Peking's actions conformed to the devil-theory of China that has grown up in the United States, the appeal of the containment policy in Asia would no doubt be much greater than it is today.

It is not surprising that a state with China's present power and long history should aspire to regional preeminence. But the task of transforming such ambitions in Asia into reality promises to be very difficult. Various forces in Asia, independent of American power, seem likely to curb Peking's influence.

The position of the Chinese state in Asia is not comparable to that of the United States in the Western hemisphere or to Russia's position in Eastern Europe. In addition to the United States, Peking confronts, in Russia, Japan, India-Pakistan, and Indonesia, large powers which, irrespective of their political order, have reason to oppose mainland China's hegemony in Asia. Russia's and Japan's interests are very different from China's, and the power complex developing in both these countries would act as a major curb on Chinese expansion in the most decisive theater, Northeast Asia, even in the unlikely event of a total withdrawal of American power. The departure of the United States from Asia would no doubt gratify Peking, but it would not clear the path for Chinese hegemony. Rather, it would set the stage for a different kind of power struggle in the area.

Since the nineteenth century, both Japan and Russia have tried to be expansionist powers at China's expense. No Chinese government is likely to rid itself of the old fear that these two powers might again take the path of aggression against China or combine against her interests in Asia. If a disengagement were ever to occur between the United States and China, it seems very probable that China's attention would turn to the older problem of opposing Russian and Japanese penetration of the Asian mainland. In the twentieth century this old three-power rivalry might take a different form than it did in the past, but the steady rise of Russian and Japanese power would continue to be a basic obstacle to Chinese hegemony. The longer and much deeper history of China's fear of Russia and Japan may one day exert a powerful influence on future Chinese leaders' attitudes toward the United States, if a major conflict between the two powers does not come to pass.

The natural direction for Chinese expansion, it is usually thought, is into Southeast Asia, where China has historically exerted influence. China's nearness and the absence of strong indigenous military powers have led to the assumption that she is destined to dominate Southeast Asia unless resolutely deterred by the United States. This fits in neatly with theories about power vacuums. But the major Southeast Asian countries themselves have strongly resisted the idea of being drawn into China's orbit (or anyone else's). All of the countries in this area, including Vietnam, share an antipathy toward Chinese pretensions to superiority and dominance, whether on the part of local Chinese populations or of the Peking government. Nearly all the countries of Southeast Asia possess impressive geographic barriers against a major Chinese invasion. Moreover, they all are well aware that Soviet and American power interests are also opposed to Chinese predominance, although not all agree with the United States about how to deal with China. Contrary to the experience of past centuries, when her spreading culture was a powerful vehicle for claims to regional predominance, China's influence as a whole has been declining in Southeast Asia. Recently excluded from the area by the Western imperial powers, China now faces the intense nationalism that has captured the successor states since World War II.

The existence of fraternal Communist parties, the most successful of which have been every bit as nationalistic as the Chinese party, has not constituted an unmixed blessing as far as Peking's search for preeminence in the area is concerned. These parties have been useful and necessary allies, as in Vietnam and Laos, in opposing the American effort to turn the 1954 Geneva agreement on Indochina into an anti-Communist and anti-China front. On the other hand, some of these highly nationalistic and ambitious Communist parties, like the Indonesian one, often complicate China's diplomatic dealings with nationalist governments. The stronger Asian Communist movements have all shown an independent temper, and this has increased their freedom to take actions contrary to China's interests.

The Chinese leaders believe that the removal of Western influence from Asia, coupled with prolonged internal instability, will eventually aid local Communist movements in coming to power. But China's leaders, no less than Russia's, are already discovering in their relations with North Vietnam and North Korea that ideological affinity and territorial proximity between Communist states do not result in the subordination of the smaller partners. Already it is evident that North Korea and North Vietnam will develop their own distinctive national personalities and forms: neither is now or is likely to become simply a small replica of "the thought of Mao Tse-tung." In the past, both regimes have shown a willingness to depart from the Chinese line on key issues. Should other Communist regimes emerge in Southeast Asia—in Vietnam, say, or possibly in Indonesia—Peking cannot assume on the basis of past experience that they will follow her lead. Actually, China must remain worried that such regimes may seek more freedom of action by currying favor with the Soviet Union—or, for that matter, with the West. Consequently, it is by no means clear at this point that China's leaders would prefer the development of stable, independent, diverse, and highly nationalistic Communist regimes in Southeast Asia in preference to the prolonged continuation of weak non-Communist regimes led by men willing to defer to China's interests in return for Peking's respect of the essential sovereignty of their countries.

None of the elites of the principal Asian nations—Japan, India, Pakistan, Indonesia—on whose political and military stance a great deal of China's ultimate position and influence in Asia depends, have shown themselves to be anybody's pawns—Russia's, China's, or America's. The United States and Russia have failed on the whole in their attempts to manipulate Asian nationalism so as to support their own state strategies in the cold war. By now it ought to be apparent that there is not going to be either an American or a Soviet solution to Asia's postcolonial problems. By its nature that goal was never really attainable, but it seemed to be a serious aspiration at one time because both Russia and America have been attracted, to a different degree and in very different ways, to the notion that they have special world ideological missions. Peking may believe China can succeed where two vastly richer and stronger superpowers failed, but the post-World War II history of Asian nationalism indicates very clearly that none of the great powers will be likely to succeed in this endeavor.

It should not be forgotten that between 1948 and 1951, during the heyday of Sino-Soviet cooperation, the Communist parties of Asia tried very hard to use armed insurrection as a means of discrediting and destroying such leaders as Nehru, Sukarno, U Nu, and others. In every instance where the non-Communist leadership could lay genuine claim to representing the force of nationalism, the Communist rebellions were crushed. So complete was the failure of these parties' assaults on nationalism that the Communist movement was forced to come to terms and to shift to policies of peaceful coexistence—a new line first championed by the Communist parties of China, India, and Indonesia, and only later by the Soviet Union. It should also be added that except for the special case of Malaya, the most politically significant defeats inflicted on Communist movements have come at the hands of non-aligned nationalist governments, and, as the recent suppression of the Indonesian Communist party again demonstrates, these defeats were brought about without the assistance of the United States.

The fear, expressed in the argument that neutralism or nonalignment is simply a temporary way station on the road to communism, that Peking and other Communists can push over popular nationalist regimes like "dominoes" once a Communist revolution succeeds somewhere else, is overwhelmingly contradicted by the proven vitality of Asian nationalism in the last twenty years. The Chinese Communists were the first to recognize, more than a decade ago, that genuine non-Communist nationalism was nobody's pushover and that efforts by local Communist parties to prove the contrary would bear bitter fruit. In Asia, it is only where an existing leadership has not earned, and therefore cannot claim, the mandate of nationalism that Communist parties have been able to make a serious challenge for power—a challenge based on their own attempt to seize power from those who either lost that mandate or never had it.

Much discussion about the threat of Chinese Communist expansion exaggerates what Peking is capable of doing both now and later and underplays the role of indigenous forces at work in neighboring countries affected by Chinese policies but clearly free from Chinese domination. This is a critical distinction to make, for the fact is that China is assigned far more responsibility than she deserves for the disturbances that lie at the roots of American anxiety about Asia. It is simply not true that Peking or any other Communist power can successfully "turn on" a Communist revolution wherever it chooses. Neither Peking's actions nor her ideological pronouncements have created the essential conditions that have energized the growth of the Communist movement in Asian countries. Local Communist parties have scored impressive gains, invariably, in those countries where native non-Communist elites have, by their own actions, failed to gain or retain their people's recognition as popular, effective nationalists. Local non-Communist elites themselves, not Peking, created the basic sources of internal discord in Laos, Vietnam, and Indonesia, where the most successful Communist movements to date have developed. Communist strength in these countries would be far less today had the non-Communist political elements subordinated their private rivalries to the larger task of national consolidation. Where the competition among the non-Communist elites has not reached the point of destroying the national fabric—for example, in Japan, Thailand, Pakistan, Burma, Cambodia, Ceylon, India, Malaysia, and the Philippines—the Communists have been unable to make a serious bid for power.

The plain fact is that Asian communism's greatest asset is not, and never has been, Communist China's potential military threat or her support of revolution. It has been, and continues to be, primarily the existence of incompetence and corruption and the lack of a genuine, socially progressive, nation-building ethic within the non-Communist elite in every country where communism has made serious advances. Conversely, the most effective deterrent to Communist gains has proved to be the existence of a non-Communist elite dedicated to solving its country's problems and therefore capable of holding the loyalty of its own people. American military power and aid, in themselves, have not proved adequate to find, to build, or to replace a dedicated, hard-working, non-Communist elite.

In the absence of indigenously inspired civil strife, gross incompetence among the non-Communists, or a foreign colonial enemy, no Communist movement in any Asian country has come even close to taking power, through either revolutionary or conventional political strategies. The political, economic, and social upheaval indispensable for a successful "people's war" cannot be manufactured abroad, and it does not burst on the scene overnight. Fundamentally, the prospects for successful Communist movements in Asia depend far less on contriving armed insurrection than on the character and ability of the non-Communist elites. Asia's non-Communists, the Chinese believe, will do the basic job of disintegrating their own societies and reputations to the point at which Communist parties can effectively exploit the situation. If the Chinese are right, and the evidence suggests that in some countries they are, the Communist threat to Asia would not disappear if Communist China's presence vanished from the scene tomorrow.

There most certainly are both immediate and long-range prospects that the kind of future the United States would like to see develop in Asia will not come about. And the nature of the threat to idealized U.S. hopes is primarily the potential rise of authoritarian or totalitarian regimes in response to a broad pattern of grievances long felt and long uncorrected. But this danger comes not from the Left alone, in the shape of communism, but also from the Right, in the form of authoritarian, oligarchic regimes representing the military, the privileged social classes, and the commercial element. There are numerous examples—Laos, Indonesia, Vietnam, Kerala—to show that when the Communist parties are likely to take power, whether through elections or revolution, the rightist classes are likely to agree on a coercive political solution of their own invention, rather than to accept one formulated in Moscow and Peking.

For a long time, United States assumptions about political developments in Asia have contained the unwarranted expectation that somehow national communities based on some form of democratic consensus ought to, or are likely to, flourish in the area, provided an assumed Communist threat to their institutions is checked and economic development is encouraged. It is quite natural that the United States, in view of her values and traditions, should act to promote economically viable and politically responsible regimes wherever there is a *clear* indication of local purpose and desire. But successful policies for the long run—not based merely on the year-to-year fluctuation in Communist fortunes—must take account of the limitations on what the United States, great though her power is, can realistically expect to achieve in a vast and varied part of the world that has very different traditions from her own. History thus far would appear to show that overt Communist military aggression can be defeated and that artificially contrived "people's wars" do not succeed in countries whose leaders command the consent and loyalty of their own people. There is, however, serious reason to doubt that any foreign power, including the United States, can redeem the image of harsh and unpopular governments or can persuade or force unwilling governments to take those measures of reform that alone can win the support of their own populations or build a nationalist following where one does not exist.

Unfortunately, the painful truth is that Asia's strongest political tradition is the very authoritarianism that stands in the way of such reforms. The variations in this authoritarian tradition have been either despotic or benevolent but have remained authoritarian. The sharing of state power under the rule of law is an alien conception in many parts of Asia. Moreover, the desirability of political Westernization is not at once obvious to most Asians, as it is to Americans. Except where Western institutions have been imposed forcibly by Western powers, there has been little lasting, indigenously sustained commitment to socially progressive or politically democratic ideas in any Asian country. There is no "free Asia" counterpart to the Western democratic traditions on which to build except in our own imagination. The United States can have hope for and can act to sustain Japan's, India's, or any other country's adoption of consensus-type political communities, but there should be no illusions. The foundations of transplanted Western political and social ideas in Asia are weak. Institutions based on them have already been overturned in Burma, Korea, Pakistan, Laos, and Indonesia; they have hardly existed in other countries of the Far East. One may even fairly doubt that Western political forms would survive in India or Japan in the event of a serious crisis.

In Asia, however, the absence of quasi-democratic, pluralistic institutions has not proved to be an insuperable obstacle to maintaining stable political communities based on the tacit or expressed consent of the governed. Indeed, some Asian societies are likely to find what they regard as the appropriate balance between the conflicting demands of progress, justice, and order best achieved within a traditional-authoritarian political system that is in harmony with their historical development. What has proved to be the indispensable condition for maintaining a stable non-Communist political order is that the government and its leaders win and retain the confidence of their people as genuine exponents of nationalism. Where this common bond of nationalism links leaders and citizens, no Communist movement in Asia has been able to sever it at the polls or on the battlefield.

All this is true even in an era when U.S. military power has been overwhelming and when vast sums have been made available for aid to any regimes that would hoist the anti-Communist banner. The United States has been at no disadvantage compared to the Communists in her resources for waging the contest in Asia. Quite the opposite is true. The real difficulties that beset the United States arise primarily from the nature of the task she has set out to achieve. That task has become, evidently, nothing less than to act as a vehicle shaping basic forces of change in a vast part of the world that not only is entering the nation-building stage of development, but is also undergoing at the same time the profound experience of total cultural transformation. But the United States has virtually no ties linking it to the traditions that are bound to govern the evolution of most Asian countries. In the context of the profound upheaval now occurring in Asia independently of great-power action, it would be well to ponder whether even the United States can reasonably expect to exert a decisive molding influence on the form or spirit of new national communities that must ultimately reflect their own diversity, peculiarities, needs, traditions, and aspirations. It is leaning on a weak reed, in truth, to base long-range policies on assumptions that the United States, or any combination of Western technological expertise and aid, will somehow be able to channel and mold the vast revolution in human attitudes and behavior that is painfully under way not only in Asia but in three-quarters of the world. But if the United States is determined to substitute American power for the absence of indigenous, non-Communist nationalism and to attempt a basic transformation of the elites and the societies of the far-off countries of Asia, let *that* true purpose be defined for what it really is, not displaced onto the myth of a Chinese Communist bogeyman.

It is primarily the evolution of nationalism, not the foreign policies or ideology of the Peking government, which frustrates the United States in Asia. The power fundamentally to change the basic indigenous forces shaping the development and character of nationalism in Asian countries lies in neither Peking nor Washington. No internal or external Communist power has yet been able to force the submission of an independent Asian country, however poor and whatever its political system, whose non-Communist leaders can justifiably claim the mandate of nationalism. It is incredible to suppose that the United States can, by the exercise of her own power, claim that mandate for any non-Communist elite that has not earned it from its own people. And until the United States comprehends the full meaning of nationalism in Asia, Communist and non-Communist alike, the gap between America's expectations and the real world around her will remain frustratingly large.

NOTES

The views expressed in this paper are those of the author. They should not be interpreted as reflecting the views of the RAND Corporation or the official opinion or policy of any of its governmental or private research sponsors.

1.   The definitive statement of the Chinese position on "peaceful coexistence" with other non-Communist states was set forth in the Sixth Comment on the Open Letter of the Central Committee of the CPSU, "Peaceful Coexistence— Two Diametrically Opposed Policies," published December 12, 1963. The full text is in *The Polemic on the General Line of the International Communist Movement* (Peking 1965), 259-301.

2.   For complete texts of Chou En-lai's three speeches at the Bandung Conference on relations with Asian countries, see *China and the Asian-African Conference (Documents)* (Peking 1955).

Part Five

SOMETHING OLD, SOMETHING NEW?:
THE 1970s

Introduction

SOMETHING OLD, SOMETHING NEW?: THE 1970s

Where does containment stand in America's arsenal of doctrines today? Richard M. Nixon, successful in his 1968 presidential bid against Vice President Hubert Humphrey, largely because the nation was tired of war and its concomitant ills at home, began a gradual withdrawal of American forces from Vietnam. "Vietnamization" was his new policy—let the South Vietnamese battle the "enemy" with American weapons and foreign aid, but not with American soldiers. He startled friends and foes alike when he announced in 1971 that he would visit the People's Republic of China, which he had always called "Red China" before. His early 1972 trip to Peking was unforgettable, especially when Nixon sipped mao-tai with Chou En-lai and quoted Mao Tse-tung himself. The Vietnamese War seemed to be winding down for Americans and the President had opened communications with the major power in Asia. Talks with the Soviets over limitations on strategic arms had also begun. Had containment been shelved?

"Probably not" argued some observers. They noted that the Nixon Administration still spoke in the vernacular of the 1940s. In his State of the Union message of January 20, 1972, the President recalled aid to Greece and Turkey, when he had voted for it as a Congressman, and applauded that 1947 decision as one which helped avoid a world war for twenty-five years. "Vietnamization" was still containment of an ill-defined "enemy," a word Nixon employed often. American economic, political, and military involvement around the globe continued under Nixon. And his administration perpetuated the heavy emphasis on military appropriations and weaponry to counter both Russia and China.

Importantly, too, Nixon and his adviser Henry Kissinger spoke in 1972 of "balance of power" and a world dominated by five units: Western Europe, Russia, Japan, China, and the United States. Each unit would supposedly have its sphere of influence and all five would balance one another off for international stability. This big power arrangement, some Americans suspected, was another device to implement containment. That is, revolution would be contained by the five units in order to maintain the balance; China and Russia would balance each other off, thereby reducing the American responsibility to contain both. The power balance idea may not work in the 1970s, especially if independent revolutionary peoples refuse to cooperate, but it may have given new life to the containment doctrine. Certainly containment has not been given the incisive reevaluation that Hoopes, Mozingo, and Kennan would desire.

Yet it does appear that America in the 1970s, if still hostile to national revolutionary movements, seems less willing to thwart them, and less willing to allow an unlimited application of global containment. In part, this is true because the United States now lacks the authority and power to shape events worldwide, as well as the national commitment from the American people to do so. Americans seem less willing to accept the Cold War image of Russia and China as deceitful expansionists gnawing at the very roots of American existence. The failure in Vietnam forced these changes.

Perhaps most students of American diplomacy would agree with Senator J. William Fulbright that the Truman Doctrine in 1972 was "frayed and tattered," but "still an influence upon our policy and outlook." Fulbright himself attempted a reexamination of containment and the Truman Doctrine in a searching, knowledgeable, and introspective article on American foreign relations since 1945 for the *New Yorker* magazine. Having served in Congress since that date and having in fact voted with Nixon for most American Cold War policies, Fulbright, unlike the President, could reflect that he was a victim of an oversimplistic analysis. "If it be granted that Stalin started the Cold War," asserted Fulbright, "it must also be recognized that the Truman Administration seemed to welcome it." Fulbright looked into the seventies with anxiety, hoping that America would never resume the earlier anti-Communist crusade.

A troubling question persists for Fulbright and other Americans in the 1970s: Will American leaders again reassert vigorously the cardinal principle of containment through intervention abroad? And will they again initiate a debate at home about the threat to be contained, the chronological and geographical limits of containment, and the means of implementation? What *is* certain is that George F. Kennan and his ideas will be central to any discussion about the future of American foreign policy.

17

The Frayed and Tattered Truman Doctrine and the Future

J. WILLIAM FULBRIGHT

For reasons still not wholly known and understood, the grand alliance of the Second World War broke up almost as soon as victory was won, and the powers that had called themselves "the United Nations" fell into the pattern of hostility, periodic crisis, and "limited" war that has characterized world politics for the last twenty-five years. At Yalta in February, 1945, the United States, Great Britain, and the Soviet Union pledged to maintain and strengthen in peace the "unity of purpose and of action" that was bringing victory in war. Just over two years later, on March 12, 1947, President Truman proclaimed the doctrine that came to be recognized as the basic rationale, from the American standpoint, for the Cold War. President Truman based the appeal he made to Congress for support of Greece and Turkey not primarily on the specific circumstances of those two countries at that time but on a general formulation of the American national interest which held that "totalitarian regimes imposed on free peoples, by direct or indirect aggression, undermine the foundations of international peace and hence the security of the United States." President Truman went on to say that at that moment in world history "nearly every nation must choose between alternative ways of life"—the one based on democratic institutions, like our own, and the other based on "terror and oppression," for which the model, of course, was the Soviet Union.

Most of us thought we knew how and why this great transition—from "unity of purpose and of action" to Truman's declaration of ideological warfare—had come about in so short a time. The cause was Soviet

J. William Fulbright, "Reflections: In Thrall to Fear," *The New Yorker,* XLVII (January 8, 1972), 41-62. Reprinted by permission; © 1972 The New Yorker Magazine, Inc.

Communist aggression, limited at the outset to Stalin's subjugation of Eastern Europe but shown by Marxist-Leninist doctrine to be universal in design, aimed at nothing less than the Communization of the world. American policy and opinion were profoundly influenced in the early postwar period by the thesis that George Kennan, signing himself "X," set forth in *Foreign Affairs* for July, 1947, which depicted Soviet policy as relentlessly expansionist, committed by a fanatical ideology to filling "every nook and cranny available . . . in the basin of world power," and "stopping only when it meets with some unanswerable force." Warning against bluster and excessive reliance on military force, Kennan nonetheless called for an American policy of "unalterable counter force," of "firm and vigilant containment," which he anticipated would "increase enormously the strains under which Soviet policy must operate," and encourage changes within Russia leading to "either the breakup or the gradual mellowing of Soviet power."

From Korea to Berlin to Cuba to Vietnam, the Truman Doctrine governed America's response to the Communist world. Tactics changed —from "massive retaliation" to "limited war" and "counterinsurgency" —but these were variations on a classic formulation based on assumptions that few really questioned. Sustained by an inert Congress, the policymakers of the forties, fifties, and early sixties were never compelled to reëxamine the premises of the Truman Doctrine, or even to defend them in constructive adversary proceedings.

Change has come not from wisdom but from disaster. The calamitous failure of American policy in Vietnam has induced on the part of scholars, journalists, and politicians a belated willingness to reëxamine the basic assumptions of American postwar policy. Induced by the agitations of the present moment, this new look at old events may well result in an excess of revision, or of emotion, but the corrective is much needed if we are to profit from experience and recast our policies. It cannot be said that the assumptions underlying the Truman Doctrine were wholly false, especially for their time and place. But there is a powerful presumptive case against their subsequent universal application—the case deriving from the disaster of our policy in Asia—and it seems appropriate to look back and try to discover how and why the promise of the United Nations Charter gave way so quickly to ideological warfare between East and West.

Until fairly recently, I accepted the conventional view that the United States had acted in good faith to make the United Nations work but that the Charter was undermined by the Soviet veto. In retrospect, this seems less certain, and one suspects now that, like the League of Nations before it, the United Nations was orphaned at birth. Whereas Woodrow Wilson's great creation was abandoned to skeptical Europeans, Franklin Roosevelt's project was consigned to the care of unsympathetic men of his own country. President Roosevelt died only two weeks before the opening of the meeting in San Francisco at which the United Nations was organized. Truman, as a new and inexperienced President, was naturally more dependent on his advisers than President Roosevelt had been; among these, so far as I know, none was a strong supporter of the plan for a world organization, as Cordell Hull had been. The Under-Secretary of State, Dean Acheson, was assigned to lobby for Senate approval of the United Nations Charter, and he recalled later that "I did my duty faithfully and successfully, but always believed that the Charter was impractical." And, with even greater asperity and candor, he told an interviewer in 1970, "I never thought the United Nations was worth a damn. To a lot of people it was a Holy Grail, and those who set store by it had the misfortune to believe their own bunk."

Disdaining the United Nations, the framers of the Truman Doctrine also nurtured an intense hostility toward Communism and the Soviet Union. Stalin, of course, did much to earn this hostility, with his paranoiac suspiciousness, the imposition of Soviet domination in Eastern Europe, and the use of Western Communist parties as instruments of Soviet policy. All this is well known. Less well known, far more puzzling, and also more pertinent to our position in the world today is the eagerness with which we seized upon postwar Soviet provocations and plunged into the Cold War. If it be granted that Stalin started the Cold War, it must also be recognized that the Truman Administration seemed to welcome it.

By early 1947—a year and a half after the founding of the United Nations—the assumptions of the Cold War were all but unchallenged within the United States government. It was *assumed* that the object of Soviet policy was the Communization of the world; if Soviet behavior in Europe and northern China were not proof enough, the design was spelled out in the writings of Lenin and Marx, which our policymakers chose to read not as a body of political philosophy but as the field manual of Soviet strategy. It is true, of course, that by 1947, with the United States virtually disarmed and Western Europe in a condition of economic paralysis, the Soviet Union might plausibly have tried to take over Western Europe through the manipulation of Communist parties, through military intimidation, through economic strangulation, and possibly even through direct military action. The fact that Stalin could have done this, and might well have tried but for timely American counteraction through the Marshall Plan and the formation of NATO, was quickly and uncritically taken as proof of a design for unlimited conquest comparable to that of Nazi Germany. Neither in the executive branch of our government nor in Congress were more than a few, isolated voices raised to suggest the possibility that Soviet policy in Europe might be motivated by morbid fears for the security of the Soviet Union rather than by a design for world conquest. Virtually no one in a position of power was receptive to the hypothesis that Soviet truculence reflected weakness rather than strength, intensified by memories of 1919, when the Western powers had intervened in an effort—however halfhearted—to strangle the Bolshevik "monster" in its cradle. Our own policy was formed without the benefit of constructive adversary proceedings. A few brave individuals, like former Vice-President Henry Wallace, offered dissenting counsel—and paid dear for it.

When Great Britain informed the United States in February, 1947, that it was no longer able to provide military support for Greece, the American government was ready with a policy and a world view. The latter was an early version of the domino theory. Knowing, as we thought we did, that Russian support for Communist insurgents in Greece was part of a grand design for the takeover first of Greece, then of Turkey, the Middle East, and so forth, we were not content simply to assume the British role of providing arms to a beleaguered government; instead, we chose to issue a declaration of ideological warfare in the form of the Truman Doctrine. It may well be true that the grand phrases were motivated in part by a desire to arouse this nation's combative spirit, and so to build congressional support for the funds involved, but it is also true—at least, according to Joseph Jones, the State Department official who drafted President Truman's appeal to Congress, under Acheson's direction—that the new policy was conceived not just as a practical measure to bolster the Greeks and Turks but as a historic summons of the United States to world leadership. "*All* barriers to bold action were indeed down," as Jones has written. Among the State Department policymakers, Jones reports, it was felt that "a new chapter in world history had opened, and they were the most privileged of men, participants in a drama such as rarely occurs even in the long life of a great nation."

The Truman Doctrine, which may have made sense for its time and place, was followed by the Marshall Plan and NATO, which surely did make sense for their time and place. But as a charter for twenty-five years of global ideological warfare and unilateral military intervention against Communist insurgencies the Truman Doctrine has a different set of implications altogether. It represents a view of Communism, of the world, and of our role in the world that has had much to do with the disaster of our policy in Asia. Even in the country to which it was first applied, President Truman's basic formulation—that "we shall not realize our objectives . . . unless we are willing to help free peoples to maintain their free institutions"—has been reduced to a mockery. But who remembers now (surely not Mr. Agnew) that the Truman Doctrine was initially designed to preserve democracy in Greece?

Acheson, who prided himself on being a realist, may not have taken all that ideological claptrap seriously, but his successors Dulles and Rusk certainly did, and they framed their policies accordingly. Whatever merit the Truman Doctrine may have had in the circumstances of early-postwar Europe, the bond with reality became more and more strained as the Doctrine came to be applied at times and in places increasingly remote from the Greek civil war. Operating on a set of assumptions that defined reality for them—that as a social system Communism was deeply immoral, that as a political movement it was a conspiracy for world conquest—our leaders became liberated from the normal rules of evidence and inference when it came to dealing with Communism. After all, who ever heard of giving the Devil a fair shake? Since we know what he has in mind, it is pedantry to split hairs over what he is actually doing.

Political pressures at home intensified the virulence of the anti-Communist ideology. In retrospect, the surprise Democratic victory in the election of 1948 was probably a misfortune for the country. The Republicans, frustrated and enraged by their fifth successive defeat, became desperate in their search for a winning issue. They found their issue in the threat of Communism, at home and abroad, and they seized upon it with uncommon ferocity. They blamed the Truman Administration for Chiang Kai-shek's defeat in the Chinese civil war; they attacked President Truman for the bloody stalemate in Korea, although they had strongly supported his initial commitment; and they tolerated and in many cases encouraged Senator Joseph R. McCarthy's attacks on reputable, and even eminent, Americans. Every American President since that time has been under intense pressure to demonstrate his anti-Communist orthodoxy.

More by far than any other factor, the anti-Communism of the Truman Doctrine has been the guiding spirit of American foreign policy since the Second World War. Stalin and Mao Tse-tung and even Ho Chi

Minh replaced Hitler in our minds as the sources of all evil in the world. We came to see the hand of "Moscow Communism" in every disruption that occurred anywhere. First, there was the conception of Communism as an international conspiracy—as an octopus with its body in Moscow and its tentacles reaching out to the farthest corners of the world. Later, after the Sino-Soviet break, sophisticated foreign-policy analysts disavowed the conspiracy thesis, but at the same time they disavowed it they said things that showed that the faith lingered on. Secretary Rusk and his associates professed to be scornful of the conspiracy thesis, but still they defended the Vietnam war with references to a world "cut in two by Asian Communism," the only difference between the earlier view and the later one being that where once we had seen one octopus we now saw two.

If you accepted the premise, the rest followed. If Moscow and Peking represented centers of great power implacably hostile to the United States, and if every local crisis, from Cuba to the Congo to Vietnam, had the Communist mark upon it, then it followed logically that every crisis posed a threat to the security of the United States. The effect of the anti-Communist ideology was to spare us the task of taking cognizance of the specific facts of specific situations. Our "faith" liberated us, like the believers of old, from the requirements of empirical thinking, from the necessity of observing and evaluating the actual behavior of the nations and leaders with whom we were dealing. Like medieval theologians, we had a philosophy that explained everything to us in advance, and everything that did not fit could be readily identified as a fraud or a lie or an illusion. The fact that in some respects the behavior of the Soviet Union and of China and North Vietnam lived up to our ideological expectations made it all the easier to ignore the instances in which it did not. What we are now, belatedly, discovering is not that the Communist states have never really been hostile to us but that they have been neither consistent nor united in hostility to us; that their hostility has by no means been wholly unprovoked; and that they have been willing from time to time to do business or come to terms with us. Our ideological blinders concealed these instances from us, robbing us of useful information and of promising opportunities. The perniciousness of the anti-Communist ideology of the Truman Doctrine arises not from any patent falsehood but from its distortion and simplification of reality, from its universalization and its elevation to the status of a revealed truth.

Psychologists tell us that there is often a great difference between what one person says and what another hears, or, in variation of the old adage, that the evil may be in the ear of the hearer. When Khrushchev said, "We will bury you," Americans heard the statement as a threat of nuclear war and were outraged accordingly. The matter was raised when Chairman Khrushchev visited the United States in 1959, and he replied with some anger that he had been talking about economic competition. "I am deeply concerned over these conscious distortions of my thoughts," he said. "I've never mentioned any rockets."

We will never know, of course, but it is possible that an opportunity for a stable peace was lost during the years of Khrushchev's power. As we look back now on the many things he said regarding peaceful coexistence, the words have a different ring. At the time, we did not believe them: at best, they were Communist propaganda; at worst, outright lies. I recalled recently, for example, the visit of Chairman Khrushchev to the Senate Foreign Relations Committee on September 16, 1959. Suggesting that we lay aside the polemics of the past, Mr. Khrushchev said:

> We must face the future more and have wisdom enough to secure peace for our countries and for the whole world. We have always had great respect for the American people. We have also been somewhat envious of your achievements in the economic field, and for that reason we are doing our best to try to catch up with you in that field, to compete with you, and when we do catch up to move further ahead. I should say that future generations would be grateful to us if we managed to switch our efforts from stockpiling and perfecting weapons and concentrated those efforts fully on competition in the economic field.

Now, in retrospect, one wonders: why were we so sure that Khrushchev didn't mean what he said about peace? The answer lies in part, I believe, in our anti-Communist obsession—in the distortions it created in our perception of Soviet behavior, and in the extraordinary sense of threat we experienced when the Russians proclaimed their desire to catch up and overtake us economically. In our own national value system, competition has always been prized; why, then, should we have been so alarmed by a challenge to compete? Perhaps our national tendency to extoll competition rather than coöperation as a social virtue and our preoccupation with our own primacy—with being the "biggest," the "greatest" nation—suggest an underlying lack of confidence in ourselves, a supposition that unless we are "No. 1" we will be nothing: worthless and despised, and deservedly so. I am convinced that the real reason we squandered twenty billion dollars or more getting men to the moon in the decade of the sixties was our fear of something like horrible humiliation if the Russians got men there first. All this suggests that slogans about competition and our own primacy in that competition are largely hot air—sincerely believed, no doubt, but nonetheless masking an exaggerated fear of failure, which, in turn, lends a quality of desperation to our competitive endeavors. One detects this cast of mind in President Johnson's determination that he would not be "the first American President to lose a war," and also in President Nixon's spectre of America as "a pitiful, helpless giant."

This kind of thinking robs a nation's policymakers of objectivity and drives them to irresponsible behavior. The distortion of priorities involved in going to the moon is a relatively benign example. The perpetuation of the Vietnam war is the most terrible and fateful manifestation of the determination to prove that we are "No. 1." Assistant Secretary of Defense for International Security Affairs John T. McNaughton, as quoted in the Pentagon Papers, measured the American interest in Vietnam and found that "to permit the people of South Vietnam to enjoy a better, freer way of life" accounted for a mere ten per cent and "to avoid a humiliating U.S. defeat" for up to seventy per cent. McNaughton's statistical metaphor suggests a nation in thrall to fear; it suggests a policymaking élite unable to distinguish between the national interest and their own personal pride.

Perhaps if we had been less proud and less fearful, we would have responded in a more positive way to the earthy, unorthodox Khrushchev. Whatever his faults and excesses, Khrushchev is recognized in retrospect as the Communist leader who repudiated the Marxist dogma of the "inevitability" of war between Socialist and capitalist states. Understanding the insanity of war with nuclear weapons, Khrushchev became the advocate of "goulash" Communism, of peaceful economic competition with the West. During his period in office, some amenities were restored in East-West relations; the Berlin issue was stirred up but finally defused, and, most important, the limited-nuclear-test-ban treaty was concluded. These were solid achievements, though meagre in proportion to mankind's need for peace, and meagre, too, it now appears, in proportion to the opportunity that may then have existed. One wonders how much more might have been accomplished—particularly in the field of disarmament—if Americans had not still been caught up in the prideful, fearful spirit of the Truman Doctrine.

Even the crises look different in retrospect, especially when one takes into account the internal workings of the Communist world. A leading British authority on Soviet affairs, Victor Zorza, has traced the beginning of the Vietnam war to a "fatal misreading" by President Kennedy of Khrushchev's endorsement of "wars of national liberation." The Kennedy Administration interpreted Khrushchev's statement as a declaration that the Soviet Union intended to sponsor subversion, guerrilla warfare, and rebellion all over the world. Accordingly, the Administration attached enormous significance to Soviet material support for the Laotian Communists, as if the issue in that remote and backward land were directly pertinent to the world balance of power. It was judged that Khrushchev must be shown that he could not get away with it. We had taught Stalin that "direct" aggression did not pay; now we must teach Khrushchev—and the Chinese—that "indirect" aggression did not pay. In Zorza's view, Khrushchev's talk of "wars of national liberation" was not a serious plan for worldwide subversion but a response to Communist China, whose leaders were then accusing Khrushchev of selling out the cause of revolution and making a deal with the United States.

In the spirit of the Truman Doctrine, the Kennedy Administration read the Soviet endorsement of "wars of national liberation" as a direct challenge to the United States. Speaking of Russia and China, President Kennedy said in his first State of the Union Message, "We must never be lulled into believing that either power has yielded its ambitions for world domination—ambitions which they forcefully restated only a short time ago." I do not recall these words for purposes of reproach; they represented an assessment of Communist intentions that most of us shared at that time, an assessment that had been held by every Administration and most members of Congress since the Second World War, an assessment that had scarcely—if at all—been brought up for critical examination in the executive branch, in congressional committees, in the proliferating "think tanks," or in the universities. Perhaps no better assessment could have been made on the basis of the information available at that time, but I doubt it. I think it more likely that we simply chose to ignore evidence that did not fit our preconceptions, or—as is more often the case—when the facts lent themselves to several possible interpretations we chose to seize upon the one with which we were most familiar: the Communist drive for world domination.

In the amplified form it acquired during the Johnson years, the conception of "wars of national liberation" as part of the Communist design for world domination became the basic rationale for the Vietnam war. All the other excuses—defending freedom, honoring our "commitments," demonstrating America's resolution—are secondary in importance and are easily shown to be fallacious and contradictory. But no one can *prove* that Mao Tse-tung and Brezhnev and Kosygin—or Khrushchev, for that matter—have not harbored secret ambitions to conquer the world. Who can prove that the desire or the intention was never in their minds? The truly remarkable thing about this Cold War psychology is the totally illogical transfer of the burden of proof from those who make charges to those who question them. In this frame of reference, Communists are guilty until proved innocent—or simply by definition. The Cold Warriors, instead of having to say how they knew that Vietnam was part of a plan for the Communization of the world, so manipulated the terms of public discussion as to be able to demand that the skeptics prove that it was not. If the skeptics could not, then the war must go on —to end it would be recklessly risking the national security. We come to the ultimate illogic: war is the course of prudence and sobriety until the case for peace is proved under impossible rules of evidence—or until the enemy surrenders.

Rational men cannot deal with each other on this basis. Recognizing their inability to know with anything like certainty what is going on in other men's minds, they do not try to deal with others on the basis of their presumed intentions. Instead, rational men respond to others on the basis of their actual, observable behavior, and they place the burden of proof where it belongs—on those who assert and accuse rather than on those who question or deny. The departure from these elementary rules for the ascertainment of truth is the essence of the Cold War way of thinking; its weakened but still formidable hold on our minds is indicative of the surviving tyranny of the Truman Doctrine.

In a decade's perspective—and without the blinders of the Truman Doctrine—it even seems possible that the Cuban missile crisis of 1962 was not so enormous a crisis as it then seemed. Khrushchev in the early sixties was engaged in an internal struggle with the Soviet military, who, not unlike our own generals, were constantly lobbying for more funds for ever more colossal weapons systems. Khrushchev had been cutting back on conventional forces and, largely for purposes of appeasing his unhappy generals, was talking a great deal about the power of Soviet missiles. President Kennedy, however, was applying pressure from another direction: unnerved by Khrushchev's endorsement of "wars of national liberation," he was undertaking to build up American conventional forces at the same time that he was greatly expanding the American nuclear-missile force, even though by this time the United States had an enormous strategic superiority. Khrushchev's effort to resist the pressures from his generals was, of course, undermined by the American buildup. It exposed him to pressures within the Kremlin from a hostile coalition of thwarted generals and politicians who opposed his de-Stalinization policies. In the view of a number of specialists in the Soviet field, the placement of missiles in Cuba was motivated largely, if not primarily, by Khrushchev's need to deal with these domestic pressures; it was meant to close or narrow the Soviet "missile gap" in relation to the United States without forcing Khrushchev to concentrate all available resources on a ruinous arms race.

Lacking an expert knowledge of my own on these matters, I commend this interpretation of Khrushchev's purpose not as necessarily true but as highly plausible. As far as I know, however, none of the American officials who participated in the decisions relating to the Cuban missile crisis seriously considered the possibility that Khrushchev might be acting defensively or in response to domestic pressures. It was universally assumed that the installation of Soviet missiles in Cuba was an aggressive strategic move against the United States—that, and nothing more. Assuming Khrushchev's aggressive intent, we imposed on the Soviet Union a resounding defeat, for which Khrushchev was naturally held responsible. In this way, we helped to strengthen the military and political conservatives within the Soviet Union, who were to overthrow Khrushchev two years later. If we had been willing to consider the possibility that Khrushchev was acting on internal considerations, we would still have wished to secure the removal of the missiles from Cuba, but it might have been accomplished by means less embarrassing to Khrushchev, such as a *quid pro quo* under which we would have removed our Jupiter missiles from Turkey.

Khrushchev had paid dear for his "softness on capitalism" in an earlier encounter with President Eisenhower. After his visit to the United States in 1959, Khrushchev apparently tried to persuade his skeptical, hard-line colleagues that Americans were not such monsters as they supposed and that President Eisenhower was a reasonable man. This heretical theory—heretical from the Soviet point of view—was shot out of the sky along with the American U-2 spy plane in May, 1960. When President Eisenhower subsequently declined the opportunity Khrushchev offered him to disclaim personal responsibility, Khrushchev felt compelled to break up the Paris summit meeting. The U-2 incident was later cited by Khrushchev himself as a critical moment in his loss of power at home. It shattered his plans for President Eisenhower to pay a visit to the Soviet Union—for which, it is said, he had already had a golf course secretly constructed in the Crimea.

There were, of course, other factors in Khrushchev's fall, and perhaps more important ones; nor is it suggested that his intentions toward the West were necessarily benevolent. The point that must emerge, however—more for the sake of the future than for history's sake—is that if we had not been wearing ideological blinders, if our judgment had not been clouded by fear and hostility, we might have perceived in Khrushchev a world statesman with whom constructive business could be done. When he fell, his successors put an end to de-Stalinization, began the military buildup that has brought the Soviet Union to a rough strategic parity with the United States, and greatly stepped up their aid to Communist forces in Vietnam.

While our response to Soviet Communism has been marked by hostility, tensions, and fear, our response to Communism in Asia has been marked by all these and, in addition, by a profound sense of injury and betrayal. Russia never was a country for which we had much affection anyway; it was the bleak and terrible land of the czars, which, when it went to the Communist devils, was merely trading one tyranny for another. But China had a special place in our hearts. We had favored her with our merchants and missionaries and our "open door" policy; we had even given back the Boxer indemnity so that Chinese students could study in America. In the Second World War, we fought shoulder to shoulder with "free" China; we were filled with admiration for its fighting Generalissimo Chiang Kai-shek, and utterly charmed by his Wellesley-educated wife.

When the Chinese darlings of our patronizing hearts went to Communist perdition, we could only assume that they had been sold or betrayed into bondage. It was inconceivable that our star pupils in the East could actually have willed this calamity; it had to be the work of Chinese traitors, abetted by disloyal Americans, joined in an unholy alliance to sell out China to those quintessential bad people the Russians. A white paper on China was issued in 1949, and Secretary of State Acheson's letter of transmittal recounted accurately the intense but futile American effort to salvage a Kuomintang regime whose officials and soldiers had "sunk into corruption, into a scramble for place and power, and into reliance on the United States to win the war for them and to preserve their own domestic supremacy." Then, having exonerated the United States from responsibility for the loss of China, Secretary Acheson wrote:

> The heart of China is in Communist hands. The Communist leaders have forsworn their Chinese heritage and have publicly announced their subservience to a foreign power, Russia, which during the last 50 years, under czars and Communists alike, has been most assiduous in its efforts to extend its control in the Far East. ... The foreign domination has been masked behind the facade of a vast crusading movement which apparently has seemed to many Chinese to be wholly indigenous and national. ...
>
> However tragic may be the immediate future of China and however ruthlessly a major portion of this great people may be exploited by a party in the interest of a foreign imperialism, ultimately the profound civilization and the democratic individualism of China will reassert themselves and she will throw off the foreign yoke. I consider that we should encourage all developments in China which now and in the future work toward this end.

In these words, the United States government enunciated what became its Truman Doctrine for Asia. By the end of 1950, we were at war with China in Korea, but even then our belief in Moscow's control of the "Communist conspiracy" or our sentimental unwillingness to believe that China of its own free will would make war on the United States, or some combination of the two, made it difficult for us to believe that the Chinese Communists had intervened in Korea for reasons directly related to their own national interest. The fact that General MacArthur's sweep to the Yalu was bringing American ground forces within striking distance of China's industrial heartland in Manchuria was not at that time widely thought to be a factor in China's intervention in the war. The view of Dean Rusk, then the Assistant Secretary of State for Far Eastern Affairs, was that "the peace and security of China are being sacrificed to the ambitions of the Communist conspiracy," and that "China has been driven by foreign masters into an adventure of foreign aggression which cuts across the most fundamental national interests of the Chinese people." Mr. Rusk went on to say, "We do not recognize the authorities in Peiping for what they pretend to be. The Peiping régime may be a colonial Russian government—a Slavic Manchukuo on a larger scale. It is not the government of China."

Nonetheless, for the first time in our history we were coming to regard China as our enemy, departing from a half century's policy of supporting a strong, independent China. One of our leading young China scholars, Warren I. Cohen, has provided this summary in his recent book, "America's Response to China":

> The great aberration in American policy began in 1950, as the people and their leaders were blinded by fear of Communism and forgot the sound geopolitical, economic, and ethical basis of their historic desire for China's well-being. Having always assumed that China would be friendly, Americans were further bewildered by the hostility of Mao's China, leading them to forsake their traditional support of Asian nationalism, not only in China, but wherever Marxist leadership threatened to enlarge the apparent Communist monolith. With the full support of the American people, Truman and his advisors committed the United States to a policy of containing Communism in Asia as well as in Europe—and in practice this policy became increasingly anti-Chinese, an unprecedented campaign of opposition to the development of a strong, modern China. There was no longer any question of whether the United States would interpose itself between China and her enemies, for the United States had become China's principal enemy.

Over the years, the notion of a "Slavic Manchukuo" gave way to a recognition of the Chinese Communists as the authors of their own deviltry. This was not a fundamental change of outlook toward "international Communism" but an accommodation to a fact that had become obvious to all save the most fanatical and self-deluded Cold Warriors: that, far from being an instrument in Moscow's hands, the Chinese· Communist leaders had become defiant and hostile toward Soviet leadership of the Communist world. Now, from the American viewpoint, there were two "Communist conspiracies," and of the two great Communist states China was judged to be the more virulent and aggressive. The Chinese had withdrawn their troops from Korea in 1958, limited themselves to a border adjustment with India in 1962 (when they could have detached a large area after defeating the Indian Army), and assumed no direct combat role in the developing conflict in Vietnam. But these facts were judged to be less important than the fact that they were Communists, who openly advocated subversion and "wars of national liberation." Communist China was not judged to be aggressive on the basis of its actions; it was presumed to be aggressive because it was Communist.

In much the same way that Khrushchev terrified us with his talk of "burying" us, the Chinese sent us into a panic with their doctrine of "wars of national liberation." While the Russians had become relatively benign, contained by America's nuclear deterrent, China claimed to be impervious to the horrors of nuclear war and was still intensely revolutionary itself, committed to the promotion and support of "wars of national liberation" throughout the world. The Kennedy and Johnson Administrations concluded that still another gauntlet had been flung down before the United States. To meet this presumed threat, our military planners invented the strategy of "counterinsurgency," which they undertook to put into effect in Vietnam.

None of this is meant to suggest that China would have been friendly to us if we ourselves had not been hostile. I do not know whether the Chinese Communists would have been friendly or not; nor, I think, does anyone else know, since we never tried to find out. Most probably, in the turmoil of revolutionary change, the Chinese Communists would have been deeply suspicious and verbally abusive of the citadel of capitalism and the leader of the Western "imperialist camp" even if the United States had been willing to come to terms with them. Be that as it may, an objective observer must admit that on the basis of their actual behavior the Chinese Communists have never proved the Hitlerian menace we have taken them to be. They have not tried to conquer and subjugate their neighbors. Nor, upon examination, does the doctrine of "wars of national liberation," as set forth by Lin Piao, constitute a charter of Chinese aggression. It stresses self-reliance and the limitations of external support. Lin Piao wrote:

> In order to make a revolution and to fight a people's war and be victorious, it is imperative to adhere to the policy of self-reliance, rely on the strength of the masses in one's own country and prepare to carry on the fight independently even when all material aid from outside is cut off. If one does not operate by one's own efforts, does not independently ponder and solve the problems of the revolution in one's own country, and does not rely on the strength of the masses, but leans wholly on foreign aid—even though this be aid from Socialist countries which persist in revolution—no victory can be won, or be consolidated even if it is won.

The sudden reversal of American policy toward China in 1971 necessarily invites our attention back to the basic causes of these two decades of conflict between the United States and the Communist countries of Asia. In the course of these two decades, we have engaged in armed conflict with all three of these countries—with Communist China, North Korea, and North Vietnam—but we have never fought a war with the Soviet Union, which is the only Communist power capable of posing a direct strategic threat to the United States. Although it was assumed from the outset of the Cold War that our real strategic interests lay in Europe rather than in Asia, it has been in Asia that we have thought it necessary to fight two wars to enforce the Truman Doctrine. Looking back, one is bound to ask whether these conflicts were inescapable. Having avoided war in the region we judged more important, and with the power we judged the greater threat, why have we found it necessary to fight in Asia, at such enormous cost in lives and money and in the internal cohesion of our own society? Is it possible that if Mao Tse-tung and Ho Chi Minh had not borne the title of "Communist" but otherwise had done exactly what they have done in their two countries, we would have accepted their victories over their domestic rivals and lived with them in peace? I think it quite possible that we would have come to terms with both. Apart from the North Korean invasion of South Korea, which was a direct violation of the United Nations Charter, the Communist countries of Asia have done nothing that has threatened the security of the United States and little, if anything, that has impaired our legitimate interests. We intervened in the Chinese and Vietnamese civil wars only because the stronger side in each case was the Communist side and we assumed that, as Communists, they were parties to a conspiracy for world domination, and were therefore our enemies. We intervened against them not for what they *did* but for what they *were* and for what we assumed to be their purpose.

There were Americans in official positions who provided a more objective, less ideologically colored view of the Chinese Communists back in the days before they won their civil war. These wartime observers in China, who included John S. Service, John Paton Davies, and Colonel David D. Barrett, were themselves sympathetic to the National government of Chiang Kai-shek, at least to the extent of urging it to make the reforms that might have allowed it to survive. Nonetheless, they reported objectively on the weakness and corruption of the Kuomintang and on the organization and discipline of the Communists in their headquarters in Yenan. They also provided information suggesting that at that time Mao Tse-Tung and his associates had no intention whatever of becoming subservient to the Soviet Union and hoped to coöperate with the United States. Not only did the observations of these men go unheeded; they themselves were subsequently denounced and persecuted. Colonel Barrett did not attain the promotion to brigadier general that his service in the Army merited, and Service and Davies were hounded out of the Foreign Service, charged with advocacy of, and even responsibility for, the Chinese Communist victory that they had foreseen. The nation was deprived thereafter of their accurate observations and valuable insights, and, what is more, their surviving colleagues in the bureaucracy got the unmistakable message that it was unhealthy to deviate from the anti-Communist line. To survive and get ahead, it was necessary to see the world as the world was defined by the Truman Doctrine.

Having been thoroughly educated in the catechism of the Cold War, we look back now with astonishment on the reports of Service, Barrett, and others from China in 1944. Barrett and Service came to know the Chinese Communist leaders well through the Dixie Mission, which was the name given to the mission of the United States Army Observer Group, headed by Colonel Barrett, at Chinese Communist headquarters in Yenan in late 1944 and early 1945. Their assignment was to assess the potential contribution of the Chinese Communists to a final assault against Japanese forces in China. They came to know and respect the Communists, not for their ideology but for their discipline, organization, fighting skills, and morale.

In his recent book "Dixie Mission," Colonel Barrett comments, "The Chinese Communists are our bitter enemies now, but they were certainly 'good guys' then, particularly to the airmen who received their help." Colonel Barrett found that as sources of information about the Japanese the Communists were "all we had hoped they would be and even more"—among other reasons, because they "could almost always count on the coöperation and support of a local population." American observers sent out into the countryside from Yenan "all expressed the belief that the Communists were being supported by the entire civil population." In retrospect, Colonel Barrett felt that he had been "over-sold" on the Communists in Yenan, but nonetheless he comments, "The overall look of things there was one which most Americans were inclined to regard with favor." American observers were impressed by the absence of sentries around the leaders, in contrast with the Nationalist capital in Chungking, where there were "police and sentries everywhere;" by the tough, well-nourished, and well-dressed troops, in contrast with the poorly nourished, shabbily uniformed Kuomintang soldiers; and by the general atmosphere of roughhewn equality and shared sacrifice. "As a whole," Colonel Barrett comments, "the Communist outlook on life was old-fashioned and conservative."

Even the flamboyant and volatile General Patrick J. Hurley—Roosevelt's special emissary and, later, Ambassador to Chungking—was at first favorably impressed by the Chinese Communists' terms for a settlement with Chiang Kai-shek. In November, 1944, Hurley flew to Yenan, where he signed an agreement with Mao Tse-tung calling for a coalition government; Hurley pronounced the agreement eminently fair, and even told Mao—in Barrett's hearing—that the terms did not go far enough in the Communists' favor. Chiang Kai-shek rejected Hurley's plan out of hand; nonetheless, Hurley thereafter supported Chiang as the sole leader of China and publicly blamed the failure of his mediation on his Embassy staff, whom he accused, in effect, of being pro-Communist. Although he contended in November, 1944, that "if there is a breakdown in the parleys it will be the fault of the Government and not the Communists," and although he told President Truman in May, 1945, that the Communists were holding back "in my opinion with some degree of reasonableness," Hurley still backed the Nationalist regime to the hilt, and in the spring of 1945 even reimposed the ban on nonmilitary travel by Americans to the Communist headquarters in Yenan. Thus began the process, culminating in the failure of the mission undertaken in 1946 by General George C. Marshall through which, without having ascertained their attitudes and intentions toward us, the United States government came to identify the Chinese Communists as enemies of the United States —presaging the policy of isolation and containment that was to endure at least until 1971.

This was not at the outset the result of decisions made at the highest level. President Roosevelt wrote to a friend on November 15, 1944, "I am hoping and praying for a real working out of the situation with the so-called Communists." And in March, 1945, in reply to a question from Edgar Snow about whether we could work with two governments in China for purposes of prosecuting the war with Japan, Roosevelt said, "Well, I've been working with two governments there. I intend to go on doing so until we can get them together." Within a few weeks after that interview, Roosevelt was dead and the conduct of American foreign policy had passed into the hands of the inexperienced President Truman. Neither Roosevelt nor Truman, however, seems in the last days of the Second World War to have given serious and sustained thought to the internal problems of China. Both Presidents were preoccupied with the defeat of Japan, and it had been clear for some time that China was unlikely to play a decisive role in bringing that about.

There was no lack of information available to the United States government in 1944 and 1945 about either the weakness and corruption of the Kuomintang or the strength and aspirations of the Chinese Communists. The views of the professional diplomats were rejected, however, árd their reports ignored—that is, until the witchhunters in the State

Department and Congress got hold of them. In June, 1944, for example, a warning was conveyed to Washington in a memorandum written principally by John Service:

> The situation in China is rapidly becoming critical. . . . There is a progressive internal breakdown. . . . The fundamental cause of this suicidal trend is that the Kuomintang, steadily losing popular support . . . is concentrating more and more on putting the preservation of its shrinking power above all other considerations.
>
> These policies, unless checked by the internal opposition they evoke and by friendly foreign influence, seem certain to bring about a collapse which will be harmful to the war and our long-term interests in the Far East.

At the same time that American observers in China were reporting the enfeeblement of the Kuomintang, they were providing detailed accounts of the growing military and political strength of the Communists. Service summed up the importance of these circumstances for the United States:

> From the basic fact that the Communists have built up popular support of a magnitude and depth which makes their elimination impossible, we must draw the conclusion that the Communists will have a certain and important share in China's future.

His colleague John Paton Davies put it even more succinctly:

> The Communists are in China to stay. And China's destiny is not Chiang's but theirs.

The Communists were not only strong but—at least, so they said —willing and eager to coöperate with the United States. In his recent book "The Amerasia Papers: Some Problems in the History of U.S.-China Relations," Service reports on a long conversation he had with Mao Tse-tung in Yenan on August 23, 1944, in which Mao emphasized that the Chinese Communists were "first of all Chinese," and appealed for American help for China after the war. "The Russians," Mao said, "have suffered greatly in the war and will have their hands full with their own job of rebuilding. We do not expect Russian help." America, he thought, could help China, and he told Service:

> China must industrialize. This can be done—in China—only by free enterprise and with the aid of foreign capital. Chinese and American interests are correlated and similar. They fit together, economically and politically. We can and must work together.

The United States would find us more coöperative than the Kuomintang. We will not be afraid of democratic American influence—we will welcome it. We have no silly ideas of taking only Western mechanical techniques. . . .

America does not need to fear that we will not be coöperative. We must coöperate and we must have American help. This is why it is so important to us Communists to know what you Americans are thinking and planning. We cannot risk crossing you—cannot risk any conflict with you.

We do not know, of course, whether Mao was sincere in his repeated appeals for American friendship. The reason we do not know is that we never tried to find out. In our postwar anti-Communist hysteria, we assumed that the Chinese Communists were hostile simply because they were Communists, and we also assumed, despite impressive evidence to the contrary, that they were subservient to the Soviet Union. We thereupon made out fateful commitment to the losing side in the Chinese civil war—the side of whose weakness and probable defeat full warning had been provided by our own highly competent observers. From these events followed two wars and a quarter century of bitter hostility, which might have been avoided if we had remained neutral in the Chinese civil war.

This is not to say that Mao might have been expected to put Sino-American relations back on their prewar basis. He most assuredly would not have done that. Certainly our pretentions to a benevolent paternalism toward China would have been given short shrift; the age of missionaries and the "open door" was at an end. But whatever our relations might have been if we had not intervened in the civil war, they would at least have been initiated on a more realistic and more promising basis. We might have long ago established a working relationship at least as tolerable, and as peaceful, as the one we have had with the Soviet Union: the sort of relationship toward which—belatedly but most commendably—the Nixon Administration now seems to be working.

The anti-Communist spirit that governed our relations with China after the Second World War also shaped—and distorted—our involvement in Vietnam. Our interest in China's civil war, though tragic in consequence, was attenuated and limited in time. Vietnam was less fortunate. In a test application of the new science of "counterinsurgency," it has been subjected to prolonged, though inconclusive, devastation. But for the American intervention, the Vietnamese civil war would have ended long ago—at infinitely less cost in lives, money, and property—in a nationalist Communist victory under the leadership of Ho Chi Minh.

In retrospect, it is difficult to understand how we could have accepted the "loss" of China but not the "loss" of the small, undeveloped countries on China's southern border. Only in the context of the assumptions of the Truman Doctrine could the Vietnamese war ever have been rationalized as having something to do with American security or American interests. Looking through our anti-communist prism, we saw Ho Chi Minh not as a Vietnamese nationalist who was also a Communist but as a spear-carrier for the international Communist conspiracy, the driving force for a "world cut in two by Asian Communism." The Johnson Administration, as Mr. Johnson's memoirs show clearly, believed itself to be acting on President Truman's doctrine that "totalitarian regimes imposed on free peoples, by direct or indirect aggression, undermine the foundations of international peace and hence the security of the United States." President Johnson and his advisers believed this despite a set of facts that did not fit the formula: the fact that the issue was not between a "free people" and a "totalitarian regime" but between rival totalitarian regimes; the fact that the war was not one of international aggression, "direct" or otherwise, but an anti-colonial war and then a civil war; and the fact that, in any case, the country was too small and the issue too indigenous to Vietnam to pose anything resembling a threat to "the foundations of international peace," much less to "the security of the United States." In practice, the issue had resolved itself into a corruption of the Truman Doctrine—into the fear of a "humiliating" defeat at the hands of Communists. It was not so much that we needed to win, or that there was anything for us to win, as that our leaders felt—for reasons of prestige abroad and political standing at home—that they could not afford to "lose." President Johnson said soon after he took office, "I am not going to be the President who saw Southeast Asia go the way China went."

The notion that a country is "lost" or "gone" when it becomes Communist is a peculiarly revealing one. How can we have "lost" a country unless it was ours to begin with—unless it was some part of an unacknowledged American imperium? To my eye, China under Mao is in the same place on the map that is was in the days of Chiang. Where, then, has it "gone"? To the moon? Or to the devil? The "lost" and "gone" concept is indicative of a virulent sanctimoniousness that is only now beginning to abate. In October, 1971, members of the Senate gave President Tito of Yugoslavia a cordial reception at an afternoon tea. In

September, 1959, a similar reception was held for Chairman Khrushchev, but one senator refused to sit in the room with him—for fear, apparently, of ideological contamination. As the President now moves toward lifting the "quarantine" of China, as we recognize at long last that there really still is a China, Communist though it may be, the tragic irrationality of the Vietnam war is thrown once again into high relief. All that bloodletting—not just for ourselves but for the Vietnamese—could have been avoided by an awareness that Communism is not a contagious disease but a political movement and a way of organizing a society.

In the case of Ho Chi Minh, as in the case of Mao Tse-tung, we might have come to this awareness twenty-five years—and two wars—ago. Ho, in fact, was a lifelong admirer of the American Revolution, of Lincoln, and of Wilson and his Fourteen Points. As a young man, in 1919, he went to the Versailles Peace Conference to appeal for self-determination for his country in accordance with President Wilson's principles, but no attention was paid to him, and Vietnam remained within the French empire. In 1945, Ho Chi Minh started his declaration of independence for Vietnam with words taken from our own: "All men are created equal." In 1945 and 1946, Ho addressed a series of letters to the United States government asking for its mediation toward a compromise with France, but none of these letters were ever answered, because Ho was, in Dean Acheson's words, "an outright Commie."

President Roosevelt, during the Second World War, had favored independence for Indo-China, or a trusteeship, but in any event he was opposed to letting the French recover Indo-China for their colonial empire. Roosevelt's attitude was spelled out in a memorandum to Secretary of State Hull dated January 24, 1944, which appears in the Pentagon Papers:

> I saw Halifax last week and told him quite frankly that it was perfectly true that I had, for over a year, expressed the opinion that Indo-China should not go back to France but that it should be administered by an international trusteeship. France has had the country—thirty million inhabitants—for nearly one hundred years, and the people are worse off than they were at the beginning.
>
> As a matter of interest, I am wholeheartedly supported in this view by Generalissimo Chiang Kai-shek and by Marshal Stalin. I see no reason to play in with the British Foreign Office in this matter. The only reason they seem to oppose it is that they fear the effect it would have on their own possessions and those of the Dutch. They have never liked the idea of trusteeship because it is, in some instances, aimed at future independence. This is true in the case of Indo-China.

Each case must, of course, stand on its own feet, but the case of Indo-China is perfectly clear. France has milked it for one hundred years. The people of Indo-China are entitled to something better than that.

British intransigence and the requirements of military strategy prevented Roosevelt from acting on his anti-colonialist preference, which was so wholly in keeping with the traditional American outlook. When the Truman Administration took office, American policy was changed, and the French were officially assured by our State Department that the United States had never questioned, "even by implication, French sovereignty over Indo-China." The United States would advocate reforms but would leave it to the French to decide when, or even whether, the people of Indo-China were to be given independence: "Such decisions would preclude the establishment of a trusteeship in Indo-China except with the consent of the French Government."

Whether this initial commitment to France—and therefore against Ho—was the result of growing anti-Communist sentiment within the Truman Administration or of friendly feelings toward the colonial powers on the part of President Truman's old-line advisers, or both, American policy was constant and firm from that time on. Later, when Acheson and his colleagues were attempting to build up France as the centerpiece of the anti-Communist coalition in Europe, the commitment to France's position in Indo-China became stronger than ever. By 1951, the United States was paying forty per cent of the cost of France's war against the Vietminh, and by 1954 eighty per cent. After the Geneva settlement, American military aid to South Vietnam averaged about two hundred million dollars a year between 1955 and 1961. By 1963, South Vietnam ranked first among the recipients of our military assistance, and only India and Pakistan received more in economic assistance. In this way, foreign aid served as a vehicle of commitment, from our initial support of French colonial rule in Indo-China to sending an American force of over half a million men to fight in a war that is still going on.

As with China, it might have been different. The Pentagon Papers show that between October, 1945, and February, 1946, Ho Chi Minh addressed at least eight communications to the President of the United States or to the Secretary of State asking America to intervene for Vietnamese independence. Earlier, in the summer of 1945, Ho had asked that Vietnam be accorded "the same status as the Philippines"—a period of tutelage to be followed by independence. Following the outbreak of hostilities in Vietnam in the early fall of 1945, Ho made his appeals to

President Truman on the basis of the Atlantic Charter, the United Nations Charter, and Mr. Truman's Navy Day speech of October 27, 1945, in which the President expressed the American belief that "all peoples who are prepared for self-government should be permitted to choose their own form of government by their own freely expressed choice, without interference from any foreign source." In November, 1945, Ho wrote to the Secretary of State requesting the initiation of cultural relations through the sending of fifty Vietnamese students to the United States. On February 16, 1946, in a letter to President Truman, Ho referred to American "complicity" with the French, but he still appealed to the Americans "as guardians and champions of world justice" to "take a decisive step" in support of Vietnamese independence, and pointed out that he was asking only what had been "graciously granted to the Philippines." On September 11, 1946, Ho communicated directly with the United States government for the last time, expressing to an American Embassy official in Paris his own admiration for the United States and the Vietnamese people's respect and affection for President Roosevelt; again he referred to America's granting of independence to the Philippines.

As far as the record shows, neither President Truman nor any of his subordinates replied to any of Ho Chi Minh's appeals. He got his answer nonetheless, clearly and unmistakably. By late 1946, with the first Vietnam war under way, American military equipment was being used by the French against the Vietnamese. As far as the United States government was concerned, Vietnam was a sideshow to the real struggle against Communism, in Europe. If the price of French support in that struggle was American support of French colonialism in Southeast Asia —and we seem never to have questioned that it was—the Truman Administration was ready to pay that price. Ho, after all, was just another "Commie." In a cable to the United States representative in Hanoi in May, 1949, Acheson said:

> QUESTION WHETHER HO AS MUCH NATIONALIST AS COMMIE IS IRRELEVANT. ALL STALINISTS IN COLONIAL AREAS ARE NATIONALISTS. WITH ACHIEVEMENT NAT'L AIMS (I.E., INDEPENDENCE) THEIR OBJECTIVE NECESSARILY BECOMES SUBORDINATION STATE TO COMMIE PURPOSES.

In February, 1950, the recognition of Ho Chi Minh's government by the Communist powers moved Secretary Acheson to declare that this recognition "should remove any illusion as to the nationalist character of Ho Chi Minh's aims and reveals Ho in his true colors as the mortal enemy of native independence in Indochina."

As with China under Mao Tse-tung, we might have got along tolerably well—maybe even quite well—with a unified, independent Vietnam under Ho Chi Minh if our leaders' minds had not been hopelessly locked in by the imprisoning theory of the international Communist conspiracy. Ho was an authentic Vietnamese patriot, revered by his countrymen. He had led the resistance to the Japanese within Vietnam and had welcomed the Allies as liberators. His unwillingness to submit to foreign domination was clear—or should have been clear—from the outset: But if the evidence of Ho Chi Minh's Vietnamese nationalism ever reached the American policymakers, it certainly did not persuade them. Acting Secretary of State Acheson instructed an American diplomat in Hanoi in December, 1946, "KEEP IN MIND HO'S CLEAR RECORD AS AGENT INTERNATIONAL COMMUNISM." In February, 1947, by which time the war between France and the Vietminh was well under way, Secretary of State Marshall conceded, in another cable, that colonial empires were rapidly becoming a thing of the past but, as to Vietnam,

> WE DO NOT LOSE SIGHT FACT THAT HO CHI MINH HAS DIRECT COMMUNIST CONNECTIONS, AND IT SHOULD BE OBVIOUS THAT WE ARE NOT INTERESTED IN SEEING COLONIAL EMPIRE ADMINISTRATIONS SUPPLANTED BY PHILOSOPHY AND POLITICAL ORGANIZATIONS EMANATING FROM AND CONTROLLED BY KREMLIN.

General Marshall's words were prophetic of what became a guiding principle—or, more accurately, a guiding aberration—of American foreign policy for at least two decades: where Communists were involved, the United States would depart from its traditional anti-colonialism and support the imperial power. Assuming as we did that Communists by definition were agents of an international conspiracy, we further assumed that a Communist leader could not be an authentic patriot no matter what he said or did. If the choice was to be—as we then rationalized it—between the old imperialism of the West and the new imperialism of the Kremlin, we would side with the former. Where possible, we told ourselves, we would support or nurture "third forces"—genuine independence movements that were neither colonialist nor Communist—and where such movements existed, as in India, we did support and welcome independence. Where they did not exist, as in Vietnam and Cuba and the

Dominican Republic, we intervened, making these countries the great crisis areas of postwar American foreign policy and, in the process, earning for the United States the reputation of foremost imperialist power.

The role is one to which we are unsuited by temperament and tradition. Until a generation ago, America was regarded throughout the world—and deservedly so—as the one great nation that was authentically anti-imperialist. It was Woodrow Wilson who introduced into international relations the revolutionary principle of "justice to all peoples and nationalities, and their right to live on equal terms of liberty and safety with one another, whether they be strong or weak." Perhaps it was a utopian dream, but Americans meant it at the time, and the world believed we meant it, and we had plans for realizing it: first the Covenant of the League of Nations and then the United Nations Charter, both purporting to introduce the rule of law into international relations, both purporting to supplant the old imperialist anarchy with the principle of trusteeship for the weak and the poor, both purporting to supplant the old balance of power with a new community of power.

The dismay and disillusion that have overtaken so many of us in America are the result, I believe, of our departure from these traditional American values. The corrosive, consuming fear of Communism has driven us into a role in the world which suits us badly and which we deeply dislike. I think that the American people have sensed this all along and are moving now to an active, conscious awareness of their own real preferences. It is no easy matter for us to knock over the household gods we have been taught for a generation to worship, but I think the American people have all along had an uneasy awareness that the dictators and warlords with whom we have been in league for so long are not really our kind of people. I suspect, too, that if Khrushchev and Mao and Ho had not had the name of "Communist" we might have recognized them as men we could respect: tough and sometimes ruthless, but patriots nonetheless; committed to an ideology we would not want for ourselves, but also committed to the well-being of their own people. With China's entry into the United Nations and the President's imminent trip to Peking, we may find that we can do business with the Chinese, just as we have done with the Russians. We may even find it possible to be cordial, as we have been with the Yugoslavs. Eventually (who knows?), we may even kick over the household gods once and for all and become friends. Huck Finn, when he helped Jim escape, knew it was a sin and knew he was going to go to Hell for it, but he liked Jim, so he did it anyway.

History is filled with turning points that are not easily identified until long after the event. It seems almost inevitable that Vietnam will prove to have been a watershed in American foreign policy, but it is by no means clear what kind. Before it can represent anything of a lasting historical nature, the war, of course, will have to be ended—not just scaled down but ended, and not just for Americans but for the tortured Vietnamese as well. One assumes that it will be ended—if not by our present leaders, then by their successors—and that when at last it is, the American people will once again in their history have the opportunity and the responsibility of deciding where they want to go in the world, of deciding what kind of role they want their country to play, of deciding what kind of country they want America to be.

The Truman Doctrine, which made limited sense for a limited time in a particular place, has led us in its universalized form to disaster in Southeast Asia and demoralization at home. In view of all that has happened, it seems unlikely that we will wish to resume the anti-Communist crusade of the early postwar years. Yet it is not impossible: memories will fade, controversies may recur, pride may once again be challenged and competitive instincts aroused. The Truman Doctrine is frayed and tattered, but it is still an influence upon our policy and outlook.

I do not think we are going to return to isolationism. I will go further: I do not think there is or ever has been the slightest chance of the United States' returning to the isolationism of the prewar years. It will not happen because it cannot happen: we are inextricably involved with the world politically, economically, militarily, and—in case anyone cares—legally. We could not get loose if we wanted to. And no one wants to. The people who are called "neo-isolationists" are no such thing; the word is an invention of people who confuse internationalism with an intrusive American unilateralism, with a quasi-imperialism. Those of us who are accused of "neo-isolationism" are, I believe, the opposite: internationalists in the classic sense of that term—in the sense in which it was brought into American usage by Woodrow Wilson and Franklin Roosevelt. We believe in international coöperation through international institutions. We would like to try to keep the peace through the United Nations, and we would like to try to assist the poor countries through institutions like the World Bank. We do not think the United Nations is a failure; we think it has never been tried.

In the aftermath of Vietnam, it is America's option—not its "destiny," because there is no such thing—to return to the practical idealism of the United Nations Charter. It is, I believe, consistent with our national tradition and congenial to our national character, and is therefore the most natural course for us to follow. It is also the most logical, in terms of our interests and the interests of all other nations living in a diverse and crowded but interdependent world in the age of nuclear weapons.

The essence of any community—local, national, or international— is some degree of acceptance of the principle that the good of the whole must take precedence over the good of the parts. I do not believe that the United States (or any of the other big countries) has ever accepted that principle with respect to the United Nations. Like the Soviet Union and other great powers, we have treated the United Nations as an instrument of our policy, to be used when it is helpful but otherwise ignored. Orphaned at birth by the passing from the political scene of those who understood its potential real usefulness, the United Nations has never been treated as a potential world-security community—as an institution to be developed and strengthened for the long-term purpose of protecting humanity from the destructiveness of unrestrained nationalism. The immediate, short-term advantage of the leading members has invariably been given precedence over the needs of the collectivity. That is why the United Nations has not worked. There is no mystery about it, no fatal shortcoming in the Charter. Our own federal government would soon collapse if the states and the people had no loyalty to it. The reason that the United Nations has not functioned as a peace-keeping organization is that its members, including the United States, have not wished it to; if they had wanted it to work, it could have—and it still can. Acheson and his colleagues were wholly justified in their expectation of the United Nations' failure; their own cynicism, along with Stalin's cynicism, assured that failure.

Our shortsighted, self-serving, and sanctimonious view of the United Nations was put on vivid display in the reaction to the General Assembly's vote to take in mainland China and expel Nationalist China. Mr. Nixon expressed unctuous indignation, not at the loss of the vote but at the "shocking demonstration" of "undisguised glee" shown by the winners, especially those among the winners to whom the United States had been "quite generous"—as the President's press secretary was at pains to add. Mr. Agnew at least spared us the pomposities, denouncing the United Nations as a "paper tiger" and a "sounding board for the left," whose only value for the United States was that "it's good to be in the other guy's huddle." The Senate Minority Leader was equally candid: "I think we are going to wipe off some of the smiles from the faces we saw on television during the United Nations voting." The revelations are striking. Having controlled the United Nations for many years as tightly and as easily as a big-city boss controls his party machine, we had got used to the idea that the United Nations was a place where we could work our will; Communists could delay and disrupt the proceedings and could exercise the Soviet veto in the Security Council, but they certainly were not supposed to be able to win votes. When they did, we were naturally shocked—all the more because, as one European diplomat commented, our unrestrained arm-twisting had turned the issue into a "worldwide plebiscite for or against the United States," and had thereby made it difficult for many nations to judge the question of Chinese representation on its merits. When the vote went against us nonetheless, the right-wingers among us saw that as proof of what they had always contended—that the United Nations was a nest of Red vipers.

The test of devotion to the law is not how people behave when it goes their way but how they behave when it goes against them. During these years of internal dissension over the war in Vietnam, our leaders have pointed out frequently—and correctly—that citizens, however little they may like it, have a duty to obey the law. The same principle applies on the international level. *"Pacta sunt servanda,"* the international lawyers say: "The law must be obeyed." The China vote in the General Assembly may well have been unwise, and it may have shown a certain vindictiveness toward the United States, but it was a legal vote, wholly consistent with the procedures spelled out in the Charter.

The old balance-of-power system is a discredited failure, having broken down in two world wars in the twentieth century. The human race managed to survive those conflicts; it is by no means certain that it would survive another. This being the case, it is myopic to dismiss the idea of an effective world peace-keeping organization as a visionary ideal —or as anything, indeed, but an immediate, practical necessity.

With the coöperation of the major powers—and there is no reason in terms of their own national interests for them not to coöperate—the conflict in the Middle East could be resolved on the basis of the Security Council resolution of 1967, to which all the principal parties have agreed, calling for a settlement based upon, among other things, the principle of "the inadmissibility of the acquisition of territory by war." Similarly, I believe that the Security Council should have interceded to prevent war between India and Pakistan. This proved impossible largely because of the self-seeking of the great powers, each of which perceived and acted upon the situation not on its merits, and certainly not in terms of human cost, but in terms of its own shortsighted geopolitical interests. Moreover, the Security Council waited until war had actually broken out and an Indian victory seemed certain before attempting to intervene. The time for the United Nations to act on the crisis in East Pakistan was many months earlier, when the Bengalis were being brutally suppressed by the armed forces of the Pakistani government. The United Nations, it is true, is proscribed by Article 2 of the Charter from intervention in "matters which are essentially within the domestic jurisdiction of any state," but Article 2 also states that "the principle shall not prejudice the application of enforcement measures" under the peace-enforcement provisions of the Charter. By any reasonable standard of judgment, the mass killing of East Bengalis and the flight of ten million refugees across the Indian border constituted a "threat to the peace" as that term is used in the Charter, warranting United Nations intervention. I do not think it likely under present circumstances that the United Nations could play a mediating role in the war in Indo-China, the disabling circumstance being that the belligerents, including the United States, almost certainly would not permit it. But, looking ahead to the time when the Vietnam war is finally ended, I think it would be feasible for the United Nations to oversee and police a general peace settlement, through a revived International Control Commission, and perhaps through the assignment of peace-keeping forces.

When a conflict presents what Article 39 of the Charter calls a "threat to the peace, breach of the peace, or act of aggression," it makes no sense to leave the issue to the caprices of the belligerents. I have never understood why it is so widely regarded as outrageous or immoral for external parties to impose a solution to a dangerous conflict. Under the United Nations Charter, the Security Council has full authority—possibly even an obligation—to impose a settlement upon warring parties that fail to make peace on their own. The very premise of the Charter is that warring nations can no longer be permitted immunity from a world police power. As far as the United States is concerned, it is worth recalling that the United Nations Charter is a valid and binding obligation upon us, ratified as a treaty with the advice and consent of the Senate. And as far as the parties to various conflicts are concerned—Arabs and Israelis, Indians and Pakistanis—it needs to be recognized that they, too, are signatories to the Charter and are therefore obligated, under Article 25, "to accept and carry out the decisions of the Security Council in accordance with the present Charter."

In this century of conflict, the United States led in the conception and formulation of plans for an international peace-keeping organization. We did not invent the idea, nor have we been its only proponents, but without our leadership the ideal embodied in the Covenant of the League of Nations and the United Nations Charter would not have attained even the meagre degree of realization it has attained. It is this idea of world organization—rather than our democratic ideology, or our capitalist economy, or our power and the responsibilities it is supposed to have thrust upon us—that entitles the United States to claim to have made a valuable and unique contribution to the progress of international relations. Coming as we did on the international scene as a new and inexperienced participant, with a special historical experience that had sheltered us from the normal pressures of world politics, we Americans pursued our conception of a rational world order with uncritical optimism and excessive fervor. As a consequence, the first encounter with disappointment, in the form of Stalin and his ambitions in Eastern Europe, sent us reeling back from Wilsonian idealism. And from the practical idealism of the United Nations Charter we reverted to the unrealistic "realism" of the Truman Doctrine in its universalized application. We made the conversion from Wilson to Machiavelli with zeal.

At no point, of course, did the leading architects of Vietnam or the Bay of Pigs or the participants in the Cuban missile crisis conceive of themselves as power brokers pure and simple. Having themselves been reared in the tenets of Wilson-Roosevelt internationalism, and having lived through the disaster of appeasement in the inter-war years, they came to regard themselves as "tough-minded idealists," as "realists with vision," and, above all, as practitioners of collective security against aggression. What the United Nations could not do the United States could and would do, with allies if possible, alone if necessary. We, after all, were the ones who bore the burden of the "responsibilities of power." It was up to us, if all else failed, to curb aggression at its outset, to accept whatever sacrifices had to be made in order to defend the "free world" against the new Communist predator. We, in effect, were the successors to an enfeebled United Nations, and were forced by fate and circumstance to endure the glory and agony of power.

In this heady frame of reference, Vietnam and its consequences might be conceived as the ripe harvest of the American era of romantic "realism." Primarily, no doubt, because of its military failures, the war in Vietnam has brought many Americans to an awareness of the sham idealism of the "responsibilities of power," and of the inadequacies of the new "realism" once it is stripped of its romantic façade. Many young Americans, and some older ones, are appalled not only by the horrors of the Vietnam war but by the deterministic philosophy, espoused by the intellectuals who came into government in the sixties, of a permanent, purposeless struggle for power and advantage. We seem to be discovering once again that without a moral purpose and frame of reference there can be no such thing as "advantage."

America may be coming near to the closing of a circle. Having begun the postwar period with the idealism of the United Nations Charter, we retreated in disillusion to the "realism" of the Cold War, to the Truman Doctrine and its consummation in Vietnam, easing the transition by telling ourselves that we were not really abandoning the old values at all but simply applying them in more practical ways. Now, having failed most dismally and shockingly, we are beginning to cast about for a new set of values. The American people, if not their leaders, have come near to recognizing the failure of romantic, aggressive "realism," although a new idealism has yet to take its place. Perhaps we will settle for an old idealism—the one we conceived and commended to the world but have never tried.

Suggestions for Further Reading

The study of international relations and American foreign policy after 1945 is an exciting and growing scholarly field. Although much research is still needed, scholars have completed books and articles which reveal the tangled roots of the Cold War. Interpretations, topics, and emphasis vary, but the curious student can pursue his curiosity and interest in the selected bibliography below. Students eager to research Cold War topics in original sources, such as Department of State documents, will find helpful the footnotes and bibliographies of the works listed here.

For general studies of post-World War II American foreign relations, see Walter LaFeber, *America, Russia, and the Cold War, 1945–1971* (New York, 1972); John Spanier, *American Foreign Policy Since World War II* (New York, 1971); Adam Ulam, *Expansion and Coexistence: The History of Soviet Foreign Policy, 1917–67* (New York, 1968); Adam Ulam, *The Rivals: America and Russia since World War II* (New York, 1971); David Horowitz, *The Free World Colossus* (New York, 1971); Robert E. Osgood, *et al., America and the World* (Baltimore, 1970); Paul Y. Hammond, *The Cold War Years* (New York, 1969); Dana F. Fleming, *The Cold War and Its Origins* (Garden City, 1961; 2 vols.); N. D. Houghton, Ed., *Struggle Against History* (New York, 1968); William Carleton, *The Revolution in American Foreign Policy* (New York, 1967); Louis Halle, *The Cold War as History* (New York, 1967); Stephen Ambrose, *Rise to Globalism* (Baltimore, 1971); Gabriel Kolko, *The Limits of Power: The World and United States Foreign Policy, 1945–1954* (New York, 1972).

Works concentrating on the origins of the Cold War and the period in which the containment doctrine was formulated, include Thomas G. Paterson, Ed., *The Origins of the Cold War* (Lexington, Mass., 1970); Lloyd C. Gardner, *Architects of Illusion* (Chicago, 1970); Barton J. Bernstein, Ed., *Politics and Policies of the Truman Administration* (Chicago, 1970); Thomas G. Paterson, Ed., *Cold War Critics* (Chicago, 1971); Herbert Feis, *From Trust to Terror* (New York, 1970);

Richard M. Freeland, *The Truman Doctrine and the Origins of McCarthyism* (New York, 1972); H. Bradford Westerfield, *Foreign Policy and Party Politics* (New Haven, 1955); John C. Campbell, *The United States in World Affairs, 1945–1947* (New York, 1947); William A. Brown, Jr., and Redvers Opie, *American Foreign Assistance* (Washington, 1953); Harold Stein, Ed., *American Civil-Military Decisions: A Book of Case Studies* (Birmingham, Ala., 1963); William A. Williams, *American-Russian Relations, 1781–1947* (New York, 1952) and *Tragedy of American Diplomacy* (New York, 1962); John Gaddis, *The United States and the Origins of the Cold War, 1941–1947* (New York, 1972).

Interpretive articles on the origins of the Cold War are numerous. Some of the most thoughtful are Norman A. Graebner, "Cold War Origins and the Contemporary Debate: A Review of Recent Literature," *Journal of Conflict Resolution,* XIII (March 1969), 123-132; H. Stuart Hughes, "The Second Year of the Cold War: A Memoir and an Anticipation," *Commentary,* XLVIII (August 1969), 27-32; Arthur M. Schlesinger, Jr., "Origins of the Cold War," *Foreign Affairs,* XLVI (October 1967), 22-52; William A. Williams, "The Cold War Revisionists," *The Nation,* CCV (November 13, 1967), 492-495; Norman A. Graebner, "Global Containment: The Truman Years," *Current History,* LVII (August 1969), 77-84; Christopher Lasch, "The Cold War: Revisited and Re-Visioned," *New York Times Magazine,* January 14, 1968, pp. 26ff; Adam Ulam, "On Modern History: Rereading the Cold War," *Interplay Magazine,* II (March 1968), 51-53; Barton J. Bernstein, "American Foreign Policy and the Origins of the Cold War," in Bernstein, Ed., *Politics and Policies of the Truman Administration* (Chicago, 1970), 15-77; Henry Pachter, "Historical 'Revisionism' and the Cold War," *Dissent,* XV (November-December 1968), 505-518.

For the crisis in the Near East and the development of the Truman Doctrine and containment, see Joseph Jones, *The Fifteen Weeks* (New York, 1955), a memoir by one of the speech writers; Stephen G. Xydis, *Greece and the Great Powers, 1944–1947* (Thessaloniki, 1963), which uses Greek sources; Theodore A. Couloumbis, *Greek Political Reaction to American and NATO Influences* (New Haven, 1966); Edgar O'Ballance, *The Greek Civil War* (New York, 1966); Leften Stavros Stavrianos, *Greece: American Dilemma and Opportunity* (Chicago, 1952); F. S. Northedge, *British Foreign Policy: The Process of Readjustment, 1945–1961* (New York, 1962); M. A. Fitzsimmons, *The Foreign Policy of the British Labour Government: 1945–1951* (Notre Dame, 1953); Richard Barnet, *Intervention and Revolution* (New York, 1968); Dimitrious Kousoulas, *The Price of Freedom* (Syracuse, 1953); William H. McNeill, *The Greek Dilemma* (Philadelphia, 1947); William Reitzel, *The Mediterranean* (New York, 1948); Frank Smothers, *et al., Report on the Greeks* (New York, 1948); Bickham Sweet-Escott, *Greece: A Political and Economic Survey, 1939–1953* (London, 1954); U.S. Senate, Committee on Foreign Relations, *Assistance to Greece and Turkey* (Washington, March 1947), hearings on the Truman Doctrine; Bernard Weiner, "The Truman Doctrine: Background and Presentations" (unpublished Ph.D. dissertation, Claremont Graduate School, 1967); William L. Neumann, "How to Merchandise Foreign Policy: British Loan and Greek-Turkish Aid," *American Perspective,* III (September 1949), 183-193; Doris A. Grabner, "The Truman and Eisenhower Doctrines in the Light of the Doctrine of Non-Intervention," *Political Science Quarterly,* LXXIII (September 1958), 321-334; Stephen G. Xydis, "The Truman Doctrine in Perspective," *Balkan Studies,* VIII (1967), 239-262; Harry N. Howard, "United States Policy toward Greece in the United Nations, 1946–1950," *Balkan Studies,* VIII (1967), 263-296; John Jay Iselen, "The Truman Doctrine: A Study in the Relationship Between Crisis and Foreign Policy-Making" (unpublished Ph.D. dissertation, Harvard University, 1964).

George F. Kennan's essay on containment is "The Sources of Soviet Conduct," *Foreign Affairs,* XXV (July 1947), 566-582. Besides the commentaries on containment *vis-à-vis* Europe in this book and in works cited above, there are Blair Bolles, "The Fallacy of Containment," *The Nation,* CLXVIII (March 19, 1949), 327-329; H. Stuart Hughes, "Containment Reconsidered,' *The Nation,* CLXXI (December 16, 1950), 564-568; B. H. Brown, "Kennanland Revisited," *New Leader,* XXXVIII (September 19, 1955), 13-16 and (September 26, 1955), 16-19; William A. Williams, "Convenience of History," *The Nation,* CLXXXVIII (September 15, 1956), 222-224; Dana F. Fleming, "Is Containment Moral?" *The Annals,* CCCLXII (November 1965), 18-27; James Burnham, *Containment or Liberation?* (New York, 1952), a vigorous attack on containment from the "liberation"—Dulles point of view; Charles Gati, " 'X' Plus 25: What Containment Meant," *Foreign Policy,* No. 7 (Summer 1972), 22-40; " 'X' Plus 25: Interview with George F. Kennan," *ibid.,* 5-21, a discussion similar to that found in his *Memoirs.*

American foreign policy and the Cold War in the 1950's can be traced in the general studies listed above and in Coral Bell, *Negotiation from Strength* (New York, 1963); Emmet John Hughes, *The Ordeal of Power* (New York, 1963); Robert J. Donovan, *Eisenhower: The Inside Story* (New York, 1956); Louis Gerson, *John Foster Dulles* (New York, 1967); Richard Goold-Adams, *The Time of Power* (London, 1962), on Dulles; Gaston Goblentz, *Duel at the Brink* (Garden City, 1960); Norman Graebner, *The New Isolationism* (New York, 1956). See also M. A. Fitzsimons, "The Suez Crisis and the Containment Policy," *Review of Politics,* XIX (October 1957), 419-445.

The questions of NATO, nuclear weapons, and the continued militarization of the Cold War produced a provocative contemporary debate. See, for example, Hanson Baldwin, *The Great Arms Race* (New York, 1958); P. M. S. Blackett, *Atomic Weapons and East-West Relations* (Cambridge, England, 1956); W. W. Kaufmann, Ed., *Military Policy and National Security* (Princeton, 1956); Henry A. Kissinger, *Nuclear Weapons and Foreign Policy* (New York, 1958); Asher Lee and Richard Stockwell, *The Soviet Air and Missile Forces* (London, 1959); C. Wright Mills, *The Causes of World War III* (New York, 1958); Klaus Knorr,

Ed., *NATO and American Security* (Princeton, 1958); Bernard Brodie, *Strategy in the Missile Age* (Princeton, 1959); Herman Kahn, *On Thermonuclear War* (Princeton, 1960); Arnold Wolfers, Ed., *Alliance Policy in the Cold War* (Baltimore, 1959); Robert Osgood, *N.A.T.O.: The Entangling Alliance* (Chicago, 1962); Bernhard G. Bechhoefer, *Postwar Negotiations for Arms Control* (Washington, 1961); Warner R. Schilling, *et al., Strategy, Politics, and Defense Budgets* (New York, 1962); Eugene J. Rose, "Mass and Attentive Opinion on Nuclear Weapons Tests and Fallout, 1954–1963," *Public Opinion Quarterly,* XXIX (Summer 1965), 280-297.

For proponents of "disengagement," see George F. Kennan, *Russia, the Atom and the West* (New York, 1958), his complete Reith lectures; Hugh Gaitskell, *The Challenge of Coexistence* (Cambridge, Mass., 1958) and "Disengagement: Why? How?" *Foreign Affairs,* XXXVI (July 1958), 539-556; Noble Frankland, Ed., *Documents on International Affairs, 1957* (London, 1960) and Gillian King, Ed., *ibid., 1958* (London, 1962), for the Rapacki Plan and Western responses; Denis Healey, articles in the March, 1958, issues of *New Republic* (vol. CXXXVIII); Eugene Hinterhoff, *Disengagement* (London, 1959); James P. Warburg, *Agenda for Action* (New York, 1957) and "Is Disengagement in Western Europe Feasible? *Foreign Policy Bulletin,* XXXVII (March 15, 1958), 100ff; Fred Warner Neal, "George Kennan's Foreign Policy," *Claremont Quarterly,* Fall, 1958, pp. 21-29; Richard Barnet and Marcus Raskin, *After 20 Years: Alternatives to the Cold War in Europe* (New York, 1965); Adam Bromke, "Disengagement in East Europe," *International Journal,* XIV (Summer 1959), 168-174; Walter Lippmann, "Mr. Kennan and Reappraisal in Europe," *Atlantic,* CCI (April 1958), 33-37. See also U.S. Senate, Committee on Foreign Relations, *Informal Meeting with George F. Kennan* (Washington, May 1959).

Other writings by George F. Kennan on the topic of Soviet-American relations in the 1950s and the opportunities for disengagement include "Americans and Russians," *New Republic,* CXXXIV (June 11, 1956), 6; "What Should We Do About Russia?" *U.S. News and World Report,* XL (June 29, 1956), 68-77, a debate with William Bullitt; "Overdue Changes in Our Foreign Policy," *Harper's,* CCXIII (August 1956), 27-33; "Fresh Look at Russia," *Foreign Policy Bulletin,* XXXVI (June 15, 1957), 145; "Disengagement Revisited," *Foreign Affairs,* XXXVII (January 1959), 187-210; "Berlin and the Geneva Meeting," *New Leader,* XLII (May 11, 1959), 3-6; "A Proposal for Western Survival," *New Leader,* XLII (November 16, 1959), 10-15; U.S. Senate, Committee on Foreign Relations, *Disarmament and Foreign Policy* (Washington, February 1959), hearings in which Kennan debates disengagement.

The critical attacks on the idea of disengagement and on Kennan were often heated. Dean Acheson led the most vigorous dissent. See his "The Illusion of Disengagement," *Foreign Affairs,* XXXVI (April 1958,) 371-382; *Congressional Record,* January 16, 1958, pp. 552-553, which carries a strongly worded Acheson commentary; and *Power and Diplomacy* (Cambridge, Mass., 1958). Other opposition to disengagement came from James B. Conant, "Against the Neutralization of a United Germany," *Western World,* No. 15 (July 1958), 35-40; M. Stanton Evans, "The Liberal Against Himself," *National Review,* II (December 22, 1956), 11-13; "Fallacy of Kennanism," *Life,* XCIV (February 3, 1958), 33; Thomas K. Finletter, *Foreign Policy: The Next Phase* (New York, 1958); Michael Howard, *Disengagement in Europe* (London, 1958); James E. King, Jr., articles in April, 1958, issues of *New Republic* (vol. CXXXVIII); Henry A. Kissinger, "Missiles and the Western Alliance," *Foreign Affairs,* XXXVI (April 1958), 383-400; Perry Laukhuff, "Germany: Four Proposals and a Dissent to George Kennan," *New Republic,* CXXXVIII (February 24, 1958), 13-15; Hans J. Morgenthau, "Should We Negotiate Now?" *Commentary,* XXV (March 1958), 192-199; D. W. Treadgold, "The Future of Communism: George Kennan's Neo-Isolationism," *New Leader,* XXXIX (September 3, 1956), 9-11.

For further discussion of disengagement, see Max Ascoli, "George Kennan Updates His Diplomacy," *Reporter,* XVIII (January 23, 1958), 17-20; P. M. S. Blackett, "Nuclear Weapons and Defence: Comments on Kissinger, Kennan, and King-Hall," *International Affairs,* XXXIV (October 1958), 421-434; James Reston, "New Proposals for Old Disposals," *New York Times Book Review,* March 2, 1958; Marshall D. Shulman, "Changing Appreciation of the Soviet Problem," *World Politics,* X (July 1958), 499-511; Kenneth W. Thompson, "The Kennan-Acheson Debate," *Commonweal,* LXVIII (April 4, 1958), 6-9; Robert C. Tucker, "Russia, the West, and World Order," *World Politics,* XII (October 1959), 1-23. For the continuation of issues centered in Europe in the 1960's, see many of the general studies of the Cold War cited above.

The deep American involvement in Vietnam in the 1960's can be understood only in the context of international relations in Asia after 1945, especially regarding China. General studies include John K. Fairbank, *The United States and China* (Cambridge, Mass., 1971); Tang Tsou, *America's Failure in China, 1941–1950* (Chicago, 1963); O. Edmund Clubb, *20th Century China* (New York, 1964); A. T. Steele, *The American People and China* (New York, 1966); Donald S. Zagoria, *The Sino-Soviet Conflict, 1956–1961* (Princeton, 1962); American Assembly, *The United States and the Far East* (New York, 1958); Edward Friedman and Mark Selden, Eds., *America's Asia: Dissenting Essays in Asian-American Relations* (New York, 1971); A. Doak Barnett, ed., *Communist Strategies in Asia* (New York, 1963); Harold C. Hinton, *Communist China in World Politics* (New York, 1966) and *China's Turbulent Quest* (New York, 1970); A. Doak Barnett and Edwin O. Reischauer, Eds., *The United States and China: The Next Decade* (New York, 1970); Peter Van Ness, *Revolution and Chinese Foreign Policy: Peking's Support for Wars of National Liberation* (Berkeley, 1970); Arthur Huck, *The Security of China: Chinese Approaches to Problems of War and Strategy* (London, 1970); J. D. Simmonds, *China's World: The Foreign Policy of a Developing State* (New York, 1970); Foster Rhea Dulles, *American Policy toward Communist China: The Historical Record, 1949–1969* (New York, 1972); John Paton Davies, Jr., *Dragon by the Tail* (New York, 1972).

For the Vietnam War, consult Noam Chomsky, *American Power and the New Mandarins* (New York, 1969); Chester Cooper, *The Lost Crusade: America in Vietnam* (New York, 1970); Theodore Draper, *Abuse of Power* (New York, 1967); Richard Falk, Ed., *The Vietnam War and International Law* (Princeton, 1968–1969; 2 vols.); Bernard Fall, *Vietnam Witness* (New York, 1966); Richard N. Goodwin, *Triumph of Tragedy* (New York, 1966); George Kahin and John W. Lewis, *The United States in Vietnam* (New York, 1969); Jean Lacouture, *Vietnam: Between Two Truces* (New York, 1966); John T. McAlister, *Viet Nam: The Origins of Revolution* (New York, 1969); Hans J. Morgenthau, *Viet Nam and the United States* (Washington, 1965); Marcus Raskin and Bernard Fall, Eds., *The Viet-Nam Reader* (New York, 1965); Arthur M. Schlesinger, Jr., *The Bitter Heritage* (Boston, 1966); Franz Schurmann, *et al., The Politics of Escalation in Vietnam* (Boston, 1966); Robert Shaplen, *The Lost Revolution* (New York, 1966); Donald Zagoria, *Vietnam Triangle: Moscow, Peking, Hanoi* (New York, 1967); John R. Boettiger, Ed., *Vietnam and American Foreign Policy* (Boston, 1968); Joseph Buttinger, *Vietnam: A Political History* (New York, 1968); Douglas Pike, *Viet Cong* (Cambridge, Mass., 1966); David Halberstam, *The Making of a Quagmire* (New York, 1965); Cabel Phillips, "Footbridge into the Quagmire," *New Republic,* CLXV (July 24, 1971), 13-15; John T. McAlister, Jr., "The Possibilities for Diplomacy in Southeast Asia," *World Politics,* XIX (January 1967), 258-305; Hans J. Morgenthau, *A New Foreign Policy for the United States* (New York, 1969); Richard M. Pfeffer, Ed., *No More Vietnams?* (New York, 1968); Robert Randle, *Geneva, 1954* (Princeton, 1969); Townsend Hoopes, *Limits of Intervention* (New York, 1969); A. Michael Washburn and Willard H. Mitchell, *Walt Rostow, Vietnam, and the Future Tasks of American Foreign Policy* (Princeton, 1967); N. Khac Huyen, "An Independent Communist Leader: Ho Chi Minh between Peking and Moscow," *Orbis,* XIII (Winter 1970), 1185-1208; Committee of Concerned Asian Scholars, *The Indochina Story: A Fully Documented Account* (New York, 1970); James C. Thomson, Jr., "How Could Vietnam Happen? An Autopsy," *Atlantic Monthly,* CCXXI (April 1968), 47-53; U.S. Senate, Committee on Foreign Relations, *Supplemental Foreign Assistance Fiscal Year 1966-Vietnam* (Washington, January-February, 1966) and *U.S. Policy with Respect to Mainland China* (Washington, March 1966), both important hearings; Chalmers M. Roberts, " 'X' Plus 25: How Containment Worked," *Foreign Policy,* No. 7 (Summer 1972), 41-53.

The Johnson Administration's case for intervention in Vietnam is made in almost every issue of the Department of State's *Vietnam: Information Notes* and the *Department of State Bulletin;* see also Eugene V. Rostow, *Law, Power, and the Pursuit of Peace* (New York, 1968); Walt W. Rostow, *The Diffusion of Power, 1957–1972* (New York, 1972); and Lyndon Johnson, *The Vantage Point* (New York, 1971). Studies by noted political critics include J. William Fulbright, *The Arrogance of Power* (New York, 1966) and Eugene J. McCarthy, *The Limits of Power* (New York, 1967). Many of the studies listed above are also critical of the American role in Vietnam. George F. Kennan expresses his dissent in the 1966 Vietnam hearings.

The prominence of the containment doctrine in the formulation of American foreign policy toward Asia is evident in the *Department of State Bulletin* (1960s) and the *Pentagon Papers* (various editions, 1971). For critical discussions of the applicability of containment to Asia, see H. Brand, "On Containment in Asia," *Dissent,* XIV (March-April 1967), 140-144; "Containing China: A Round-Table Discussion," *Commentary,* XLI (May 1966), 23-41; Roger D. Masters, "Goals for American Power," *Yale Review,* LV (Spring 1966), 365-388; John F. Melby, "The Cold War—Second Phase: China," *International Journal,* XXIII (Summer 1968), 421-434; Lawrence D. Messier, "The Feasibility of a Containment Policy in Southeast Asia," *Towson State Journal of International Affairs,* IV (Spring 1970), 104-120; Hans J. Morgenthau, "U.S. Misadventure in Vietnam," *Current History,* LIV (January 1968), 29-34; David P. Mozingo, "Containment in Asia Reconsidered," *World Politics,* XIX (April 1967), 361-377; Richard J. Powers, "Containment: From Greece to Vietnam—and Back," *Western Political Quarterly,* XXII (December 1969), 846-861. Dana F. Fleming, "Can We Escape from Containing China?" *Western Political Quarterly,* XXIV (March 1971), 163-177; Sir Robert Thompson, "The Truman Doctrine Now," *Quadrant,* XIV (May/ June 1970), 37-39; Edmund Stillman, " 'Containment' Has Won, But . . .," *New York Times Magazine,* May 28, 1967, pp. 23ff; Norman Graebner, "Whither Containment?" *International Journal,* XXIV (Spring 1969), 246-263; Richard Barnet, *Intervention and Revolution* (Cleveland, 1968); Carl Oglesly and Richard Shaull, *Containment and Change* (New York, 1967); Thomas G. Paterson, "After Peking, Moscow: New Levers of Containment," *The Nation,* CCXIV (April 24, 1972), 531-532.

George F. Kennan figured prominently in most of the foreign policy debates after 1945. His list of speeches and writings is extensive. Besides his well-known commentaries on containment in 1947, disengagement in 1957, and Vietnam in 1966, noted above, there are numerous other statements which have also stirred discussion and which reveal his intellectual development. The Department of State's *Foreign Relations of the United States* for the years 1945 and 1946 contain Kennan's reports from his post as Chargé of the American Embassy in Moscow. Other Kennan statements include "United States and the United Nations," *Vital Speeches,* XV (November 15, 1948), 68-70; "International Situation," *Department of State Bulletin,* XXI (September 5, 1949), 323-324; "Foreign Aid in the Framework of National Policy," *Proceedings of the Academy of Political Science,* XXIII (January 1950), 448-459; "Is War with Russia Inevitable?" *Department of State Bulletin,* XXII (February 20, 1950), 267-271; "Current Problems in the Conduct of Foreign Policy," *ibid.,* XXII (May 15, 1950), 747-751; "Russia and the United States," *New Republic,* CXXII (June 26, 1950), 12-16; "The Situation in the Far East," *University of Chicago Roundtable,* August 27, 1950, pp. 14-17; "Lectures on Foreign Policy," *Illinois Law Review,* XLV (January-February 1951), 718-742; "Let Peace Not Die of Neglect," *New York Times Magazine,* February 25, 1951; "America and the Russian Future," *Foreign Affairs,* XXIX (April 1951), 351-370; "How New

Are Our Problems," *Foreign Service Journal,* XXVIII (Octooer-November 1951), 20; "National Interest of the United States," in H. F. Harding, Ed., *Age of Danger* (New York, 1951), pp. 80-85;

See also Kennan's "Soviet-American Relations," *Vital Speeches,* XIX (February 15, 1953), 268-272; "Hope in an Age of Anxiety," *New Republic,* CXXVIII (June 1, 1953), 14-16; "Climate of Current Investigations of Communism," *Vital Speeches,* XIX (June 15, 1953), 539-541; "Did Stalin's Death Change Anything?" *Reporter,* IX (July 7, 1953), 32-35; "Nature of the Challenge," *New Republic,* CXXIX (August 24, 1953), 9-12; "Communism and Conformity," *Bulletin of Atomic Scientists,* IX (October 1953), 296-298; *Realities of American Foreign Policy* (Princeton, 1954); "Illusion of Security," *Atlantic,* CXCIV (August 1954), 31-34; "For the Defense of Europe: A New Approach," *New York Times Magazine,* September 12, 1954; "Role of Morality in Foreign Policy," *America,* XCII (November 6, 1954), 146-147; "Totalitarianism in the Modern World," in Carl Friedrich, Ed., *Totalitarianism* (Cambridge, Mass., 1954); "Speak Truth to Power," *The Progressive,* XIX (October 1955), 5-18; "Foreign Policy and Christian Conscience," *Atlantic,* CCIII (May 1969), 44-49; "Peaceful Co-existence: A Western View," *Foreign Affairs,* XXXVIII (January 1960), 171-190; "Japanese Security and American Policy," *Foreign Affairs,* XL (October 1964), 14-28; "Fresh Look at Our China Policy," *New York Times Magazine,* November 22, 1964; *On Dealing with the Communist World* (New York, 1964); "Europe in East-West Relations," *Survey,* No. 58 (January 1966), 118-127; "The Russian Revolution 50 Years After: Its Nature and Consequences," *Foreign Affairs,* XLVI (October 1967), 1-21; "The Legacy of Stalinism," *Massachusetts Historical Society Proceedings,* LXXIX (1968), 123-134; *Democracy and the Student Left* (Boston, 1968); "To Prevent a World Wasteland: A Proposal," *Foreign Affairs,* XLVIII (April 1970), 401-413; "Hazardous Courses in Southern Africa," *ibid.,* XLIX (January 1971), 218-236; "Note on Russian Foreign Policy," *Encounter,* XXXVI (February 1971), 53-54.

Kennan has always believed in a professional diplomatic corps largely free from the changing winds of whimsical public opinion. In his *American Diplomacy, 1900–1950* (Chicago, 1951), he complained of American moralism-legalism in foreign policy. That is, American leaders too often followed unreliable emotion, sometimes thrust upon them by public opinion, against American national interest. His eagerness to create an elite foreign service is expressed in a number of his writings: "Training for Statesmanship," *Atlantic,* XCI (May 1953), 40-43; "The Future of Our Professional Diplomacy," *Foreign Affairs,* XXXIII (July 1955), 566-586; "America's Administrative Response to Its World Problems," *Daedalus,* LXXXVII (Spring 1958), 5-24; "Diplomacy as a Profession," *Foreign Service Journal,* XXXVIII (May 1961), 23-26.

Kennan's own career as a diplomat can be traced in his autobiographical works: *Memoirs, 1925–1950* (Boston, 1967); *From Prague After Munich: Diplomatic Papers, 1938–1940* (Princeton, 1968); *Memoirs, 1950–1963* (Boston, 1972). These books reprint a number of Kennan's incisive memoranda. Kennan has also taped an interview, which is deposited at the John F. Kennedy Library. His own private papers have been placed in the Princeton University Library.

Kennan has also distinguished himself as an historian of Russia and its foreign policy. See his "History and Diplomacy as Viewed by a Diplomatist," *Review of Politics,* XVIII (April 1956), 170-177; *Russia Leaves the War* (Princeton, 1956); *The Decision to Intervene* (Princeton, 1958); "American Troops in Russia," *Atlantic,* CCIII (January 1959), 36-42; "Walter Lippmann, the New Republic, and the Russian Revolution," in M. W. Childs and James Reston, Eds., *Walter Lippmann and His Times* (New York, 1959); "Our Aid to Russia: A Forgotten Chapter," *New York Times Magazine,* July 19, 1959; "Soviet Historiography and America's Role in the Intervention," *American Historical Review,* LXV (January 1960), 302-322; "Experience of Writing History," *Virginia Quarterly Review,* XXXVI (Spring 1960) 205-214; *Soviet Foreign Policy, 1917–1941* (Princeton, 1960); "Russia and the Versailles Conference," *American Scholar,* XXX (Winter 1960–1961), 13-42; *Russia and the West under Lenin and Stalin* (Boston, 1961); "Price We Paid for War," *Atlantic,* CCXIV (October 1964), 50-54; "Reflections: Custine," *New Yorker,* XLVII (May 1, 1971), 46ff; "The Historiography of the Early Political Career of Stalin," *Proceedings of the American Philosophical Society,* CXV (June 17, 1971), 165-170.

A man of Kennan's stature usually draws attention from journalists, scholars, and other publicists. Kennan is no exception. Observers have studied his ideas and his life as a diplomat, scholar, and philosopher. Particularly relevant for discussions of the moralism-legalism theme are Myres S. McDougal, "Law and Power," *American Journal of International Law,* XLVI (January 1952), 102-114; Dexter Perkins, "American Foreign Policy and Its Critics," in Alfred H. Kelly, Ed., *American Foreign Policy and American Democracy* (Detroit, 1954), pp. 65-88; Dwight J. Simpson, "New Trends in Foreign Policy: A Criticism of the 'Kennan Thesis,'" *World Affairs Quarterly,* XXVII (January 1957), 327-343; R. H. S. Crossman, "Strange Case of Mr. X — George Kennan," in Crossman, *Charm of Politics and Other Essays in Political Criticism* (New York, 1958), pp. 128-133; R. C. Good, "National Interest and Political Realism: Niebuhr's 'Debate' with Morgenthau and Kennan," *Journal of Politics,* XXII (November 1960), 597-619; Jonathan Knight, "George Frost Kennan and the Study of American Foreign Policy: Some Critical Comments," *Western Political Quarterly,* XX (March 1967), 149-160; Lloyd C. Gardner, "1900–1921: A Second Look at the Realist Critique of American Diplomacy," in Barton J. Bernstein, Ed., *Towards a New Past* (New York, 1968), pp. 203-231.

Other studies of Kennan's views and career include Max Lerner, "Mr. X, Mr. L and Mr. S," in Lerner, *Actions and Passions* (New York, 1949), pp. 301-304; Edgar A. Mowrer, "Who Will Counsel the Counselor?" *Saturday Review of Literature,* XXXIV (September 29, 1951), 6-8, 37-40; G. W. Herald, "Mister X in Quest of Peace," *United Nations World,* VI (March 1952), 17-20; Alice Widener, "The Real George F. Kennan," *American Mercury,* LXXIV (March

1952), 8-18; Joseph G. Whelan, "George Kennan and His Influence on America. Foreign Policy," *Virginia Quarterly Review,* XXXV (Spring 1959), 196-220; M. J. Lasky, "A Conversation with George Kennan," *Encounter,* XIV (March 1960), 46-57; Louis J. Halle, "World of George Kennan," *New Republic,* CXLV (August 7, 1961), 21-23; Henry M. Pachter, "George Kennan: The Perils of History," *Dissent,* VIII (Autumn 1961), 473-479; William A. Williams, "Foreign Policy and the American Mind," *Commentary,* XXXIII (February 1962), 155-159; Christopher Lasch, "Historian as Diplomat," *Nation,* XCV (November 24, 1962), 348-353; Louis J. Halle, "The Turning Point," *Survey,* No. 58 (January 1966), 168-176; Marvin Kalb, "Vital Interests of Mr. Kennan," *New York Times Magazine,* March 27, 1966, pp. 30ff; Richard J. Powers, "Kennan Against Himself?" (Unpublished Ph.D. dissertation, Claremont Graduate School, 1967); George Kateb, "George F. Kennan: The Heart of a Diplomat," *Commentary,* XLV (January 1968), 21-26; Henry Pachter, "The Intellectual as a Diplomat: A Critical Discussion of George F. Kennan," *Dissent,* XV (March–April 1968), 161-170; P. Podlesny, "History Calls to Account," *International Affairs* (Moscow), XV (January 1969), 96-98; Louis J. Halle, "George Kennan and the Common Mind," *Virginia Quarterly Review,* XL (Winter 1969), 46-57; Edmund F. Kallina, Jr., "A Conservative Criticism of American Foreign Policy" (Unpublished Ph.D. dissertation, Northwestern University, 1970); Lloyd C. Gardner, *Architects of Illusion* (Chicago, 1970), pp. 270-300; Robert E. Hindle, "George F. Kennan and the Beginnings of Containment" (Unpublished Ph.D. dissertation, Claremont Graduate School, 1970).

For a complete bibliography on the topics and individuals discussed in this book, the curious should consult the bibliographies of the works cited above, as well as such references as the *New York Times Index* and the *Guide to Periodical Literature.* The history of American foreign policy after the Second World War invites more research.

This book and this bibliography only nibble at the vast amount of historical material available, but should serve as a beginning for further reading, research, and interpretation. The foreign policy debates of the 1940s, 1950s, and 1960s are too important—for the 1970s—to let die of neglect.